D1002232

H46 654 438 4

Gavin Mortimer is an award-winning writer and journalist. He is the author of *A History of Football in 100 Objects* (published by Serpent's Tail), Puffin's *Ultimate Guide to Cricket*, and *Fields of Glory*, which was voted one of the best books of 2001 by Robin Marlar of *The Cricketer*. He is the sport correspondent for *The Week*.

A HISTORY OF
CRICKET
IN 100 OBJECTS

GAVIN MORTIMER

First published in 2013 by Serpent's Tail,
an imprint of Profile Books Ltd
3A Exmouth House
Pine Street
London EC1R 0JH
website: www.serpentstail.com

ISBN 978 1 84668 940 6
eISBN 978 1 84765 959 0

Designed and typeset by sue@lambledesign.demon.co.uk

Printed in Great Britain by
Clays Ltd, St Ives plc

10 9 8 7 6 5 4 3 2 1

For Margot, when she comes of cricket age

Contents

Introduction

We've done it! A history of cricket in 100 objects. If we had a helmet on we'd remove it, kiss the badge and then wipe our brow. Instead we'll raise our pen in recognition of reaching three figures because it's been no easy task. How can you chronicle in 100 objects a sport that has been played for more than 500 years? Initially we came up with a list of more than 200 objects before cutting as lavishly as Sachin Tendulkar until we were down to a ton of cricketing trivia.

No doubt some will question our object selection the way they might question Kevin Pietersen's shot selection as he lofts a catch to deep square leg on 97. But in selecting our century of objects (of which all had to be inanimate) we have endeavoured to chart how cricket spread from being the most English of pastimes to become a sporting obsession from Barbados to Brisbane to Bombay.

We have followed the changes in laws, tools, technology, attitudes and format, but we have also, we hope, shown that over the centuries one aspect of this great game has remained constant – the spirit in which cricket is played.

We accept that some will disagree with our final choice of objects, but then isn't questioning selectors' decisions one of cricket's core appeals? So, as we retire to the pavilion to enjoy a cheese-and-pickle sandwich and a nice cup of tea, we'll leave you to carry on the innings. Good luck, and watch out for the googlies.

Roundhead helmet

'Hundreds of pages have been written on the origin and early history of cricket,' explained A.G Steel, a former teammate of W.G. Grace's in the England side of the 1880s, and the Hon. Robert Henry Lyttelton in their tome on the game entitled *Cricket*. 'The Egyptian monuments and Holy Scriptures, the illuminated books of the Middle Ages, and the terra-cottas and vases of Greece have been studied, to no practical purpose, by historians of the game.'

And they wrote that in 1888! One hundred and twenty years later tens of thousands of trees have been felled in printing books which attempt to unravel the origins of cricket, but still the mystery remains.

One of the principal points on which cricket historians disagree is whether cricket is derived from the medieval game of club-ball. The Reverend James Pyecroft was sure on the subject, writing in the nineteenth century that 'club-ball we believe to be the name which usually stood for cricket in the thirteenth century'. But a contemporary of Pyecroft's, Nicholas Felix, pooh-poohed the idea, commenting that club-ball was a 'very ancient game and totally distinct from cricket'.

Nor is much credence given these

days to the idea that a young Edward II played a form of cricket, passed down to him by his grandfather, Henry III, King of England from 1216 to 1272.

Things become clearer towards Tudor times, all thanks to a fifty-nine-year-old gentleman called John Derrick. In 1598, the fortieth year of Elizabeth's reign, Derrick was embroiled in a legal dispute over a plot of land in Guildford. Called to testify in a Guildford court, Derrick explained that, as a local schoolboy, 'hee and diverse of his fellows did runne and play there at creckett and other plaies'.

So there we have it, cricket was definitely being played on village greens in the mid-sixteenth century. Perhaps Henry VIII was a fan, what with his reputation for maidens. By the early seventeenth century references to cricket were common. In 1611 'boyes played at crickett' with a 'cricket-staffe', while Maidstone in Kent was damned as a 'very profane town' in the 1630s on account of 'morris dancing, cudgel playing, stoolball, crickets, and many other sports openly and publickly on the Lord's Day'.

More to contend with than a few dozen peasants playing cricket on a Sunday

Such a sentiment reflected the increasing spread of Puritanism throughout England in the first half of the seventeenth century. As its joyless influence grew, so cricket lovers were persecuted for their passion; eight players in Sussex were fined for playing the game in 1637 and seven men of Kent were ordered to pay two shillings each after admitting they'd taken guard on the Sabbath.

But soon England had more pressing matters to contend with than a few dozen peasants playing cricket on a Sunday. In 1642 civil war erupted between the Royalist supporters of Charles I and Oliver Cromwell's Roundhead army, culminating in the execution of the king in 1649. Cromwell became Lord Protector of the Commonwealth of England, Scotland and Ireland and, even though he was rumoured to have played cricket in his youth, his government had no time for the game. 'Puritanism was tough on recreation and it is unsurprising that cricket was targeted,' wrote John Major, who, like Cromwell, represented the constituency of Huntingdon while a Member of Parliament. 'The austere piety of the Puritans' belief, and their determination to make people devout, was bound to be in conflict with the exuberant joy of a ball game.'

Consequently, many well-heeled Royalist sympathisers retired from London to their country seats in Kent and Sussex. Here they were exposed for the first time to cricket, taking up the game out of sheer boredom, and when they returned to the capital following the Restoration in 1660 they brought with them their new pastime.

Cromwell was dead, Charles II was king and England was no longer in thrall to the Puritans. Theatres and taverns reopened, gambling and prostitution thrived and cricket began to take hold among the great and the good of London. 'In a year or two it became the thing in London society to make matches and to form clubs,' wrote cricket historian Harry Altham. 'Thus was inaugurated that regime of feudal patronage which was to control the destinies of the game for the next century or more.'

And, as we shall see in our next chapter, one of the staunchest patrons of cricket in the eighteenth century was a man who was as much a playboy as Cromwell was a Puritan.

House of Hanover coat of arms

What, you may ask, is a German coat of arms doing in a history of cricket? Well, it's a curious tale but one that bears telling. Hanover was the royal dynasty that ended with the death of Queen Victoria in 1901 and which included, nearly two centuries earlier, Frederick Louis, Prince of Wales.

Freddie was many things, a fop and a philanderer among them, but he was also a lover of cricket, and without his royal patronage the sport wouldn't have gained such cachet among the English nobility of the eighteenth century.

Frederick was born in Hanover in 1707, the same year that in London the English capital stages its most illustrious cricket match to date, a clash between a London XI and a team of gentlemen from Croydon at Lamb's Conduit Fields in Holborn.

As we saw in our last chapter, cricket had been brought to the capital on the back of the Restoration, and in the half-century following the succession of Charles II the game took a firm hold in the south-east of England.

There was still bear-baiting, cock-fighting and bare-knuckled boxing, but cricket offered the more discerning Englishman something a little less bloody. Patrons began cropping up, wealthy enthusiasts who used their money to spread further the appeal of cricket. Edward Stead was a prominent one in Kent, forming his own XI in the 1720s and challenging teams from London and Surrey. In 1728 his side took on the Duke of Richmond's XI for a 'large sum of money', and a few months later Stead's men defeated a Sussex team sponsored by Sir William Gage.

Gambling was at the heart of these matches, which is why the aristocracy were so attracted. Richmond wasn't the only cricketing duke. There were Newcastle, Dorset and Bedford, the latter regularly staging matches at his sprawling estate at Woburn Park against sides that included an Earl of Sandwich XI.

But no earl or duke could match the passion of a prince for cricket. Quite why 'Poor Fred' developed such a love for the game is unknown. Originally he may have adopted the game as a means of proving his 'Englishness', conscious that a blue-blood from Hanover was always going to have a hard time winning over the locals. But Frederick clearly developed a genuine love for cricket and was a regular at Kennington and other grounds across the country from 1731 onwards.

It was said that after a match between Surrey and Middlesex in 1733 the prince was so impressed by the quality of cricket that he paid each player a guinea. Two years later he sponsored a Surrey XI against London in a match played at Moulsey Hurst, and then he began playing himself. The Duke of Marlborough's XI was defeated by the prince and his men in 1737, HRH winning a 'considerable sum' in the process.

Though Frederick had a venomous relationship with his father, George II, he was on better terms with his younger brother, Prince William, Duke of Cumberland, himself a cricket lover when he wasn't butchering Scots. The pair were present at the Artillery Ground in 1744 to see Kent play an All-England XI, a contest won eventually by Kent. It was hailed by the contemporary press

as 'the greatest cricket match ever known', and the poet James Love dipped his quill in ink to mark the occasion, beginning:

Hail, cricket! Glorious, manly, British Game!
First of all Sports! Be first alike in Fame!

By the mid-eighteenth century cricket's roots were thick, deep and growing, thanks to its aristocratic patrons. From Sussex to Kent to East Anglia, clubs were being founded, such as the one in Norwich, which advertised in the *Norwich Mercury* for 'lovers of cricket' to join.

Hail, cricket! Glorious, manly, British Game!

When Dr Johnson published *A Dictionary of the English Language* in 1755 he defined cricket as 'a sport of which the contenders drive a ball with sticks in opposition to each other'. He would have known, having played the game while studying at Oxford in 1729.

By then, however, the Prince of Wales was dead. It was said he was injured by the ball during a game of cricket at his Buckinghamshire home in 1749. Two years later, while dancing at Leicester House, he collapsed and died from a burst abscess on the lung, some in the medical profession attributing the abscess to the blow from the cricket ball.

Killed by a cricket ball – it's the way the prince would have wished to go.

Cricket bat

**As we've just seen, Dr Johnson in his dictionary
described cricket as a game played 'with sticks'. When
cricket laid down its first set of laws in 1744 the bat was
not a priority. Any shape, size and style was permitted,
though most gentlemen used a long bat which was
curved at the bottom, a hybrid of a hockey stick and a
golf club.**

'A big proportion of the weight was in the curve,' wrote
H.J. Henley in a 1937 essay for a book celebrating the
150th anniversary of the Marylebone Cricket Club,
'planned to block or scoop away the primitive bowling in
vogue, which was of the fast underhand variety, the type
known in later years as "sneaks", "grubs"', "grounders"
and "daisy cutters".'

The man credited with making the first significant
alteration to the shape of the bat was John Small, described
by a contemporary as 'a remarkably well-made and
well-knit man, of honest expression and as active as a
hare'. His 1773 bat had square shoulders from handle to
blade, not the wine-bottle shoulders of previous designs.
At around the same time (historians disagree on the exact
date) Thomas 'Shock' White of Reigate took guard in a

game against Hambledon, armed with what Henley described
as a 'monstrosity wider than the wicket'. Nonetheless there was
nothing in the laws of the game to punish White's innovative
impertinence, not until the laws were amended in 1774 to restrict
the width of the bat to 4½ inches. Subsequently its maximum
length was set at 38 inches.

Though the width and the length haven't changed in nearly
250 years, the weight and the shape have altered drastically.
Up until the mid-nineteenth century bats were made all in one piece
until, in 1853, handles with two strips of whalebone inside the cane
were introduced. This absorbed the shock of leather on willow and
handles made from India rubber helped batsmen grip the bat better.

The biggest change in shape was in the early twentieth century.
Where once bats had been the same thickness from splice to base,
'gradually they were given
a bulge in the part where
the ball is met by a correctly
executed stroke'. In writing
these words in 1937
H.J. Henley expressed his
doubt that the extra weight

> In 1853 handles with
> strips of whalebone
> inside the
> cane were
> introduced

made much of a difference. 'The great players of the [eighteen]
eighties made drives which carried as far as those of present-day
cricketers, but men who have had practical experience of both the
"thin" blade and the "fat" say that the latter puts more force into a
purely defensive stroke.'

For W.G. Grace balance was the overriding factor in choosing
a bat. 'I play with a bat weighing 2lb 5oz, which, I think, is heavy
enough for anybody,' he wrote in 1899. 'But a few ounces make
very little difference if the bat is really well balanced.'

Grace also mentioned the other dimensions he looked for in his
bats. 'The ordinary and best length is 34½ inches, the blade 22 and
the handle 12½,' he advised. 'Some cricketers prefer thick handles
and others like thin ones, this point must be determined by the size
and length of the hand.'

Grace's advice was followed by the next great of the game, Don Bradman, whose bat weighed 2 pounds 4 ounces, but one of the Don's Australian teammates, Bill Ponsford, became famous in the 1920s for his 'Big Bertha' bat, a mighty club of some 2 pounds 9 ounces.

That's the average weight of an international player's bat in the twenty-first century, though the power-hitting required for Twenty20 has led some batsmen to take a 3-pound bat to the wicket. Despite various attempts to tamper with the composition from the traditional white willow – which won out over red willow in the nineteenth century because it is softer – cricket bats remain essentially the same as they did in Grace's time.

Bat manufacturers can go on as much as they want about 'enlarged sweet spots', 'low impact areas' and 'perimeter weighting', but what it comes down to is how the piece of willow feels in the batsman's hands. 'I am repeatedly asked whose bats are the best, and what maker's I play with,' a famous cricketer said in the past. 'My answer is I play with any good bat I can get hold of, never minding who is the maker, as long as the bat is not too heavy and is well balanced, and suits me to handle.'

The cricketer's name? W.G. Grace.

Hambledon monument

**We saw in our second chapter how cricket was spread in
the first half of the eighteenth century by the aristocracy,
the likes of the Duke of Richmond and Frederick Louis,
Prince of Wales. Poor Fred died in 1751, a year after the
subject of our next object came into existence.**

The commemorative stone erected in 1908 on
Broadhalfpenny Down marks the site where the
Hambledon Club was formed circa 1750. The club didn't
last long – within half a century they had drawn stumps
– but in the years of its existence its influence was such

that Hambledon became
known as the 'cradle of
cricket'.

Of course, in reality it
was no such thing. Cricket
pre-dates the formation
of the Hambledon Club by
a good 200 years, but the
myth of the Hampshire
club took root when in
1833 John Nyren wrote
The Young Cricketer's Tutor.
Nyren was the son of
Richard, who captained
Hambledon in its
formative years as well as
running the Bat and Ball
Inn on Broadhalfpenny

Down. John Nyren could spin a yarn like Shane Warne could a ball, and his book immortalised Hambledon and exaggerated its influence. Nevertheless, for a brief period in the second half of the eighteenth century, Hambledon was the foremost club of its day, attracting the leading players, gamblers and spectators to the picturesque Broadhalfpenny Down.

As many as 20,000 people were said to have attended the really big games, terrible for the Down's wildlife but a boon for the myriad stallholders who erected their colourful tents around the ground's boundary.

John Nyren could spin a yarn like Shane Warne could a ball

Richard Nyren was the driving force behind Hambledon Cricket Club. A left-handed bowler of some repute, he organised and promoted the matches, and afterwards, when the match was complete, he invited everyone back to the Bat and Ball Inn. There they drank punch, at twopence a pint, strong enough, said his son, 'to make hair curl'.

Word of the Hambledon Club spread across southern England, attracting players who would become cricket's first 'characters'. There was Tom Brett, strong as an ox and a demon fast bowler; behind the stumps was dashing Tom Sueter, a pet of all the neighbourhood and the man credited with mastering the 'cut' as an attacking shot; John Small, a shoemaker turned batmaker, used his own tools to accumulate vast scores.

Two of the men who would leave a lasting impression on cricket arrived late on in Hambledon. William 'Silver Billy' Beldham played his first game for the club in 1785, when he was nineteen, the start of a cricketing career that would redefine the art of batting. David Harris did something similar for bowling when he replaced Tom Brett as Hambledon's main strike bowler in the 1770s. Harris was the first bowler to understand the importance of a good line and length, the pioneer of a skill that every subsequent bowler has striven to master.

As Harris's career blossomed, so the fortunes of Hambledon began to wilt. Their finest afternoon had come one glorious June day in 1777 when they thrashed 'a fully representative eleven of England' by an innings and 168 runs in a match that received much publicity.

Soon more and more young men took up the game, many of them wealthier and better connected than the bucolic batsmen and bowlers of Hambledon. In 1787, ten years after the club's most famous victory, the Marylebone Cricket Club was formed. 'More and more did London become the centre of cricket,' wrote Harry Altham, 'and steadily the membership [of Hambledon] declined and the players were lured away by the golden magnet.'

Ironically, one of the last matches of importance that Hambledon played was in 1793 at Lord's, the ground that had usurped Broadhalfpenny Down as the 'cradle of cricket'. Three years later the club was dissolved, and though an attempt was made to resurrect it a few years later, Hambledon's day had passed. Marylebone was now the pre-eminent club in England, and Hambledon became just an extra on the scorecard of history.

The publication of Nyren's book in 1833 first restored Hambledon's reputation and then embellished its importance in the early history of cricket. It also awakened in Englishmen a romantic longing for the past, for a pre-Industrial Revolution England, when they perceived life to be purer. In reviewing Nyren's book in *The Gentlemen's Magazine*, the Reverend John Mitford wrote:

> *Farewell, ye smiling fields of Hambledon and Windmill Hill! Farewell, ye thymy pastures of our beloved Hampshire, and farewell, ye spirits of the brave who still hover over the fields of your inheritance. Great and illustrious eleven! Fare ye well! In these fleeting pages at least, your names shall be enrolled. What would life be, deprived of the recollection of you? Troy has fallen, and Thebes is a ruin. The pride of Athens is decayed, and Rome is crumbling to the dust. The philosophy of Bacon is wearing out; and the victories of Marlborough have been overshadowed by fresher laurels. All is vanity but cricket; all is sinking in oblivion but you. Greatest of all elevens, fare ye well!*

Laws of the game

Ah, the laws of cricket! Arcane to some, absurd to others, but for most of us the anchor that ensures the game never loses it nobility.

The earliest known laws were drawn up in 1744 by a band of distinguished 'Noblemen and Gentlemen' who used the Artillery Ground in London. This was the venue for what was described as 'the greatest cricket match ever known', a game in which Kent beat an All-England XI in front of the Prince of Wales. When in 1937 *The Times* newspaper published a book celebrating the 150th anniversary of the MCC, it wrote that 'it is conceivable that [the laws'] object was to lay down precisely the conditions that were to govern play in the great match'.

So what were the most significant laws agreed upon by the noblemen and gentlemen of the Artillery Ground and subsequently published in a pamphlet in 1755?

There was a two-stump wicket with a single bail, measuring 22 inches by 6 inches, and two creases were cut into the ground with the popping crease 46 inches in front of the wicket. A batsman could be out any number of ways: bowled, caught (off the bat or his hands), stumped, run out, handling the ball, obstructing the field or 'wilfully' hitting the ball twice. A batsman couldn't be given out leg before wicket – this issue wouldn't be addressed until 1774 – nor did the 1744 rules stipulate the size of a bat (though they did the ball, as we'll soon see).

An over comprised four balls (this increased to five in 1889 and six in 1900, and in Australia it rose to eight in 1924 before returning to six in 1979) and the only no-ball was when the bowler's foot strayed over the crease.

And a quick note about the crease. The distance between the bowling crease and the popping crease (the crease over which the bat could be popped for safety) is 46 inches, which in Tudor times was the same measurement as an ell, an ell being the length of an arrow. It's probable that an arrow was used to measure out the distance the batsman should stand in front of the stumps.

Today the only claim the MCC has on the laws of cricket is the copyright

This would then have then been cut or scratched out in the ground, the word scratch being derived from old English 'crease'.

In 1774 the laws were further revised at the Star and Garter in London, the principal changes to arise from the meeting being the introduction of the lbw law and the maximum length and width of a bat. In 1788 the laws were once more tinkered with, presumably to give the newly formed Marylebone Cricket Club a feeling of importance. Rolling, watering and mowing of the pitch were permitted by mutual consent of the captains, and the lbw law was updated.

Three significant changes to the laws arose from a meeting of the MCC in 1798: the size of the wicket increased from 22 inches in height to 24, and from 6 inches in breadth to 7; a new ball could be demanded at the start of each innings, and if a fielder stopped the ball with his hat the batting side would be awarded five runs.

The laws continued to be tweaked throughout the nineteenth century. Leaving aside the monumental changes to the bowling action and lbw law (examined in chapter 9), cricket in this century witnessed the following significant alterations:

1810 Toss for choice of innings.

1811 Wides added to the score but called 'byes' until 1828 when 'wides' used for the first time.

1819 Height of wicket increased from 24 to 26 inches, and popping crease extended from 46 to 48 inches.

1823 Height of wicket increased from 26 to 27 inches, now 8 inches in breadth.

1835 The 'follow-on' is introduced compelling a team 100 runs or more in arrears after the first innings to bat again (or 'follow' its innings 'on'). The margin was reduced to 80 runs in 1854 and raised to 120 in 1895

1836 The bowler is credited with every wicket which falls to his bowling – previously the custom had been to credit the fielder who took a catch and not the bowler who delivered the ball.

1838 A third stump is added to the wicket.

1848 Leg-byes first recorded as such.

1849 It is permitted to sweep and roll the pitch between innings.

The MCC continued to be the sole guardians of cricket's laws well into the twentieth century, and when it celebrated its 150th birthday in 1937 *The Times* proclaimed: 'They have never set out to be dictators to the game but to be its servants; they welcome suggestion and will always conform to what they find to be the preponderance of considered and reasonable opinion.'

Today the only claim the MCC has on the laws of cricket is

the copyright. In 1968 it ceded its authority as the ruling body of English cricket to the Test and County Cricket Board, forerunner of today's England and Wales Cricket Board. The MCC in the twenty-first century has prestige but little power.

Then in 1993 what power remained was transferred to the International Cricket Council and what is now the England and Wales Cricket Board. The ICC's Executive Board meets regularly to discuss the laws and in 2011 made changes to a number of them, including the abolition of runners, an alteration to the run-out law and Powerplays in one-day internationals. Not everyone was impressed. 'I don't think there's enough foresight with the framing of all the laws,' said former Australia captain Ian Chappell. 'You need to think of the laws occasionally, but we are having major changes all the time, which means you haven't thought through the rules properly at first.'

Umpire's white coat

Who'd be a professional umpire today? If it wasn't already a thankless task, the advent of high-tech television equipment has enabled players and public to scrutinise every decision made by an umpire. With all the pressure they face out in the middle it's a wonder the umpires are the ones wearing the coats rather than the men leading them gently away towards a padded cell.

The word 'umpire' comes from the Old French *'nonper'*, which meant not (non) equal (per) and was the word used to describe an impartial arbiter of a dispute between two parties. It's believed the 'n' of *nonper* was attached to the indefinite article ('a nonper' becoming 'an onper') in the second half of the fifteenth century to give us 'an oumper', which in time became 'umpire'.

As we saw with our previous object, cricket's laws were first promulgated in 1744 and then published in a pamphlet eleven years later, which had this to say about the role of the umpires:

They are sole judges of all Outs and Ins, of all Fair and Unfair play or frivolous delays, of all hurts whether real or pretended, and are discretionally to allow what time they think proper before the game goes on again.

They are sole judges of all hindrances, crossing ye Players in running and standing unfair to strike and in case of hindrance may order a notch to be scored. They are not to order any Man out unless appealed to by any one of ye Players. These laws are to ye Umpires jointly.

Each Umpire is ye sole judge of all Nips and catches, Ins and Outs, good or bad runs at his own Wicket and his determination shall be absolute and he shall not be changed for another umpire without ye consent of both sides.

For most of the nineteenth century each team supplied its own umpire (usually an ageing former player), until 1883, when the law was amended making it compulsory for umpires to be neutral in county matches. The change met with the approval of A.G. Steel when he wrote his history of the game in 1888. 'However honest and free from suspicion a man might be, his opinion, at a critical stage of the game, could not fail to be unconsciously biased in favour of the side with whose name his own had long been associated. Many men became alarmed at the idea of obtaining a reputation for giving partial decisions, and would go to the other extreme, and decide against their own side oftener than the facts justified.'

Neutral umpires averted this crisis of conscience. Not that it made their task any easier. 'The duties of an umpire are most laborious and irksome; they require for their proper performance the exercise of numerous qualifications, and yet it is always the lot of every man who dons the white coat... to receive certainly no thanks and, too frequently, something which is not altogether unlike abuse.'

One hundred and twenty years later umpires were still coming in for abuse, as West Indian Steve Bucknor discovered during a tempestuous Test match between Australia and India at the Sydney Cricket Ground in 2008. Most of the abuse came in the press and not out on the pitch, and the *Sydney Morning Herald* felt compelled to come to Bucknor's defence. The paper, arguing against transferring more decisions from the hands of the umpires to television replays, admitted that Bucknor had made mistakes but added that 'right or wrong, umpiring controversies are part of the Test match tradition. Cricket history would not be the same without them.'

It's a wonder the umpires are the ones wearing the white coats

The paper was adamant that electronic certainty should not supersede human fallibility as cricket's most powerful arbiter. After all, it added, we've been here before with umpiring controversies – and indeed, it wasn't even the first inceident of its kind at the SCG. During a match between the touring England side and a New South Wales XI in February 1892, the tourists had an appeal for a catch turned down by E.J. Briscoe, an umpire 'well known for his powers of retort and his sense of unflinching duty'.

'You will give no one out,' bellowed W.G. Grace, the incredulous England captain. 'It is unpardonable. You must be blind!'

Briscoe, reported the *Sydney Morning Herald* the following day, refused to take any further part in the match and was replaced by one of the NSW players.

Cricket ball

It's small, red and since the earliest laws of cricket were published in 1744 it's weighed between 5 and 6 ounces. Though much has changed about cricket down the centuries, the shape and size of the ball today would be instantly recognisable to the young men who bowled and batted in Tudor times.

The eighteenth-century painter and diarist Joseph Farington mentioned in his diary of 1811 that the Duke family of Penshurst in Kent had been making cricket balls for 250 years. Such a claim is greeted with scepticism by some cricket historians, though what is known for certain is that the Dukes company first began producing cricket balls in 1760 from its premises in Tonbridge, a couple of miles east of Penshurst, and twenty years later were manufacturing the six-seam balls of today.

By then cricket's lawmakers had already decreed that the ball – unlike the bat – had to conform to certain specifications; namely that it 'weigh between five and six ounces'. The balls were made from layered cork and yarn encased in smooth white leather, but at some point between the promulgation of the 1744 rules and the publication in 1843 of Charles Dickens' *Martin Chuzzlewit*, they began to be dyed red; in describing the ledgers of the Anglo-Bengalee Disinterested Loan and Life Assurance Company, Dickens writes they possessed 'red backs like strong cricket balls beaten flat'.

Colour wasn't the only aspect of the ball to have changed in the second half of the eighteenth century. In 1774 the laws were revised to ensure the ball should not weigh more than 5 3/4 ounces and no less than 5½ ounces, and in 1838 there was a further amendment to its size, this stipulation requiring that the ball's circumference 'measure not less than nine inches nor more than nine and a quarter in circumference'.

The last tampering with the ball (in a regulatory sense, at least) was in 1927, when the permitted circumference was changed to between $8^{13}/_{16}$ and 9 inches.

Despite the attempt at uniformity, balls can still be as inconsistent as the English weather. 'It requires much knowledge and experience to tell a good ball from an indifferent one,' wrote W.G. Grace in 1887. 'They are all pretty much the same in appearances, size and weight, and it is only after a hard knock or two that a bad one begins to show its true nature.' In Grace's opinion, the ball-makers were to blame for these

> The ball today would be instantly recognisable to the young men of Tudor times

vagaries, and he advised cricket enthusiasts to 'buy only from those who have earned the right to be classed amongst the best makers. A badly made ball is dear at any price.'

Opinion is divided among today's cricketing nations as to which manufacturer makes the best ball. England and Australia, for example, rely on different ball-makers, with the former opting for the tried-and-trusted Dukes ball and the Aussies preferring their own Kookaburra brand. To look at they appear almost identical, though the Dukes ball is a marginally darker shade of red. As the BBC discovered prior to the start of the 2010/11 Ashes series between Australia and England, however, there is another small but significant difference: the seam, the stitching around the middle of the ball that allows the spinner to turn it and the seamer to swing it. 'A brand new Kookaburra swings immediately whereas the Dukes probably swings more from about six to ten overs old,' the former Australia fast bowler Jason Gillespie explained to the BBC. This is because the seam on the Kookaburra is flatter and a little wider; the seam of a Dukes ball, by contrast, 'feels thinner but tends to not wear down as quickly as the Kookaburras'.

The other factor at play is the surface of rock-hard Australian pitches, which take a greater toll on the ball's sheen than the softer English wicket.

Ultimately, however, it's the bowler who has the last word on the ball. 'At the end of the day it is just a cricket ball,' said Duncan Fletcher. 'Bowl it in the perfect area and then see what happens.'

MCC tie

Any cricket fan worth his salt will recognise this next object – the scarlet-and-gold tie of the Marylebone Cricket Club. The tie's colours are colloquially called 'eggs and bacon', and it was at the tea gardens at White Conduit House in Islington that the club had its origins.

When Lord Martin Bladen Hawke, one of the great players of cricket's 'Golden Age', wrote an essay about the origins of the MCC in 1937, he traced the club's roots to the tea gardens in 1780. 'By 1782 they had become known as the White Conduit Cricket Club,' explained Lord Hawke. 'From this aristocratic, if haphazard, beginning 150 years ago sprang the Marylebone Cricket Club.' Beyond this, though, His Lordship wasn't able to provide much in the way of specifics as to how and when exactly the MCC was born, nor have subsequent historians. What is known is that the White Conduit Cricket Club inaugurated their new ground at Lord's (see chapter 28) with a match between the Mary-le-Bone club and the Islington Club on 30 July 1787. In all probability the Mary-le-Bone club was the White Conduit Club rechristened, a nod to the location of their new ground.

What was certain, however, was that the MCC soon became cricket's sole arbitrator. Just a year after its formation, the club was asked to resolve a dispute between Leicester and Coventry concerning a batsman who in defending his wicket had struck the ball twice with his bat. The teams appealed to the MCC, 'the first reputed cricket society in the Kingdom'.

This authority went unchallenged for nearly 100 years until 1867 – the year after the MCC had purchased the freehold of Lord's Ground – when a letter was published in the *Sporting Life* proposing the establishment of a Cricket Parliament to replace the MCC as the game's supreme court. The plan was motivated by a feeling of southern bias; that the MCC was a London club and was unrepresentative of English cricket now that the game had spread north to Lancashire and Yorkshire. The proposition called for a parliament of cricket legislators to be elected each year from across the country, but the demagogue's cry fell on deaf ears.

One hundred and fifty years later the MCC remains arguably the most prestigious sports club in the world, but its influence on cricket has waned. In 1993 it ceded most of its power to the ICC, what *Wisden* described as a 'notably unwelcome passage in their history'. In future the MCC would be like a twelfth man – people were aware of his presence but he could do little to influence the outcome of the match.

In all probability the Mary-le-Bone club was the White Conduit Club rechristened

That was followed five years later by a bitter row over the question of admitting women members. For 211 years the MCC had resisted, and when it went to a vote in February 1998 members once more voted to keep the status quo. They were universally ridiculed as a result, the New Zealand *Sunday News* labelling the club's members 'dinosaurs of world cricket'. The British government suggested the 18,000 members of the MCC might like to vote again. When they did in September 1998 the MCC succumbed to pressure and voted in favour of admitting female members. More recently, in 2012, the club turned on itself in a dispute over a proposed £400 million redevelopment of Lord's, prompting John Major to resign from the main committee.

Increasingly, the MCC is to cricket what the Royal Family is to Britain – a benign figurehead, a symbol of another age and a bulwark against the brasher aspects of life. For many cricket fans the sight of an eggs-and-bacon tie is strangely reassuring, like an England batting collapse, restoring order to a chaotic world.

As for the origins of the MCC colours, they too are shrouded in mystery. According to the club's historian, Glenys Williams, until the 1860s the club played in light blue. The red and gold made their first appearance in the 1860s, the same decade one of the club members, William Nicholson, advanced the money required to purchase the freehold of Lord's Ground. Nicholson made his money from the family's gin company, the colours of which were red and yellow. As Williams says: 'Although no written proof has yet been found there is a strong family tradition that the adoption of the red and gold was MCC's personal thank you to William Nicholson for his services to the club – sport's first corporate sponsorship deal perhaps?'

Not a bad deal, and what are the chances that Nicholson also threw in a couple of cases of gin to keep the members content?

Batsman's leg guard

'The striker is out if [he] puts his leg before the wicket with a design to stop the ball, and actually prevents the ball from hitting his wicket by it'

The Laws of Cricket, 1774

And so we have the first reference to the method of dismissal known today as leg before wicket – or what every cricket buff refers to by its acronym, lbw.

When the original laws were framed in 1744 a batsman could be bowled, caught, stumped or run out, but being dismissed on account of his legs received no mention.

This was because of the type of bat used by players. As we saw in our third chapter, in cricket's salad days the bats were curved, a cross between a hockey stick and a golf club. The custom was for batsmen to stand to one side of the wicket and wield their bat almost like a scythe. In addition the bowling was invariably along the ground, what we call today 'daisy-cutters'.

But as bats lost their curve in the late 1860s and bowling

began to take off, so batsmen changed their stance and used their legs as a second line of defence, bringing to an end what Teresa McLean described in her book *The Men in White Coats* as 'cricket's crude innocence'.

The two men who most effectively exploited this loophole in the laws were the Hambledon batsman Tom Taylor and his friend Joey Ring, whose actions were deemed 'shabby' even by their own teammate William 'Silver Billy' Beldham. By the early 1770s, though, it wasn't just Taylor and Ring – everybody was at it.

According to an account left by Beldham, 'the bowlers found themselves defeated' in the face of these underhand tactics, so in 1774 the law proscribing the practice was introduced. 'Lbw,' writes McLean 'has been a thorn in umpires' sides and a psychological burden from that day to this.'

Soon batsmen throughout southern England were spluttering in indignation at being given out leg before wicket, incredulous that an umpire could believe them so ungentlemanly as to by 'design' block the ball with their legs. Umpires were abused for casting aspersions on the integrity of batsmen, and so when the laws were updated in 1788 by the newly formed Marylebone Cricket Club, the wording of the lbw law was altered. The word 'design' was removed and a batsman would be given out if he was hit by a ball which 'pitched in a straight line to the wicket, and would have hit it'.

Being dismissed lbw was no longer guaranteed to end a man's prospects of a good marriage and entry into civilised society, but it seems there was for many years still a stigma attached to having the ball hit one's legs in front of the wicket. 'It did not appear on any surviving scorecards until 1795,' explained McLean, 'though this does not mean that umpires were abstaining from lbw convictions; rather the scorers were not distinguishing lbw dismissals from bowled out, any more than most of them distinguished stumped out, "catched out" and run out from bowled out.'

The first batsman to be officially given out leg before wicket was the Hon. John Tufton, batting for an England side against Surrey at

Moulsey Hurst in 1795. (The bowler was John Wells.) The following year Tufton was elected Member of Parliament for the borough of Appleby in Westmorland. Presumably to escape the shame – or perhaps because he now felt he had the qualities required for politics.

In 1823 the lbw law was further revised so that a batsman could be out if a ball delivered in a straight line to the wicket struck any part of his body, but in 1839 the law reverted to its 1788 definition, when the emphasis was put on the pitch of the ball and not its line.

For nearly 100 years there were no major alterations to the lbw law, but in 1926 the Hon. R.H. Lyttelton wrote to Sydney Pardon, editor of *Wisden*, expressing his growing concern at the number of lbw dismissals. He backed up his disquiet with some research that Pardon found 'startling'. In the 1870 season, of 1,772 first-class dismissals, only 44 had been lbw, a ratio of 1 in 40. By 1910 451 of 6,704 dismissals were lbw, a ratio of 1 in 14. In 1923 921 of 7,919 dismissals were given out leg before wicket, a ratio of 1 in 8.

> Umpires were abused for casting aspersions on the integrity of batsmen

It took the MCC nearly another ten years to do something about it. In 1935 they introduced an experimental law in which a batsman could be given out lbw if the ball pitched outside the line of the off stump. This removed the need for the ball to pitch in line with the wickets if the umpire judged that the ball would go on to hit the stumps. This time the change was written into cricket's statute book in 1937.

The law was modified once more in 1970, the authorities still concerned at the number of batsmen using their pads to play the ball in a defensive and negative manner. Now a batsman could be given out lbw if a ball – which the umpire judged to be heading for the stumps – pitched in line with the wickets or 'outside a batsman's off stump and in the opinion of the umpire he made

no genuine attempt to play the ball with his bat'. So in effect a
batsman would not be given out lbw if the ball pitched outside off
stump, provided he was playing a shot.

Wisden welcomed the change, its editor commenting in
the 1972 edition that it 'gave the batsmen more freedom and
consequently led to more attractive cricket'. Others
weren't so satisfied, and the Australian Cricket Board
– concerned at the sharp fall in lbw decisions –
proposed a return to the pre-1970 law but with
a clause stating that 'if no stroke is offered to a
ball pitching outside the off stump which in the
opinion of the umpire would hit the stumps, but
hits the batsman on any part of his person other than
the hand, then the batsman is out, even if that part of the
person hit is not in line between wicket and wicket'.

> The most perplexing and disagreeable law of the whole code

The proposal was accepted, and the lbw law has remained the
same ever since, surviving intact when the MCC revised the laws
of the game in 1980 and again in 2000. The twenty-first century,
and the television technology that it has unleashed on cricket (see
chapter 97), has exposed the lbw law to more scrutiny than ever
before. But 'twas ever thus. As Charles Box wrote in his book *The
Theory and Practice of Cricket*, the lbw law is the 'most perplexing
and disagreeable of the whole code. Many ingenious theories have
been planned for simplifying it, but at present without success.'
And that was in 1868!

Hoop skirt

Possibly no other sport stirs the soul quite like cricket. Certainly no other sport can match its romance, the gladiatorial duel to the death between batsman and bowler. This romance extends to its history, as we have seen with Hambledon and its reputation as the 'cradle of cricket'.

Yet of all cricket's lilies that have been gilded down the years, none has been gilded quite as much as our next object – the hooped skirt of Christiana Willes. She was the woman who, according to legend, invented the art of overarm bowling. Miss Willes' brother, John, was a keen Kent cricketer in the habit of having his sister throw him a few balls so he could practise his batting. The problem was, so the myth goes, Christiana's massive hooped skirt prevented her bowling the customary underarm delivery. So she improvised, and threw the ball to her brother in a round-arm style that was soon being copied across southern England.

John Major called it a 'charming though dubious' tale. Harry Altham didn't even deign to mention it in his own history of the game, such was his scepticism. The flaw in the story, the rabbit in the batting order, if you like, is the timeline. John Willes was indeed the pioneer of round-arm bowling, first using it playing for Kent against an England side in 1807. 'The straight-armed bowling, introduced by John Willes, Esq., was generally practised in this game,' recorded the *Morning Herald*, 'and proved a great obstacle against getting runs.'

Yet in 1807 hooped skirts had been out of fashion for years. The voluminous panniers of the eighteenth century had died out in the 1780s with women turning to simpler, slender dresses that took their inspiration from the garments of Ancient Greece. It wasn't until the 1820s that skirts once more began to grow with the caged crinoline dresses that became synonymous with the Victorian era. The Willes were a wealthy landowning family from Kent; no way would Christiana have bucked fashion by continuing to wear an outdated pannier dress.

The young Miss Willes received scant attention from the Reverend James Pycroft when he wrote his 1851 book *The Cricket Field*. Though he conceded that John Willes was the first round-arm bowler to make an impact in cricket, the reverend claimed it was an innovation whose roots lay in Sussex.

Kent claimed otherwise, insisting they were the inventors of round-arm bowling, but whichever county was the originator of the art it soon caught on elsewhere, and a decade into the nineteenth century underarm bowling, like a certain style of ladies' skirt, was no longer the height of fashion.

But though an increasing number of the bowling fraternity had embraced the new style, batsmen remained bitterly resistant to its charms. Suddenly they were faced with much quicker deliveries, far greater bounce and many more bruises to their unprotected legs – the first pads weren't worn until the 1830s.

In 1816 the MCC banned round-arm bowling, stating in a new Law 10 that only underarm bowling was permitted. John Willes, and many others, ignored the new ruling and continued to take wickets with their round-arm style. Until, that is, one fateful July day in 1822 when Willes was no-balled at Lord's playing for Kent against the MCC. 'Willes threw down the ball in disgust,' wrote Harry Altham in 1926, 'jumped on his horse, and rode away out of

Lord's and out of cricket history.' Actually Willes did dismount his horse eventually, becoming a coach and teaching a new generation of cricketers how to bowl round-arm.

In the meantime the art had found two new champions in James Broadbridge and William Lillywhite, the man David Frith has described as 'the truculent little "giant" who gave evolution its momentum'. So determined – and so effective – was he in bowling round-arm that eventually the MCC tinkered with Law 10 in 1828 so as to allow the hand to be raised as high as the elbow.

This still wasn't enough for Lillywhite and Broadbridge, whose hands went as high as their shoulders, and so in 1835 the MCC gave way once again, this time altering the wording of Law 10 so that it now read: 'The ball must be bowled, and if it be thrown or jerked, or if the hand be above the shoulder in the delivery, the umpire must call "no ball".'

Underarm bowling was no longer the height of fashion

Bowlers became faster throughout the 1840s and 1850s, and with speed came an evolution of technique as players searched for an extra yard of pace. On the evening of 27 August 1862 Edgar Willsher of Kent ran into bowl for England against Surrey at the Oval, unaware that he was also running into history. Up came his left arm, past his elbow, past his shoulder and practically over his head. 'No ball!' cried the umpire John Lillywhite (ironically, the son of William). When he was no-balled for the fifth time, Willsher and eight of his England teammates stormed off the Oval in protest.

Lillywhite was only applying the letter of the law, but the fact was that more and more bowlers were guilty of bringing their arm above the level of their shoulder. By no-balling Willsher in the showpiece match of the year, wrote Harry Altham, the MCC was forced once more to take action. 'Two years later, Law 10 was finally revised, and the long battle of the bowler for liberty was won.'

Underarm bowling was still permitted (the last recorded case in a first-class match was by Trevor Molony of Surrey in 1921) but it had been overtaken by overarm.

A quill

As cricket began to spread throughout the southern counties of England in the late eighteenth century, it became popular at Eton and Westminster – much to the displeasure of their respective headmasters. In 1796 the Eton XI were soundly thrashed on and off the pitch, first losing to Westminster by 66 runs on Hounslow Heath and then receiving six of the best from their masters upon their return to College, punishment for playing the game without permission.

The arrival of Harrow on the cricketing scene weakened the opposition of the Eton authorities. Dr Thomas Thackeray, great-grandfather of William, the celebrated

novelist, was instrumental in championing cricket at Harrow, and, seeing illustrious backers on the Harrovian side, Eton's masters relented in their opposition.

The first official match was in the summer of 1805 after Harrow issued Eton with a challenge: 'The gentlemen of Harrow School request the honour of trying their skill at cricket with the gentlemen of Eton, on Wednesday July 31 at Lord's Cricket Ground. A speedy answer, declaring whether the time and place be convenient, will oblige.'

Eton accepted, though the match at Lord's was pushed back to 2 August – perhaps to allow time for Lord Byron to talk his way into the Harrow team. J.A. Lloyd, the Harrow captain, wrote after his side had lost by an innings and 2 runs that 'Byron played very badly... he should never have been in the XI had my counsel been taken'.

The Eton XI received six of the best from their masters upon their return to College

Byron's club foot must have impeded his batting, and it appears that his eye – not to mention his memory – wasn't up to much either. Writing to a friend two days after the match, the then seventeen-year-old Byron explained: 'We played the Eton and were most confoundly beat. However, it was some comfort to me that I got 11 notches in the first innings and 7 in the second, which was more than any of our side except Brockman and Ipswich could contrive to hit.'

But the scorebook never lies; and in fact Byron made just 7 and 2, some way short of fifteen-year-old Lord Ipswich, who top-scored in both innings with 21 and 10. Poetic licence, perhaps.

The evening after the match Byron did what crestfallen cricketers have done since time immemorial – he went on a spree, leaving the first account of what we now lovingly call the post-match piss-up. 'Later to be sure we were most of us very drunk and we went together to the Haymarket Theatre where we kicked up a row, as you may suppose when so many Harrovians and Etonians meet in one place,' wrote Byron. 'I was one of seven in a single Hackney, four Eton and three Harrow fellows, we all got into the same box, the consequence was that such a devil of a noise arose that none of our neighbours could hear a word of the drama, at which not being highly delighted they began to quarrel with us and we nearly came to a battle royal.'

The camaraderie of the evening evaporated in the days that followed as Eton dispatched a rhyme to their vanquished foe:

Adventurous boys of Harrow School,
Of cricket you've no knowledge.
You play not cricket, but the fool,
With men of Eton College.

Harrow's reply – attributed to the goose-feather quill of Byron – was swift:

Ye Eton wits, to play the fool
Is not the boast of Harrow School;
No wonder, then, at our defeat –
Folly like yours could ne'er be beat.

As sport's influence grew in English public schools throughout the nineteenth century, an antidote to the triple vices of drinking, gambling and masturbation, so the Eton versus Harrow match grew in prestige. In 1857 *The Times* said of the fixture: 'It is important to secure a race of young Englishmen who, in days to come when our bones have mouldered away, shall retain the grasp of England upon the World.'

By the end of the nineteenth century crowds of 30,000 were common at Lord's to watch the two sides; and Harrow produced two greats of cricket's 'Golden Age' – F.S. Jackson and Archie Maclaren, both of whom captained England.

One hundred years later the fixture had diminished in stature. In 1982 the three-day match was reduced to a one-day fixture and the crowds had also been pared. Writing in the *Daily Mail* in 1993 Ian Woolridge lamented the fact, saying it did 'little for the status of public school cricket. Eton and Harrow, the oldest of all matches at Lord's, are now the last school teams to play there.'

The irascible Woolridge also found scant consolation in the behaviour of the Lord's crowd, mostly made up of ex-pupils, whose behaviour reflected the 'boozy strains of terrace culture in this age of yob rule'.

Boozy strains? Lord Byron knew all about cricket and booze. Perhaps not so much has changed: boys will always be boys.

Fort George, Bombay

It's a question that has baffled many historians. Why did India, having won independence from the British in 1947, still insist on playing cricket, the sport above all other synonymous with 'the hated imperialists'?

To understand why cricket took such a hold in the country one has to go right back to the beginning, to 1721, when there is definite evidence (from naval dispatches) that British sailors were playing cricket while stationed at Cambay, to the north of Bombay.

For the next half-century and more cricket, like life in general for the colonials, moved slowly, but as the expatriate community began to grow in the latter half of the century, turning from traders to imperialists, so cricket spread, with the province of Bengal, in the east of India, the most enthusiastic followers of the game.

The first Indian cricket club to be formed was Calcutta in 1792, making it in all likelihood the second-oldest club in the world after the MCC, which was then five years into its existence. Be that as it may, it was 1,200 miles on the other side of the country, in what was then called Bombay, that cricket really took hold.

For despite the formation of the Calcutta Cricket Club and despite the fact that 1804 witnessed the first recorded organised game of cricket in India (and the first century, scored by Robert Vansittart), the sport was played only by the English. The only Bengalis present were the small number in the crowd, and they were clearly not inspired to take up the game. This, writes Mihir Bose in *A History of*

Indian Cricket, was because of the 'Bengali distrust of team games, reflecting not only a highly individualistic approach but also a definite social barrier between the rulers and the ruled'.

Not so to the west where in Bombay the Parsis wasted no time in picking up bat and ball. The Parsis had fled Iran in the seventh century, settling in western India, where they were left unmolested by the king on the condition they didn't proselytise. They didn't, but nor were they ever accepted by the Hindu population; indeed, when the British arrived, the Parsis viewed them not as invaders but as fellow outsiders. The Parsis had always had a sharp eye for business, and they saw in the British the means to improve their standing in India – and not just through trade.

The Parsis wasted no time in picking up bat and ball

What better way to ingratiate oneself with an invader than by adopting their customs and their love of cricket? In his 1897 book *A Chronicle of Cricket*, Shapoorjee Sorabjee described how the Parsis began playing cricket:

> *'Some enthusiastic boys at first only gleefully watched from a distance the game played at Fort George, and then hunted after and returned the balls from the field to the players. For such gratis services rendered heartily and joyfully the officers sometimes called them to handle the bat, which was done with extreme pleasure and delight... thus were learnt the initiatory practical lessons in cricket by the Parsis.'*

This vast forty-acre playing field outside Fort George (it had been cleared by the British to provide soldiers with a clear field of fire from the fort) was known as the Esplanade Maidan. It hosted myriad sporting activities, and it was here that the Parsis began playing among each other. The enthusiasm with which the Parsis embraced cricket didn't escape the Hindu elite. Not wishing to see their rivals steal a march on them with the British, the Hindus formed their own club in Bombay in 1866 called the Bombay Hindu Union Cricket Club. In 1875 – fifteen years after the demolition of Fort George – the British established the Bombay Gymkhana ('Club' in Hindi) and shamefully sectioned off a part of the Maidan so it was out of bounds to dogs and Indians. They did deign to play a Parsi XI and, though they won, the British didn't have quite the easy ride they'd expected.

In 1886 the Parsis formed their own Gymkhana club, and the same year they toured England under Dr D.H. Patel. According to the official BCCI website, the squad was given a rousing send-off by Pherozeshah Mehta, 'one of the eminent Indians of the time'. He told the players: 'As artists go to Italy to do homage to the Great Masters, or as pilgrims go to Jerusalem to worship at a shrine, so now the Parsis are going to England to pay homage to the English cricketers, to learn something of that noble and manly pastime in the very country that is cricket's chosen home.'

The tourists performed creditably in England, losing nineteen and drawing eight of their matches, though the tour was unsuccessful financially. When the Parsis toured again in 1888 under P.D. Kanga they returned to India having won eight, lost eleven and drawn twelve and without having sustained so great a financial loss.

In 1890 an English touring side sailed to India under the captaincy of George Vernon, the main aim being to play teams of fellow Englishmen. Lord Hawke was among the party but His Eminence was struck down with a severe case of gastritis not long after arriving in India. According to Hawke's biographer, James Coldham, by the time he was fit enough to rejoin the squad 'the tourists had completed nine fixtures, winning seven and losing only one, against a surprisingly capable Parsi XI in Bombay'. The Parsis had won by four wickets, Mehallasha Edulji Pavri the star turn with match figures of nine wickets for just 37 runs.

It was the Englishmen's only defeat of the eleven-match tour, and Indian cricket had won its respect.

Duke of Wellington's hat

The fact that the Iron Duke's hat makes our cut of cricket artefacts isn't because of the famous quip the Duke of Welllington was alleged to have made about the Battle of Waterloo being won on the playing fields of Eton. Cricket – or indeed any organised sport – was not played regularly at Eton at the time Napoleon's army was put to the sword at Waterloo.

Nonetheless, Wellington would have known all about cricket at the time of Waterloo. On Monday 12 June 1815, six days before the battle, officers from the Brigade of Guards played a match among themselves at Enghien, around 20 miles south-west of Brussels.

> The Napoleonic Wars erupted as cricket was becoming the sport of the people

According to the Belgium Cricket Association, Wellington watched the match, accompanied by the Fourth Duke of Richmond's sixteen-year-old daughter Lady Jane Lennox. The duke, one of the founding members of the MCC who also helped fund the purchase of Lord's (see chapter 28), took part in the match, and the family's tutor later described the occasion in a letter to a friend: 'The family are at present gone of Enghien to a cricket match among the gentlemen of the guards in which the Duke [of Richmond] takes part. You have of course heard of his fame as a cricketer; he was I believe considered one of the two best in England, the other is Ld. Frederic Beauclerc.'

Wellington may have enjoyed watching cricket, but his influence on the game was unintentionally damaging. The Napoleonic Wars erupted as cricket was becoming the sport of the people. What had been for much of the eighteenth century a pastime for the privileged was increasingly becoming a game played by the poor as well as the prosperous at the end of that century. But suddenly young men were called to the Colours, and cricket clubs suffered as a consequence.

The MCC, for example, played twenty-four matches in 1800 and just two in 1812, while the Harrow versus Eton match, first staged in 1805, wasn't contested again until 1818. Though all these institutions quickly began to thrive again after the British (and Prussian) triumph at Waterloo, the consequences of years of war had a disastrous effect on Britain's working class.

More than 300,000 soldiers and sailors returned home penniless and jobless to find the country ravaged by poor harvests and economic depression. Playing cricket was the last thing on these young men's minds. So while cricket soon picked up again among the well-off, the game stagnated among the poor. Some of these desperate souls turned to crime to find food and soon found themselves being transported in irons to Australia. Here, if and when they eventually gained their freedom, they would help establish cricket as the pre-eminent sport in Australia.

Back in England, meanwhile, cricket remained for the first half of the nineteenth century a sport predominantly played by a clique of well-off young men in southern England.

Tall black hat

At the risk of turning this book into a history of millinery, our fourteenth object is also a hat. This hat is tall, black and fashionable, as worn by William Clarke's All-England XI when they toured the country in the late 1840s.

Few people had as much impact on nineteenth-century cricket as William Clarke. Such was his influence that

in Harry Altham's 1926 book, *A History of Cricket*, the author bracketed Clarke alongside William Lillywhite and W.G. Grace when it came to cricket 'immortality'.

So who was William Clarke? When William Denison published his *Sketches of Players* in 1846 he shed some light on the man. Born in Nottingham on 24 December 1798, he was 5 feet 9 inches and a touch under 14 stone. His sturdy proportions might have had something to do with the fact he was a 'licensed victualler'. Denison continued:

'He kept the celebrated Trent Bridge Cricket Ground, about a mile out of the town of Nottingham, and has long been known in the matches played in all the Northern and Midland districts of England, as a cricketer of no mean capabilities.' Underarm bowling was Clarke's forte, and Denison noted that in the 1845 season he had taken 106 wickets in twelve matches, 'producing an average of 8¾ per match'.

Denison's book was published in the same year, 1846, that Clarke found the team where he would make his name and warrant his place among cricket's immortals. The seeds of the side had been sown the previous year when Clarke staged a match at the Trent Bridge ground he managed between his Nottinghamshire XI and a team billed as 'England'. The game was a commercial triumph, and Clarke saw an opportunity not only to popularise cricket throughout England, but also to make himself rich.

Clarke was a man of sturdy proportions, a 'licensed victualler'

He moved to London, wheedled his way into the capital's cricket community – even bowling to MCC members – and fine-tuned his plan for a touring team of professional players. Clarke called it the Eleven of England, but it soon came to be known as the All-England XI. 'There had, of course, been England sides before,' explained Altham. 'But they had been elevens selected either by the MCC or by private backers... never before had anyone thought of organising and maintaining in the field for a series of matches, and over a period of years, a side that represented the very cream of English cricket.'

The idea took a while to gather momentum. Their first match was in August 1846, a five-wicket defeat against Twenty of Sheffield. It was another year until their next match, but then the All-England XI began to capture the public imagination, owing in no small part to Clarke's promotional strategy. Asked by James Dark, proprietor of Lord's at the time, why he was taking his team to Newcastle instead of playing all his matches in the south of England, Clarke replied: 'I shall play sides strong or weak, with numbers or with bowlers given, and I shall play all over the country too – mark my words – and it will make good for cricket.'

The All-England XI did indeed 'make good for cricket'. Clarke assembled the best players in the English game, described by John Major as 'the forerunners of Kerry Packer's cricket circus one and a quarter centuries later' (see chapter 62). Among the players were: Alfred Mynn, nicknamed 'The Lion of Kent' and the Ian Botham of his day; Nicholas Felix, a brilliant left-handed batsman and the man credited with inventing batting gloves; an ageing William Lillywhite, signed up more for his reputation than his prowess; and John Wisden, the best all-rounder of his day and the man who founded the eponymous cricket almanack. The players dressed like the stars that they were, in white shirts with red stripes, black boots and tall fashionable hats.

Between 1846 and 1849 Clarke's All-England XI toured the country, winning twenty-seven of its fifty-one matches and losing just eleven. As their fame spread so their fixture list became ever more crowded – by 1851 they were playing thirty-four matches in the season, and the demands on the players were becoming intolerable.

The stagecoach was still the standard mode of transport and travelling was prodigious

In an age when the stagecoach was still the standard mode of transport for long distances, the travelling was prodigious. 'Often the eleven would travel down from the North all through the night to play in one of the big fixtures in London, or find themselves condemned to a five or six hours' coach drive in the dark through the muddy lanes of Devonshire and Cornwall, or over the bleak flats of Lincolnshire,' wrote Altham.

In return the players were paid between three and five guineas a match, not much considering they were the best in the land. They asked for more, but Clarke wouldn't budge; he even took a cut from any sponsorship deal a player might land. Yet he was becoming a very rich man, acculmulating wealth from the thousands of cricket fans who paid to watch their heroes at grounds up and down the country.

Eventually the players revolted, led by John Wisden, who in 1852 established the United All-England XI to rival Clarke's side. Most of the players Wisden recruited were those who had narrowly missed out on selection for the All-England XI – good enough, in other words, to pose a serious threat to the hegemony of Clarke.

Nonetheless, Clarke's XI continued to tour. In 1854 they were in Bristol, and a five-year-old boy was taken by his father to watch them. All he remembered in his later years was that the players 'wore top hats'. The boy's name was William Gilbert Grace.

Clarke died two years later, two months after he had played his last game for the All-England XI against Whitehaven. Yet he had set in train an idea that continued for thirty more years until the emergence of an official England Test XI finally made the all-star teams redundant.

'They were truly missionaries of cricket,' wrote Harry Altham, 'winning to knowledge and appreciation of the game whole districts where hitherto it had been primitive and undeveloped.'

Kit bag

The cricketer's kit bag, or the 'coffin' as it's euphemistically known in the trade, contains all the essentials – trousers, shirt, boots, pads, gloves and cap.

In essence it's changed little over the last 100-odd years, save for the invention of polyester shirts and boots that come with 'Climate Control' features. 'Piffle!' as W.G. Grace might have exclaimed. Then again, he would probably have donned a pair of climate-control boots, complete with 'Thermo Plastic Heel Counter' and 'Ultra Lightweight "Nickel Plated" Spikes' – provided the price was right. Grace was never one to turn down an opportunity to make a quick buck and, given the chance, he would have put sponsors' cash before sartorial elegance.

As it is, he had to make do with what was on offer, so we thought it only fair we let the good doctor describe for himself the contents of the cricketer's kit bag. He was writing at the end of 1887, in an essay published in *Cricket* by A.G. Steel and R.H. Lyttleton, but his words ring true today.

He began his essay in characteristically forthright fashion, declaring: 'I propose to say something about everything that is needful in the outfit of a cricketer, beginning with his personal clothing.'

Shirts: 'It was no unusual sight ten or twenty years ago to find an eleven or country twenty-two dressed in all the colours of the rainbow. White is now usually worn, and it certainly looks better and cooler than any other colour.'

Trousers: 'Be sure to try on every new pair of trousers when sent home from the tailor's, or you may find out when too late to rectify the mistake that they are either too small or too large, and are completely useless. A revelation of this kind when you arrive on the cricket field and are getting ready to go in is destructive alike to high scoring and sweetness of temper.'

Caps: 'I think indispensable and preferable to any kind of hats, unless in very hot weather under a broiling sun, when some protection to the neck and back of the head is necessary. 1887 was one of the hottest seasons I ever played through, but only once did I change my cap for a hat with a large brim.'

Sweaters: 'Jackets and jerseys, or "sweaters", as they are commonly called, have their place in the outfit of a cricketer... a jersey or sweater is preferable; it fits closer to the body, is much pleasanter, and in the field on a very cold day it helps to keep you warm...'

Socks: 'They are better made plain, not ribbed, and in natural colours they are more comfortable and do not mark the feet.'

Boots: 'Have them made of brown or white leather. It is rather difficult to say what is the best thickness for the sole... I always wear thick soled boots with low flat heels; by having the heels low and flat you are not nearly so likely to sprain or twist your ankle as you would be with high and narrow ones. To prevent slipping it is necessary to wear spikes or nails in your boots or shoes. Be careful what sort of spikes or nails you use; I prefer short spikes, which are made in different sizes and can be screwed into the boots in a very short time... I should advise all cricketers who play often to have two pairs of boots, one with short spikes or nails which will hold and prevent

> Grace would have donned a pair of climate-control boots – provided the price was right

slipping on a hard dry ground, and the other with longer spikes for a soft, wet spongy ground.'

Pads: 'When choosing pads see that they are exactly your size and fit well, for large, heavy and uncomfortable pads will do as much to tire you out in a long innings as hard hitting.'

Gloves: 'When purchasing gloves... see that the rubber on the fingers of the right-hand glove comes down slightly over the tops of the fingers, and on the side of the thumb instead of the back.'

And finally W.G. had this to say about the cricketer's kit bag:

One made of good leather is preferable to any other sort. Mind you have it large enough to hold everything you can possible require. Have a strong lock and key for it, and straps as well. Have your name inscribed in the brass round the lock, and your initials painted in plain bold letters on the side. In the hurry of hand-shaking and bustle to catch a train the wrong bag has been often taken for want of this simple precaution.

No need for Grace to paint his name on the side of his kit bag; the sight of the initials W.G would have been enough to strike the fear of God into any absent-minded player.

Redgum tree

You'll remember that in chapter 13 we discussed the increasing number of wretched working-class men and women transported from England to Australia in the early years of the nineteenth century.

They were joined there by voluntary emigrants, an intrepid breed brave enough to gamble on a better life in a prison colony on the other side of the world. Yet while they had left the Old Country behind, those sunburned settlers brought with them to Australia some reminders of their previous lives, cricket being one of them.

The Hobart Cricket Club was formed in Tasmania in 1832, followed six years later by the Melbourne Cricket Club. According to Alf Batchelder's *Pavilions in the Park*, from the mid-1840s onwards Melbourne played their matches close to what is today the site of Crown Casino. 'It was an attractive location, with the Yarra flowing between lovely green banks shaded by gum trees,' writes Batchelder, who added that the club had 'squatted' on the ground.

In 1847 the Melbourne Cricket Club began playing matches against Geelong, and four years later they met Launceston in Tasmania in what is regarded as the inaugural first-class match in Australian cricket. In March 1852 the Tasmanians came to Victoria for a reciprocal fixture, by which time Melbourne's cricketers were already in search of a new home. The problem with their existing ground was the drainage, or lack of it. In November 1849, for example, the Yarra burst its banks and flooded the cricket pitch while a game was in progress.

The ground they selected for their new home was an area of 'undulating, well-timbered bushland' that separated Melbourne from Richmond, a suburb containing hundreds of small tenements belonging to those families not rich enough to live in the city centre.

The bushland was the home to the Wurundjeri Aborigine tribe, two of whose scarred trees remain near the present-day MCG, but that was of no concern to the white settlers. In 1853 Lieutenant-Governor Latrobe authorised the club to take up residence on the Aboriginal land, and soon labourers were cutting down redgums and carting them off to be burnt.

By September 1854 the new Melbourne Cricket Ground – complete with pavilion – was hosting matches, the first on the thirtieth of the month between teams of members led by William Philpott and George Cavenagh, editor of the *Herald* newspaper.

The new ground accelerated the popularisation of cricket in Victoria. The state boasted seventy clubs by 1861, while Tasmania, South Australia and New South Wales had also fallen in love with the game. On Christmas Eve that same year the first party of cricket tourists to visit Australia from England landed in Melbourne, led by H.H. Stephenson and promoted by Messrs Spiers and Pond. The entrepreneurs enticed some of the country's best players with a fee of £150 plus all expenses covered.

In 1849 the Yarra burst its banks and flooded the cricket pitch while a game was in progress

Over 19,000 people greeted the tourists in Melbourne; and the clamour to see them in the flesh continued, forcing the players to drive 'some miles to a secret destination in the bush, in order that they might have some peace from the attentions of their admirers'.

They played their first match on New Year's Day, at the Melbourne Cricket Ground, defeating the host team by an innings and 36 runs in front of 15,000 spectators. The Englishmen liked what they saw of the Melbourne Ground, regarding its water supply, pavilion and grandstand capable of seating 6,000 as far superior to anything back home.

There were signs on the pitch that Australia would soon be a force in cricket. Of the twelve matches the tourists played, they won six, four were drawn and there were two defeats – against Castlemaine and a combined NSW & Victoria team. One of the party, Charles Lawrence of Surrey, was so taken with Australia that he remained there, accepting an offer to coach cricket at the Albert Club in Sydney.

When Lawrence did eventually return to England, in 1868, he took with him a party of thirteen Aboriginal tourists. They were the first Australian cricket team to visit England, and though they were patronised by the press and public alike – crowds were as interested in their boomerang throwing as they were their bowling – the Aborigines won fourteen and drew nineteen of their forty-seven matches.

In between the 1861 tour to Australia and the visit of the Aboriginal party to England there had been a second tour Down Under led by George Parr in 1863/64. This did not enjoy the success of the first, at least not off the field, where the Englishmen were regarded as on the make and more interested in money than cricket. A further ten years would pass before an English team would return to Australia, by which time the young country was able to compete with a side including the likes of W.G. Grace. 'We may one day see an Australian XI at Lord's,' declared a haughty *Bell's Life* in reviewing the tour.

Indeed they would, but before that there would be humiliation on a grand scale – and at the Melbourne Cricket Ground of all places.

1859 photograph

England against Australia. The Ashes. Just the mention of the word gets the spine tingling. Yet it might have been so different had the subject of our next object, captured in this photograph, taken to cricket. Evidence exists that the United States of America were playing cricket decades before anyone in Australia picked up a bat with a New York XI beating a side from London as early as 1751.

Nearly a century later, in 1844, the United States met Canada in New York in what is generally accepted to be the first ever international cricket match. Canada batted first and were all out for 82, 18 more than the Americans made as David Winkworth and Freddy French ripped through the home side's batting order.

An estimated 15,000 spectators watched the match, and the following year the USA travelled to Canada for the rematch.

In 1859 George Parr, who four years later would lead the second England touring party to Australia, skippered a side on a tour of Canada and the USA. The tour was three years in the planning, money being the primary issue at stake. Eventually the Montreal Club guaranteed to pay the twelve players £50 each plus all expenses.

USA was playing cricket decades before anyone in Australia

The party sailed out on the SS *Nova Scotian*, posing for a photo on deck which we've chosen as our seventeenth object. It wasn't a particularly agreeable crossing; rough weather confined most of the squad to their quarters, but their mood was soon brightened upon landing in Canada. 'The opening match at Montreal was well patronised,' wrote Harry Altham in *A History of Cricket*, 'especially by the fair sex.'

The tourists were too strong for the home side, winning by eight wickets and, after a royal feast in the prestigious St Lawrence Hotel, they departed for New York. Two thousand people were waiting for the tourists when they arrived, and a further 23,000 came to the game to see England crush New York by an innings and 64 runs.

The excitement continued in Philadelphia, where a thousand young women looked on daintily from the ladies' stand as the tourists won by seven wickets.

Parr's side won their remaining two matches and reached Liverpool on 11 November after what everyone agreed was a successful tour. As well as winning all their matches and becoming acquainted with many wholesome young ladies, the players pocketed nearly £100 each from their two-month trip.

Cricket had clearly taken root in the United States, and more than a few of the tourists expected to return in the near future on a second tour. But within eighteen months of the tour, the USA descended into civil war. Instead, as we've just seen, England's cricketers took up offers to tour Australia.

Peace returned to the States in 1865, but cricket never again enjoyed the levels of popularity that it had pre-war. John Major has suggested that 'it was perhaps too leisurely a sport for such a young and thrusting nation'. But if this were true, why did cricket find such success in Australia, even younger and arguably more thrusting than America?

The truth is that more and more immigrants came to America in the second half of the nineteenth century. What self-respecting Irish, German or Italian would want to play cricket, a sport seen as representative of the British Empire? Instead they played baseball, and where cricket did survive in the States – notably in Philadelphia (the club was founded in 1854) – it was played by men of British descent. But even here cricket gradually died out, and in 1924 the Philadelphian club disbanded its cricket team.

Nearly three-quarters of a century later, the club was resurrected by the Philadelphia Sporting Club's director of tennis – a New Zealander!

Eden Gardens

Eden Gardens in Kolkata has been described as 'cricket's answer to the Coliseum' and few who have experienced the atmosphere inside the stadium would disagree.

When South Africa returned to international cricket in 1991 following their sporting isolation, captain Clive Rice led them to India for a series of three one-day internationals, the first time the two countries had met. 'On the day of the [first] match, we walked into our first "Wall of Sound",' recalled Rice in an interview with the *Indian Express* in 2011. 'It was the most unbelievable experience of my life. And I don't think I will have another day like that.'

The history of Eden Gardens, with a 90,000 capacity the second-largest cricket stadium in the world behind the 100,000-seater Melbourne Cricket Ground, began in 1864.

Seventy-two years earlier, in 1792, the Calcutta Cricket Club came into existence, its first match reputed to be a match between the Gentlemen of Calcutta and the Gentlemen of Barrackpore on 23 February 1792.

For the next half-century the site of the present stadium was open land to the north of Fort William and at the western corner of the Esplanade, overlooking the Strand on the Hooghly. Then in 1840 the then Governor-General of Calcutta, Lord Auckland, a green-fingered ruler, decided to turn the scrubland to the north of Fort William into a garden and park. Once complete the park was known as the Auckland Circus Gardens, but it was rechristened Eden Gardens by the early 1850s, and, according to an article in Calcutta's *Telegraph* newspaper, in 1856 'a Burmese pagoda of exquisite beauty was installed in the park by Lord Dalhousie [and] a band of musicians was in attendance every evening to entertain the prominent citizens who came to enjoy the fresh breeze'.

In 1864 the eastern perimeter of Eden Gardens' parkland was expanded so that the Calcutta Cricket Club could play matches without disturbing those enjoying the 'exquisite beauty' of the gardens. A thatched hut was erected as a pavilion, replaced in the early 1870s by a permanent structure measuring 125 by 25 feet and constructed of the finest teak transported from Burma. Now the British felt they had a ground of which to be proud, one that wouldn't have looked out of place in Sussex or Surrey.

When George Vernon brought an English touring side to India in the winter of 1899/90, their first match was against the Calcutta Club at Eden Gardens, and when they played a Bengal XI in their next fixture the same venue was used. By now cricket in Calcutta was spreading among the local population as it had among the Parsis and Hindus in Bombay. 'The locals were thrilled at the sight of Englishmen playing cricket, which resembled indigenous games such as danguli and pittu,' explained the *Telegraph*. 'The princely families of Cooch Behar and Natore and, to an extent, the zamindars of Rangpur, Jessore, Murapara and Mymensingh patronized the game with the fervour of crusaders.'

> The zaminders of Rangpur patronized the game with the fervour of crusaders

In 1926 England sent a team under Arthur Gilligan to play thirty-four matches in India, Ceylon and Burma. No Tests were played, but when the tourists returned in 1933/34 – led by Douglas Jardine of Bodyline infamy – they played three, including the second at Eden Gardens which ended in a draw.

Riots, stampedes and crowd disturbances have blighted Eden Gardens in the last fifty years, leading to the famous old stadium's recent facelift. Gone is some of its unique sprawling charm, replaced by concrete and bucket seats. 'The days of cucumber-tomato sandwiches and luchi-alurdom gulped down with fresh oranges and endless cups of tea are over,' wrote Raju Mukherji in 2011. Yet despite all the modernisation, 'the same spirit still remains, the spirit that overcomes barriers. Eden Gardens will continue to weave its spell on generations of cricket lovers and cricket players in the days to come.'

Wisden

Where would the humble cricket fan be without our next object? Groping in the dark, most probably, like a nightwatchman seeing out the last over of the day.

Wisden first hit the shops in 1864, and 149 years later it's still unbeaten, surviving two world wars and a late-twentieth century technological revolution that has swept away so many venerable publications.

That wasn't envisaged when John Solan looked into cricket's crystal ball in the 1964 edition of *Wisden* to imagine how the game might possibly alter by the time the Almanack celebrated its 200th anniversary. 'Fashions will have changed, no doubt, but not cricket,' proclaimed Solan. He believed the average reader, while 'oiling his bat and debating whether it's going to be the Moon again for a holiday this year', would be 'the only sporting figure in the world, or in outer space, to be dressed in long trousers and, in moments of retrospection, will be harbouring dark thoughts that cricket is not what it was'.

FIFTEENTH EDITION.

JOHN WISDEN'S

Cricketers' Almanack for 1878:

A RECORD

OF

THE FULL SCORES AND BOWLING SUMMARIES

OF THE

PRINCIPAL MATCHES PLAYED IN 1877,

WITH

OTHER INFORMATION USEFUL AND INTERESTING

TO CRICKETERS.

LONDON:

PUBLISHED AND SOLD BY JOHN WISDEN AND CO.,

AT THEIR

CRICKETING AND BRITISH SPORTS DEPÔT,

21, *Cranbourn Street, near Leicester Square, W.C.*

ONE SHILLING.]   [POST FREE 1s. 1½D.

Entered at Stationers' Hall.

Cricket might not be what it was forty-nine years on, but *Wisden* most certainly is. The 1864 edition of cricket's yellow bible ran to 112 pages, nearly 1,000 fewer than the 1,055 pages of *Wisden*'s centenary issue. The 2012 edition was a whopping 1,648 pages, the first to be edited by Lawrence Booth and one which was warmly reviewed by cricket author Duncan Hamilton, who captured the essence of sport's most illustrious tome. 'What constitutes a "good" *Wisden* must be the joint creation of poets and manual workers: a judicious, lyrical mix of contemporary issues, historical reflection and cold statistics,' wrote Hamilton. 'The Almanack's 149th edition... fulfils these criteria.'

Those cold, hard statistics have been the staple of *Wisden* ever since it was first published. Whether it's scorecards from Test matches, record fifth-wicket partnerships or results from every nation's domestic league, you'll find it in *Wisden*. So what better way to honour *Wisden*'s comprehensive contribution to cricket than by returning the favour with six stats of our own.

1. *Wisden* has been its current size ever since the inaugural edition, and its initial price of one shilling remained in place until 1915. The 2012 edition cost £50.

2. The first advertisement to appear in the Almanack was in 1867 when John Wisden promoted his sports company's patent catapult, 'the principle of working which will be shown at No2, New Coventry Street, Leicester Square'.

3. The *Wisden* cover motif of two gentlemen in top hats playing cricket first appeared on the 1938 issue, the same year it adopted its distinctive yellow colour. The motif is based on a wood cutting by Eric Ravilious, killed four years later while serving with the RAF as a war artist.

4. The obituary section began in 1872, recording the deaths the previous year of fifteen cricketers. Prominent among the deceased was Henry Mills Grace, father of W.G., who had nurtured his son's love of the game as a child. Only when

Sydney Pardon became editor in 1891, however, was a full obituaries section commissioned.

5. In 1889 editor Charles Pardon initiated a new feature in *Wisden*, commissioning 'new portraits, specially photographed by Hawkins of Brighton, of six of the most prominent and skilful [bowlers]'. The idea proved a hit with readers, resulting in a second edition of *Wisden* being printed for the first time, and by 1897 'it had developed into that much-loved and delightfully argumentative feature, Five Cricketers of the Year'.

6. *Wisden* has retained the 'Almanack' nomenclature even though it stopped devoting serious attention to non-cricketing events, phenomena and anniversaries in 1879. This was in marked contrast to early editions when, as the 1964 edition explained, readers were informed that the 'British Museum closes on January 1st and... carpets were first manufactured in Kidderminster'. From 1879 *Wisden* contained a single-page calendar, but this was curtailed in 1941, leaving future generations of readers clueless about the quality of Kidderminster's carpets.

W.G. Grace's beard

William Gilbert Grace, aka W.G., was the most famous English cricketer of all time and the most popular sportsman in Victorian Britain. He was Ian Botham and Freddie Flintoff wrapped into one enormous girth, a larger-than-life character who appealed to rich and poor, young and old, male and female.

In fact, the only people Grace didn't much appeal to were umpires – and that was because he preferred his own judgement to theirs.

But where do you start in trying to describe his impact on cricket? We're going for the beard, synonymous

with the big man thanks to Archibald John Stuart Wortley's oil painting that hangs in the National Portrait Gallery.

If the truth be told, it's a little unfair to W.G. that his name now conjures up an image of ample girth and ample beard. For in his youth he was one of the finest athletes in England; unfortunately that was an era before film, and no one captured him running the 440 yards in seventy seconds in the National and Olympian Association meeting at Crystal Palace, less than twenty-four hours after he had scored 224 not out for an All-England team against Surrey. Nor are there any photographs of his 6-feet-2-inches and 12-stone frame playing football for the Wanderers, nor of his hunting or running with beagles. Instead, what we have to remind ourselves of England's most famous cricketer is the beetle brow above the bushy beard.

But enough of appearance and more of achievements, for this is why W.G. makes our list (and this isn't the time or the place, by the way, to dwell on his various misdemeanours, which, like his beard and his girth, were ample).

On the centenary of his birth, in 1948, the annual Gentlemen vs Players Match at Lord's was dedicated to his honour, the same ground where in 1923 the Grace Gates were erected. A special scorecard was issued for the match, on the back of which was printed a list of Grace's achievements, including:

- 54,896 runs scored and 2,876 wickets taken in forty-four seasons of first-class cricket (1865 to 1908).

- On his last appearance for the Gentlemen, in 1906, at the Oval, he made 74 on his fifty-eighth birthday. In eighty-four matches against the Players he scored over 6,000 runs and took 271 wickets.

- In 1880 he scored 152 against Australia in the first Test match played in this country.

- In 1876 he scored 839 runs in three consecutive innings against Kent, Nottinghamshire and Yorkshire.

- On fourteen occasions he scored a century and took ten or more wickets in the same match.

At the end of the 1887 season – Grace's most prolific of the decade, in which he scored 2,062 runs at an average of 54 – he contributed a chapter to *Cricket* co-authored by A.G. Steel and R.H. Lyttleton. Grace's chapter was 'How To Score', and he had this to say to his readers:

I cannot recollect many of my big innings that were not the results of strict obedience to the rules which govern the training for all important athletic contests. Temperance in food and drink, regular sleep and exercise, I have laid down as the golden rule from my earliest cricketing days. I have carefully adhered to this rule, and to it in cricket history, and the measure of health and strength I still enjoy.

Grace died in 1915, seven years after his last game of cricket. But in those seven years, oh, how the world had changed. Man reached the North and South Poles, the first American–European radiotelegraph service was established, an aircraft flew over the English Channel, the *Titanic* went down and then, in 1914, the world went to war. A year later, as German airships began to bomb southern England, chased by the aircraft of the Royal Flying Corps, a friend bumped into Grace in the street. He was haggard and drawn, glancing nervously towards the sky. 'You can't be frightened by aeroplanes,' the friend chided. 'You, old man, who had Ernest Jones [a great Australian fast bowler] bowling through your beard.' Grace looked at his friend and replied: 'That was different. I could see that Jones and see what he was at. I can't see the aeroplanes.'

On the centenary of Grace's birth the great cricket writer Neville Cardus explored his continued hold on our imagination. Why Grace? Why not any of those other great names from cricket's Golden Age? Of course, there was his brilliance – Cardus described Grace as 'the father of all modern batmanship'. But there was more to it than that; he was a link to the Victorian age when indeed there were no aeroplanes, no radio and little sports photography. So much more was left to the imagination. So much more seemed romantic, so that even Grace's gamesmanship, his sledging and his downright cheating became somehow gentler.

But above all, concluded Cardus, Grace is so woven into the tapestry of cricket, and of English cricket in particular, because of his beard. 'Those whiskers were crucial,' declared Cardus. 'They created the sense of authority. The present age has yielded much by taking to the razor.'

Gold medal

The last time we were in Australia, W.G. Grace was captaining a tour party that played fifteen matches, none of which was given first-class status. That trip had been plagued by division within the tourists' camp, the professionals and amateurs not mixing well.

So when England accepted an invitation to visit Australia in 1876, captain James Lillywhite took only professionals. The amateurs were left at home – as was W.G. Grace, studying for his medical exams – all of which would form a convenient excuse following events at the Melbourne Cricket Ground in March 1877.

Gold medals were struck by the Victoria Cricket Association to mark the first ever official Test match between Australia and England, the player's name on the reverse and on the obverse a pair of crossed cricket bats, stumps and a ball.

England arrived in Melbourne on 15 March after a whistlestop tour of New Zealand, during which they'd played eight matches and lost the services of their wicketkeeper, Ted Pooley, thrown in jail for 'dastardly conduct' after a betting scandal.

Australia, however, had problems of their own in selecting their strongest XI for the inaugural Test. A row between the Victoria and New South Wales cricket boards spilled over into the dressing room with fast bowler Fred Spofforth refusing to play because of selection issues. Frank Allen was nominated as Spofforth's replacement, but he turned down the invitation, preferring to visit a local fair instead.

The MCG looked a picture on 15 March as the Australian openers walked out to bat. The ground that had so impressed the first party of English cricketers fifteen years earlier had been further developed in recent years. A second stand had been built at the northern end, capable of holding 2,000 spectators, and it was known as 'Reversible Stand' because in the winter the seating could be reversed so people could watch football in Yarra Park.

Play began shortly after 1 p.m. with Alfred Shaw bowling the first delivery to Charles Bannerman, regarded as Australia's finest batsman. Not long into his innings Bannerman was dropped – 'a sitter', as one of the Englishmen said later. By the time he retired hurt with a damaged finger Bannerman had scored 165 out of Australia's 240 for seven. England wrapped up the tail for just a further five runs and then went out to bat. Harry Jupp top-scored with 63, but the tourists were dismissed for 196. Australia failed to capitalise on their 49-run lead, collapsing to 104 all out with Alfred Shaw taking five of their wickets in front of a crowd of 10,000 on the third day.

England's Ted Pooley was thrown in jail for 'dastardly conduct'

That left England requiring 153 for victory. They were in trouble from the start, losing opener Allen Hill for a duck, and were eventually all out for 108. The Australians had won by 45 runs (by a quirk of fate exactly the same winning margin when the two nations contested the Centenary Test in 1977) and the press went wild. It was, declared *The Australian*, 'no ordinary triumph', and it was down to the fact that the 'combined team worked together with the utmost harmony and goodwill'.

It was more than just a sporting triumph for Australia. The victory gave the young nation self-confidence – if not yet a swagger, then certainly a belief in its own abilities and a realisation that England wasn't invincible.

The two sides met again a fortnight later, also at Melbourne, and this time the English gained revenge, winning by four wickets thanks to two half-centuries from Yorkshireman George Ulyet. Nonetheless, the Australian press and public viewed the series as a triumphant success, even taking into account that Bannerman and two of his teammates were English born. 'It shows that in bone as muscle, activity, athletic vigour, and success in field sports, the Englishmen born in Australia do not fall short of the Englishmen born in Surrey or Yorkshire,' commented one paper.

James Lillywhite returned to England impressed by what he had seen of Australian cricket. Within a few months he began making plans to bring an Australian side to the Old Country for a tour; cricket rivalry between Australia and England was about to become even more intense.

Iron safe

In 1882 this particular iron safe had an adornment: the derrière of one Charles Alcock, who was sat upon it, head in his hands, weeping at the death of English cricket, whose obituary was subsequently displayed in the *Sporting Times*.

History has allowed the name Charles Alcock to slip through its hands like a thick outside edge from a tail-ender. For here was a man who helped shape both cricket and football for decades, even centuries, to come through a combination of foresight and deft administration. So what was it Alcock contributed to cricket in the latter half of the nineteenth century? Born in 1842 and schooled at Harrow, Alcock's first love was football. He and his brother John founded the Forest Club (later the Wanderers FC) in 1859, and both men were instrumental in establishing the Football Association in the 1860s. Establishing the FA was one thing, but it was Alcock who popularised football in the early 1870s with the introduction in 1872 of the FA Cup, a tournament won in its inaugural year by Alcock's own Wanderers (he captained them in the final against the Royal Engineers in front of 2,000 fans at the Oval).

In fact, 1872 was a momentous year for Alcock: aside from leading Wanderers to victory in the FA Cup he umpired the first official football international between England and Scotland, and he was appointed secretary of Surrey Cricket Club. This was a masterstroke on the part of Surrey Cricket Club, for Alcock was a visionary who saw the potential of the Oval, sporting and financial.

Throughout the 1870s the Oval hosted England at football and rugby union, staged FA Cup Finals and was the venue for tennis matches. In 1878 the ground welcomed the touring Australians, a crowd of 20,000 (who were charged double the ordinary admission fee by Alcock – a shilling instead of sixpence) enjoying the sight of Alec Bannerman and Fred Spofforth in their prime.

As well as nurturing football and cricket, the indefatigable Alcock also founded and edited two magazines – *Football Annual* and *Cricket* – through which he spread his visions for both sports.

History has allowed Charles Alcock to slip through its hands like a thick outside edge from a tail-ender

Foremost among Alcock's beliefs was that the best way to promote a sport was through competition. Never a fan of rugby union, Alcock couldn't warm to a sport where most matches (at club level, at least) were meaningless friendlies. Having given football the FA Cup, Alcock proposed creating a one-day competition for cricket. Rebuffed on this front, he turned his attention to Test cricket.

When Billy Murdoch's Australian side arrived in England in 1880 they found fixtures hard to come by. Their predecessors of two years earlier had sullied the reputation of Australian cricket with their 'commercial spirit' and few counties were willing to play them. But while others shied away, Alcock stepped forward, seizing upon the tourists' blank schedule to suggest an inaugural Test match between England and Australia to be staged at the Oval.

The Aussies were keen, so too, surprisingly, was Lord Harris, the 'premier cricket-playing peer', who usually had the last word on cricketing fixtures in England. His Lordship skippered the side (was that how Alcock won him over?) and W.G. Grace forfeited a week's shooting to open the batting in what would be his first Test.

He duly scored a ton on his debut as England racked up a daunting 420 in their first innings. Australia were skittled out for 149 in reply (Fred Morley taking five for 56), though they fared better in following on, scoring 327, with Murdoch making a sparkling century. But England knocked off the runs to win the first Test match on English soil.

Two years later the Aussies were back and intent on revenge (as we shall see shortly), and though Alcock was left sitting on his safe with his head on his hands, the feeling of despair was fleeting. He continued to innovate for the rest of the century, turning Surrey into the strongest county in England and in 1885 averting a civil war in football by persuading the FA to vote for the professionalisation of the game.

Alcock has been hard done by history, ignored while others with grander titles or bigger mouths have claimed the credit for much of his work. As John Major says: 'Alcock deserves a higher place in the mythology of the game than history has yet given him.' So here's our small contribution in elevating Alcock – a safe, rather fitting for a man whose perspicacity enriched both football and cricket.

Ashes urn

> In Affectionate Remembrance
> of
> **ENGLISH CRICKET**
> which died at the Oval
> on
> **29th August, 1882**
> Deeply lamented by a large circle of
> Sorrowing Friends and Acquaintances
> R.I.P.
> N.B. – The body will be cremated,
> and the Ashes taken to Australia

So ran the obituary notice in the *Sporting Times*, composed by journalist Reginald Brooks a few days after Australia had left Charles Alcock sitting on his safe with his head in his hands. Australia's victory by seven runs in a low-scoring match (the only score of note was Australian opener Hugh Massie's 55 in the second innings) stunned the whole of England. In the final half-hour of the match, as England chased their target in front of a crowd of 20,000, 'one spectator dropped down dead, and another with his teeth gnawed out pieces from his umbrella handle'. Nerves were as taut in the hosts' dressing room as England ran inexorably out of batsmen. One batsman went out to bat, 'ashen grey' and trembling from head to foot. He didn't last long, another victim of the incomparable Fred Spofforth, who finished with match figures of fourteen wickets for 90 runs after taking offence at the start of the match to derogatory comments about Australians (or 'Cornstalks', the English nickname for colonials because their children grew fast and thin). The 6-feet-3-inch Australian, nicknamed the 'Demon', was carried shoulder-high from the ground at the end of the match, and later immortalised by *Punch*:

> *Well done, Cornstalks, whipt us*
> *Fair and Square.*
> *Was it luck that tripped us?*
> *Was it scare?*
> *Kangaroo land's 'Demon' or our own*
> *Want of devil, coolness, nerve, backbone?*

Australia departed leaving behind an England in turmoil. Three years previously her army had been humiliated in battle by the Zulus at Isandlwana (incidentally, some of the British officers had in their trunks their 'cricketing outfits' at the time their camp was overrun by the Zulus), and now her cricketers had experienced the ignominy of defeat to Australia. Was the nation in irreversible decline? Something had to be done, and it was – a touring party led by the Honourable Ivo Bligh was dispatched to Australia to restore England's prestige within weeks of the Oval defeat.

England sailed for Australia minus several of her stars, W.G. Grace, George Ulyett and Alfred Lyttelton among those missing, and there was a further setback when fast bowler Fred Morley broke several ribs when the squad's ship collided with another vessel 350 miles from Colombo.

Upon arriving in Australia Bligh declared it his intention to 'regain the ashes', and he got his chance to play for something tangible following a friendly match at Sunbury in Victoria in Christmas 1882. At the post-match reception, held at the home of Sir William Clarke, a group of ladies burned either a stump or a bail (historians disagree on what exactly it was), scooped the ashes into a small terracotta urn and handed it to Bligh. Bligh clearly appreciated the jape – he later married one of the ladies – and upon winning the third match against Australia he stated that the Ashes had indeed been won back. It's believed that the urn was formally presented to Bligh and his team at the conclusion of the Test series, by which time two labels had been pasted on. The top label read 'The Ashes' and underneath was, a verse from the *Melbourne Punch* of 1 February 1883 (probably published out of respect to the earlier London rhyme), which ran:

> *When Ivo goes back with the urn, the urn;*
> *Studds, Steel, Read and Tylecote return, return;*
> *The welkin will ring loud,*
> *The great crowd will feel proud,*
> *Seeing Barlow and Bates with the urn, the urn;*
> *And the rest coming home with the urn.*

Bligh, later Earl Darnley, kept the urn as a memento in his home at Cobham Hall, presumably not just of the cricket but of the day he met his future wife, and it wasn't until his death in 1927 that cricket's most famous trophy found its way to the MCC. The urn has been at Lord's ever since, housed in the museum (replicas are held aloft by winning captains at the end of each Ashes series), though in 2006 it went on a fourteen-week tour of Australian museums. The 4$\frac{1}{3}$-inch-high urn had its own business-class ticket for the 26,000-mile journey and was accompanied by three MCC minders, one of whom was Adam Chadwick, the curator of the Lord's Museum. 'I used to be an auctioneer so I'm used to putting prices on things that are unique,' Chadwick told reporters when

The urn had its own business-class ticket for its 2006 tour

asked for how much it had been insured. 'While we've settled on a seven-figure sum for the urn, if it got lost, broken or destroyed, no amount of money could fill the hole.'

In the 131 years since the *Sporting Life* mourned the death of English cricket, there have been 310 Ashes Test matches (up to the end of 2012) with Australia winning 123 to England's 100. Australia have enjoyed the greatest period of unbroken dominance, a nineteen-year period between 1934 and 1953 which included Don Bradman's Invincibles of 1948 (see chapter 46). England have had the upper hand in the last decade, but whatever the outcome of the back-to-back Ashes series in 2013 and 2014 there will be many more unforgettable matches to laud between Test cricket's oldest protagonists. 'The fight for the Ashes has produced more magical moments through its twisting and winding paths of fortune and anguish than any other sporting endeavour,' wrote Gordon Ross in his 1972 book *A History of Cricket*. 'Let us cherish those Australian ladies for what they did nearly ninety years ago.'

Scoreboard

In 2008 a new scoreboard was installed at Lord's, one which, as the press release explained, had 'three new permanent, state-of-the-art colour LED replay screens... each made of 88 modules that have been specially imported from Hong Kong'.

What was more, bragged the press release, 'the new screens are also more environmentally friendly, using less energy to power them. Around one-third of the power is required for all three new LED screens compared to the energy used by the pair of old bulb-based scoreboards.'

It was at Lord's where cricket's first scoreboard was installed, way back in 1846, when W.G. Grace was but a glint in his father's eye. Before then, all but the most keen-eyed spectators were ignorant of the state of the game – except when the scores were level, for then the two scorers stood up to indicate the fact.

Scorers, on the other hand, had been around for years. The earliest known scorecards were printed by a man called Pratt in 1776, scorer to the Sevenoaks Vine Club in Kent, but it took many years for his invention to catch on. Most scoring at this time was still done by men sitting on vantage points cutting 'notches' (runs) on tally sticks, as it had been for years. In 1706 William Goldwyn wrote a couplet about such an event:

Two trusted friends squat on the rising floor
To notch with knives on sticks, the mounting score.

The introduction of the scoreboard, however, revolutionised scoring. Now everyone could keep track of the day's play, and the first to fully exploit this enthusiasm for scoring was Fred Lillywhite of the famous cricketing family. In 1848 he used a portable printing press at grounds to print updated scorecards. So attached to scoring was Lillywhite that, when he toured North America with George Parr's side in 1859 (see chapter 17), he took 'his precious scoring-booth on wheels' with him and became a 'little querulous' with the way it was handled by the shipping company on the voyage across the Atlantic.

A year before that tour, in 1858, the Kennington Oval had introduced the first mobile scorebox, 'a house on rollers with figures for telegraphing on each side'. On the other side of the world, at the Melbourne Cricket Ground, a further innovation was unveiled in 1881 when a scoreboard appeared at the western end of the ground which gave the batsman's name and how he was out.

> Most scoring before 1776 involved cutting notches on tally sticks

Scoreboards at the main international stadiums today, like the one at Lord's, show colour action replays as well as keeping punters up to date with the score. When the refurbished Sydney Cricket Ground is unveiled in 2013 it will include an eye-boggling 3,000-square-foot video screen doubling as a scoreboard. 'The bigger and improved screen will provide even more enjoyment for fans with replays... plus full match scoring,' said an SCG spokesman. 'Modern day spectators the world over demand a large, high-resolution video screen to enhance their match day experience.'

Pith helmet

Hats and helmets have long been a tradition in cricket, but the reason for the inclusion of this particular type of headgear has little to do with the game itself.

We saw in chapter 23 that, after the Isandlwana massacre of British soldiers by Zulu forces in January 1879, alongside the regulation pith helmets of the fallen men were found cricket whites. When the British war correspondent H. Rider Haggard later visited the scene of the massacre, he 'walked over the battlefield finding the occasional relic of the battle: crushed cartridge cases and a broken cricket stump and bail'.

But it was an earlier generation of British redcoats who brought cricket to the broiling South African sun. There is questionable evidence that the unfortunately named Charles Anguish (he later committed suicide) was the first to play cricket in the country when he took up a post with the civil service in the late 1790s.

That can't be corroborated, but what is for certain is that a match was staged in January 1808 between officers of the 60th Regiment and Officers of the Colony. The game was advertised in the Cape Town *Gazette and Africa Advertiser*, and at stake was a large sum of money.

Cricket remained the preserve of the British military and civil service for the first half of the nineteenth century, and where they were posted so cricket took root. The oldest cricket club in South Africa is Port Elizabeth, founded in 1843, and within twenty years there were clubs as far afield as Cape Town, Bloemfontein, Pretoria and Johannesburg. Matches were staged in this decade between 'Mother Country' XIs and teams composed of 'Colonial Born' players. Again, there is evidence that the Bantus and Khoikhoi may have played cricket in the 1840s, but to all intents and purposes it remained a sport for the white settler – and the privileged white settler at that. Describing the Western Province Club, A.G. Steel writes that in the 1860s its matches were 'very social functions, regularly enlivened by a military band, and often graced by the presence of the Governor and his staff'.

The matches may have been enlivened by bands, but on the hard, dry pitches of South Africa the batsmen got all the exhilaration they needed from the unpredictable bounce of the ball. Indeed, no first-class match would be played on turf in South Africa until the 1926/27 season, matting being considered safer.

Nonetheless, cricket continued to spread, and in 1876 the colony staged its first organised tournament – the Champions Bat Competition – at Port Elizabeth, featuring teams from Cape Town, Port Elizabeth, Grahamstown and King William's Town.

The tournament continued on and off for the next fourteen years until in 1889 cricket in South Africa was transformed by the arrival of an English touring party led by Aubrey Smith, later to become a Hollywood actor. The visitors played nineteen matches, winning thirteen and losing four with two unfinished. According to *Wisden*, 'all the beatings were sustained in the early part of the trip, and it is no libel to say that for a time generous hospitality had a bad effect upon the cricket'.

Two Test matches were among England's victories, the first at Port Elizabeth in March 1889, when England won by eight wickets, and the second at Cape Town a fortnight later. England won again, but Bernard Tancred helped himself to a small slice of cricket immortality when he became the first Test batsman to carry his bat, the opener finishing unbeaten on 26 out of South Africa's total of 47.

Two of the tourists, Smith and Monty Bowden, remained in the colony at the end of the tour, and that wasn't the only thing that stayed in South Africa. Prior to their departure from England, the squad had been given a cup by a Scottish shipping magnate called Sir Donald Currie. His instructions were for the cup to be given to the best provincial side that the tourists played. Kimberley were handed the cup, and the following year they were challenged to a match by Transvaal. The cup – soon christened the Currie Cup – was won by Transvaal, and thereafter the cup became the jewel in the domestic crown of South African cricket.

In 1894 a team of South Africans embarked on a tour of England, playing mostly second-class fixtures, though they did beat an MCC side in which an ageing W.G. Grace was present. South Africa's first tour overseas 'excited little interest' in England, according to one cricket historian. Yet even before the tourists had left the colony there was a foretaste of the trouble that lay ahead for cricket, and South Africa in particular. One of the players selected for the tour was Krom Hendricks, a fast bowler of Malay extraction considered the '[Fred] Spofforth of South Africa' by the coach of Western Province. When Cecil Rhodes found out he vetoed the idea, the prime minister of the Cape Colony saying it would be 'impolitic' to include him in the squad.

Where the British military set foot, so cricket took root

A year later Rhodes attended a dinner and sat next to Pelham Warner, a Middlesex player and later captain of England. 'They wanted me to send a black fellow called Hendricks to England,' Rhodes informed Warner. Warner said he had heard Hendricks was a very fine bowler. 'Yes, but I would not have it,' replied Rhodes. 'They would have expected him to throw boomerangs during the luncheon interval.'

Surrey badge

Nottinghamshire were the first county side to dominate English cricket, winning outright or sharing the County Championship title eleven times in the 1870s and 1880s. Trouble was, the County Championship in those days wasn't much of a championship at all, and when it did become a proper competition along came Surrey to steal Nottinghamshire's thunder.

Though a championship of sorts had first been contested in 1865, by 1870 the regular county fixtures numbered just twenty-two. Eventually, in 1872, a meeting was held in London at which nine county representatives thrashed out some basic rules to govern the championships. It's interesting to note that the driving force behind this meeting was the secretary of Surrey, a man who we last met in chapter 22. Charles Alcock had been the brains behind the introduction of the Football Association Cup the previous year, a tournament specifically designed to add some spice to the football season, and now here he was hoping to do something similar for cricket.

Alcock hosted a further meeting of the nine counties at the Oval in April 1873. Present were representatives from Derbyshire, Gloucestershire, Kent, Lancashire, Middlesex, Nottinghamshire, Surrey, Sussex and Yorkshire. When the meeting broke up they had all agreed on the following rules:

1. *That no cricketer, whether amateur or professional, shall play for more than one county during the season.*

2. *Every cricketer born in one county and residing in another shall be free to choose at the commencement of each season for which of those counties he will play, and shall, during that season, play for that county only.*

3. *A cricketer shall be qualified to play for any county in which he is residing and has resided for the previous two years, or a cricketer may elect to play for the county in which his family home is, so long as it remains open to him as a place of residence.*

4. *That should any question arise as to the residential question, the same should be left to the discretion of the Marylebone Club.*

5. *That a copy of these rules be sent to the Marylebone Club, with a request that they be adopted by the club.*

Perfect. So cricket had its own form of the FA Cup. Well, no, not exactly. The nine protagonists had overlooked one rather important point – how exactly the winner would be decided. So the press took it upon themselves to issue a merit table at the end of each season, awarding the championship to the side that lost the fewest matches. From 1887 onwards the press adopted a new system, awarding sides one point for a win and half a point for a draw. This was the same year, incidentally, that Derbyshire dropped out of the championship, exasperated at a shambolic competition that saw them play six matches that season compared with Surrey's sixteen. And this was the inherent problem with the championship – not unlike the wicket at Lord's, it lacked shape and consistency.

Fortunately that all changed in 1889, the year Lancashire, Nottinghamshire and Surrey produced a three-way tie. The county secretaries met and formulated a new system of awarding points: losses to be deducted from victories and drawn matches to be ignored. This, declared *Wisden*, was the moment the 'now officially recognized competition for the championship' began.

Surrey won the inaugural championship title under the new rules, and in 1891 Somerset were invited to join the competition. But they, like the other seven counties, were in thrall to Surrey, who went on to claim a further four titles in the five seasons that followed.

In Thomas Bowley, George Lohmann, John Sharpe and Bill Lockwood, Surrey had a quartet of bowlers too good for the rest of the country. Three of the four were outsiders, enticed south by Charles Alcock, who did so much to turn Surrey into the dominant side of the late nineteenth century. 'It must have been a bitter business for the men of Notts to watch the success of Bowley, Sharpe and Lockwood, all of them Nottingham born,' mused Harry Altham in 1926. 'But allowed by the home authorities to drift South in search of the regular employment that they could not find at Trent Bridge.'

Nottinghamshire, so imperious in the early unofficial days of the County Championship, didn't win their first official title until 1907. By then the competition had been bolstered by the addition of Essex, Derbyshire, Leicestershire, Warwickshire and Hampshire in 1895, the inclusion of Worcestershire four years after that date and the admission in 1905 of Northamptonshire. Glamorgan would join in 1921, and seventy years later Durham became the eighteenth county to join.

> The nine protagonists had overlooked how exactly the winner would be decided

The championship today is divided into two divisions, the system of points scoring a world away from what they decided at the Oval in 1893. But Nottinghamshire fans will feel a sense of satisfaction that in the last ten years they've won the championship twice, and Surrey haven't at all.

The Sheffield Shield

From Surrey to Sheffield for our next object, though we're not talking Yorkshire but rather Australia.

The Sheffield Shield measures 43 inches by 30, is constructed from gold, silver and copper and was designed in 1892 by Phillip Blashki, a Polish immigrant who had a reputation as one of Melbourne's leading silversmiths of the late nineteenth century.

The £150 the Shield cost to create was donated by Lord Sheffield, Conservative politician and patron of cricket. In 1883 His Lordship had established a cricket nursery at his country seat in Sussex, and later he took a touring party to Holland. Characterised as 'genial, jovial, hearty and a thorough sportsman', the cricket-mad aristocrat 'cares little for vanity of wearing apparel, but dresses himself for comfort and in a style all his own'.

In 1891/92 Lord Sheffield was the man responsible for organising and financing England's tour to Australia, even agreeing to pay W.G. Grace £3,000 for his time. According to the *Melbourne Age*, reflecting in 2004 on the success of the Sheffield Shield: 'Australian cricket was ailing at the time [Australia had not won a Test series in ten years], and this is said to have been the main reason Lord Sheffield decided to organise and underwrite the tour: he wanted to give Australian cricket a lift.'

Sheffield succeeded, though England failed to win the Test series, going down 2–1 to their hosts. 'Before the matches began the Australians had a very modest opinion of their own powers,' wrote Harry Altham. 'Before they

were over, confidence had returned in measure all the greater for
having been so long in abeyance.'

Before Lord Sheffield sailed for home he deposited a cheque for
£150 in the hands of Australian cricket with instructions to design
a trophy for a national cricket competition. While the game's
authorities discussed the finer points of the putative competition,
Blashki got down to work in his studio. What he crafted was
described in the pages of *The Australasian* in 1892: 'The shield is
of silver, the centre-plate representing the Sheffield Park Cricket
ground where so many Australian teams have played. On either
hand is a bowler and a batsman in action. In the centre-piece
the men are shown in the field and the wickets, bat and ball will
be of gold as well as some sixteen little tablets which are to bear
the names of the winning teams. The Australian arms and the
Sheffield Arms will be correctly enamelled in colours and rest on
the shoulders of the shield.'

It was agreed that Victoria, South Australia and New South
Wales would contest the Shield for the first time in the 1892/93
season. Victoria triumphed, and the following year South Australia
lifted the Shield. By the time they won it again, in 1910, the
Sheffield Shield had become the Holy Grail of Australian domestic
cricket, engendering what one provincial newspaper called
'remarkable public interest between the colonies'.

In 1926 Queensland began contesting the Shield, then Western
Australia in 1947 and Tasmania thirty years later. Though New
South Wales boasts the most number of victories with forty-five,
no state has ever truly dominated, with NSW the last to win four
consecutive titles in the early 1960s.

In 2006 a team of Brisbane jewellers spent more than 200
hours restoring the battered old Shield, dismantling it into 150
pieces before reassembling it with a timber backing in place of
the original blue-felt background. The Queensland craftsmen
also removed some of the graffiti that had accrued over the years,
including the legend: 'Queensland never to win'.

They have, by the way, seven times.

The Lord's Pavilion

Lord's is the undisputed home of cricket, where the sweet lullaby of leather on willow – chorused by the pop of champagne corks and the snores of sozzled members – has been heard for well over 200 years.

Lord's has been part of the fabric of English sporting life since long before the twin cathedrals of Twickenham and Wembley opened their doors to worshippers, and St John's Wood has become synonymous with cricket as a result.

Yet it could have been so different, and for that we have the runaway snobbery of two men to thank – the Earl of Winchilsea and Charles Lennox, subsequently the duel-fighting Fourth Duke of Richmond. The pair were members of the Star and Garter, a club in Pall Mall where London's most fragrantly powdered gentlemen

were wont to hang out in the late eighteenth century. According to Harry Altham in *A History of Cricket*, it was in 'about 1780 the cricket enthusiasts among the members began to play the game together in the White Conduit Fields of Islington'. The fields were public, managed by the landlord of a local pub with a good head for business. 'Bats and Balls for Cricket and a convenient field to play in,' ran an advert he placed in the London papers.

The trouble was Islington was a little, how can one put it, downmarket for some of the more discerning members of the Star and Garter. 'It seems that a section of the White Conduit Club began to resent the public and rather primitive surroundings of the Islington matches,' wrote Altham. 'And accordingly two of its members, the Earl of Winchilsea and Charles Lennox, took active steps to secure a new private ground, more worthy of their club's pretensions.'

Leather on willow has been heard at Lord's for over 200 years

Good! cried the locals, who resented their manor being invaded by aristocrats. As the *Daily Universal Register* noted on 22 June 1785, the cricketers received a 'severe rebuke... from some spirited citizens whom they insulted and attempted *vie et armis* to drive from the footpath, pretending it was within their bounds'.

The man tasked with finding more suitable accommodation for the cricket enthusiasts was Thomas Lord, a thirty-year-old Yorkshireman, described by a contemporary as in possession of a charming personality, a handsome face and a brain for business.

Lord chose a seven-acre field north of Marylebone Road on what is now part of Dorset Square. There were one or two murmurs of discontent from members at the unevenness of the field but Lord assured them a heavy roller would do the trick. On the plus side there was plenty of space for spectators and for the refreshment tents from which the club could make money.

Lord's hosted its first match on 21 May 1787, between the White Conduit Club and Middlesex, and for the next twenty-three years the Dorset Fields Ground was the premier venue for cricket in England.

In 1810 the lease expired, and Lord, by now portly, prosperous and middle aged, rented two fields from the Eyre family on the St John's Estate, just around the time that the government decided to build the Regent's Canal right through the area. 'Undaunted Lord applied for and obtained from the same Eyre family a new parcel of land, situated some half-mile north of the old ground,' wrote Altham. 'And on June 22nd 1814 the first match, MCC v Hertfordshire, was played on the third, and, we may surely believe, last "Lord's Ground".'

Not that the new ground was an instant success. In 1825 a fire broke out, razing the wooden pavilion despite the best endeavours of passers-by, who doused the flames with water from the trough for the sheep which grazed on the outfield. The presence of livestock may have been one reason why Lord's gained a reputation for its poor playing surface, wags commenting that 'the only respect in which its pitch resembled a billiard table was the pockets'.

The pavilion that emerged from the ashes of 1825 (itself demolished in 1889) was likened to 'an Indian railway station' and caused much grumbling among MCC members; like their forefathers 100-odd years earlier they thought their club deserved better. The architect commissioned to build the new pavilion was Thomas Verity, an expert in his field who had helped in the design of the Royal Albert Hall and the redevelopment of Piccadilly Circus.

> The only respect in which its pitch resembled a billiard table was the pockets

The pavilion was opened on 1 May 1890, to the delight of members, who particularly enjoyed the building's rain stops, gargoyles in appearance, that were reputedly caricatures of members of the MCC Committee.

Subsequent MCC Committees have been accused of failing to move with the times, but in developing Lord's they have always proved far sighted and flexible. In the last thirty years much of the ground has been redeveloped, always with an eye to aesthetics, and the 1999 Media Centre – the first all-aluminium, semi-monocoque building in the world – won a major architectural award for its design.

Floodlights were introduced in 2009, and in 2012 Lord's hosted the archery competition of the London Olympics, resulting in the Games' purple and pink logos being plastered across the home of cricket. Worse, the pavilion's Long Room was defaced with sponsors' logos, leaving Donald Bradman and W.G. Grace to stare down disapprovingly from their portraits.

As the BBC noted, MCC head of cricket John Stephenson 'had the look of a man forced to sleep in the spare room while the guests were staying'.

Lord's knows what Thomas Lord would have made of it all.

A tennis ball

'On no!' exclaimed Bernard Bosanquet when asked if he thought his bowling was illegal. 'Only immoral.'

The ball that 'Bosie' bequeathed to cricket was the 'googly', first delivered to a googly-eyed Sam Coe of Leicestershire during a match in the summer of 1900. More than a century later the googly is still going strong, a tribute to the long hours Bosie spent perfecting his devilish delivery with a tennis ball.

Saqlain Mushtaq of Pakistan invented his own 'googly' in the 1990s, which came to be called the 'doosra' (though Australians claim their own Jack Potter beat him to it by thirty years), while Sri Lanka's Muttiah Muralitharan and Shane Warne had their own tricks of the trade with which they teased, tormented and terminated scores of befuddled batsmen.

But what exactly is a googly, a doosra or what the Aussies call a wrong 'un? Simply put, it's an off-break delivered by a (right-arm) leg-spin bowler. In other words, a ball that the batsman expects to break (spin) from leg to off, which in fact does the reverse and breaks from off to leg. To do this requires two things: plenty of practice and wrists strong and flexible enough to twist at the moment the ball is delivered so that the axis of spin is altered.

Nothing in Bernard Bosanquet's early cricket career suggested he would be the man to break with orthodoxy. Of Huguenot stock, he was born in Enfield, Middlesex, in 1877, and at both Eton and Oxford made a name for himself as a fast-bowling batsman. He also represented the university at hammer-throwing and billiards, and it's said he first began turning his wrist with billiard balls. As Bosanquet would later admit, there were already spin bowlers on the first-class circuit in England who were bowling leg-break deliveries that came straight on to the batsman. But Bosie wanted more; he wanted the ball to spin from off to leg. This he achieved for the first time in 1897, in circumstances fittingly anarchic. 'I was playing a game with a tennis ball, known as "Twisti-Twosti",' he later recalled. 'The object was to bounce the ball on a table so that your opponent sitting opposite could not catch it... After a little experimenting I managed to pitch the ball which broke in a certain direction; then with more or less the same delivery make the next ball go in the opposite direction! I practised the same thing with a soft ball at "Stump-cricket". From this I progressed to the cricket ball...'

For the next two years Bosanquet kept his ball under his cap, so to speak, producing it now and again during practice sessions in Oxford. From there he plucked up the courage to bowl a couple of googlies in minor matches until, in July 1900, he decided to unleash his secret weapon playing for Middlesex in a county match against Leicestershire. The left-handed Sam Coe had scored an effortless 98 when Plum Warner brought Bosanquet into the attack. His eyes probably lit up as Bosie tossed up a flighted delivery. Contemporary accounts report Coe took a big stride down the wicket, looking to hit the ball for four through the on side. But the ball spun out of Coe's reach and wicketkeeper William Robertson whipped off the bails. It's said Bosanquet feigned surprise as Coe trudged back to the pavilion, wondering aloud what could have caused the ball to do such a thing.

But as David Frith wrote in *The Slow Men*: 'Bosanquet knew what he was doing all right... this convivial and good-humoured man's nature had sufficient of a dark side to it for him to pretend that this and further successes were all mysterious accidents, and he even persuaded his captain, P.F. Warner, not to put it about that the science of bowling was in the process of having a fresh chapter written.'

Bosanquet later recalled that 'it took any amount of perseverance but for a year or two the results were more than worth it'. In 1902 he claimed his first Australian victim, trapping Jim Kelly lbw when the tourists played Middlesex at Lord's.

The next year Bosanquet took his googly Down Under as part of the England squad touring Australia and New Zealand. Most of the matches were played in New Zealand, but there was a brief visit to Australia, long enough for Bosquanet to come face to face with Victor Trumper in a match against New South Wales. The greatest batsman of his age was then in his prime and carted the tourists' bowling to all four corners of the ground. Then on came Bosanquet. The first two balls to Trumper were ordinary leg-breaks; Trumper played them with consummate ease. The third ball from Bosanquet's wrist was a googly, which removed Trumper's middle stump.

Bosanquet continued to take Test wickets for the next three seasons, but he became increasingly reluctant to deliver his googly. Press criticism hurt him, this intelligent, sensitive man, and he took the last of his twenty-five Test wickets against Australia in 1905. Two years later the *Oxford English Dictionary* noted the first use of google as a sporting verb – as used by *Badminton Magazine* in its September 1907 issue: 'The googlies that do not google.'

Bosanquet may have retired from the international scene by then, but his science had been enthusiastically embraced by a quartet of South African bowlers, including Reggie Schwarz and Aubrey Faulkner. After the war (which claimed the life of Schwarz and unbalanced the mind of Faulkner), the Australian pair of Arthur Mailey and Clarrie Grimmett became adept practitioners of Bosanquet's art. On meeting Grimmett during Australia's 1930 tour of England Bosanquet is reputed to have remarked: 'Am I responsible for you?'

As for who is responsible for the word googly, that's a question that continues to baffle. There were rumours that the word was of Maori origin, picked up by Bosanquet when he toured New Zealand in 1903, but others suggest googly is a mishmash of 'goo' – as in baby noises – and 'guile'. That sounds suitably confusing; let's leave it at that.

The ICC

We can't say this object is our favourite, and while it's not as unsightly as W.G.'s beard it's a darned sight denser and infinitely more impenetrable.

The International Cricket Council celebrated its centenary in 2009, and *Wisden* marked the occasion by commissioning Australian author and broadcaster Gideon Haigh to write an essay on cricket's governing body. Entitling the essay 'Imperial... International... Independent?', Haigh mercilessly flailed the ICC to all four corners of the ground.

He began the essay as he meant to go on: 'Weak, ineffectual, a sham democracy, a rubber stamp for the powerful...' If the ICC had been an opening bowler it would have been taken off there and then.

But strident as Haigh was in his attack he was also fair, reminding readers that when South African Abe Bailey had proposed the establishment of an 'Imperial Board of Control' in June 1909, he envisioned a 'shop for talk not action'.

And that was very much how the ICC was run for its first fifty years. The name the founders settled on was the Imperial Cricket Council, and in the first few years of its existence membership comprised England, South Africa and Australia, the latter pair coming to Lord's for 'an annual beano... putting on their best suits for a day of hospitality'.

Even after India, New Zealand and the West Indies were admitted to the ICC in 1926 there was scant distinction between it and the MCC, with the chairman and secretary of the latter also fulfilling the same roles within the Imperial Cricket Council.

After the Second World War the Council remained at the crease, ineffective but immovable, like an ageing village-green batsman who just won't give a chance. During England's Ashes tour to Australia in 1958/59 a controversy erupted over the action of Victorian fast bowler Ian Meckiff. There were calls in some quarters for Meckiff to be banned for throwing, and England tour manager Freddie Brown met with Syd Webb of the Australian Cricket Board. Shouldn't the matter be left in the hands of the ICC? asked Webb. 'The Council has no power,' replied Brown. 'It is the place where opinions can be ventilated.'

What ultimately blocked the ICC's ventilation system was South Africa. In 1965 the West Indies and India both made clear their disapproval of England's plan to host a South African touring party given that the Republic had lost its ICC status having left the Commonwealth four years earlier. New Zealand and Australia sided with England, but that same year the ICC welcomed its first intake of what have become known as 'associate members', non-Test-playing nations that included Ceylon (now Sri Lanka), Fiji and the United States. In 1966 Bermuda, Denmark, East Africa and Holland were admitted to the ICC, which had now rebranded itself the International Cricket Conference.

> Not as unsightly as W.G.'s beard but infinitely more impenetrable

An attempt to readmit South Africa to the ICC in 1981 – proposed by New Zealand and seconded by England – was voted down, and in 1983 it was India's turn to win the World Cup. Emboldened by their success on the pitch, the Indian Board in the summer 1984 tabled a proposal that Haigh described as 'unforeseeably momentous'.

At the ICC meeting Indian Board president N.K.P. Salve proposed that the 1987 World Cup be held in India and Pakistan, breaking with the tradition of staging the tournament in England.

The English weren't happy, but cold hard cash won out, the Indian bid being twice as lucrative as their adversaries'. As Salve noted later: 'For the first time a battle had been successfully fought in ICC... India and Pakistan and their friends had shown England and her allies that they were no longer supreme in the matters of cricket administration.'

Thirty years later cricket's administrative power lies squarely in the hands of India, with their giant financial clout, and the ICC remains – in the eyes of many – as impotent as ever. On the question of that great blight on the modern game – match-fixing – the ICC has been reactive rather than proactive. The first scandal, which broke in 2000 and brought down Hansie Cronje

> **Cricket's administrative power now lies squarely in the hands of India**

and Mohammad Azharuddin, led to former Metropolitan Police Chief Commissioner Lord Condon overseeing a cricket Anti-Corruption Unit. He wasn't impressed with the sport's leadership, saying the ICC lacked 'an infrastructure to meet the financial and governance requirements of the modern game'.

More recently it took the now defunct *News of the World* to expose Pakistan's spot-fixing ring in 2010 and an Indian TV station to break allegations of corruption among umpires two years later.

Gideon Haigh concluded his excellent essay in the 2009 *Wisden* by caustically noting that 'where the I in ICC once stood for Imperial, and now for International, there seems no danger it will ever stand for Independent'.

Indian, maybe, but definitely not Independent.

Statue of Maharaja Bhupinder Singh

You will recall that we left Indian cricket in 1888, as P.D. Kanga and his side returned from England after an encouraging tour in which they won eight of their matches. The next man to lead an Indian side to England was Maharaja Bhupinder Singh.

Kanga, by all accounts, was a bit of a character, but no one could compare with the Maharaja. He was nineteen

when chosen to captain the 1911 Indian side to tour the British Isles; nineteen but already a Sikh prince with a harem that would eventually number 300. It's amazing that he found time to play any cricket; actually, he didn't play much on the tour to Europe, but we're getting ahead of ourselves.

Back to the planning of the tour, which was some eight years in the pipeline. The first attempt to send a team that was 'perfectly representative of Indian cricket' to England failed in 1903. Prominent Parsi,

Hindu and Muslim members of Bombay's cricketing community
had been unable to agree on the squad's make-up. So six years later
they tried again, the driving force behind the idea one J.M. Framji
Patel, Bombay's most important cricket administrator. Addressing
a meeting of the game's great and good in Bombay in 1909, Patel
declared: 'There are many links that bind us together as citizens of
the greatest Empire the world has ever seen, and among those the
Imperial game of cricket is not the least... cricket, in the end, will
kill racial antagonism.'

Patel was talking not just about religious rivalry within India,
but also the increasing tension seeping into Indo-British relations.
Nationalism was making the British shift uncomfortably on their
colonial seat, so the idea of a cricket tour was seized on by them.
Sir George Clarke, the governor of Bombay, thought it 'would be
most beneficial' to re-establishing 'happy relations' between the
two countries. The MCC was similarly effusive, secretary Francis
Lacey believing that a cricket tour would 'do much to remove
prejudices and promote friendship'.

Then there was the question of what the tour could bring
to Indian cricket. One newspaper quoted a 'native thinker',
who announced: 'In an eleven consisting of Hindus, Parsis and
Moslems, each one will instinctively feel that he is an Indian first,
and a member of his own race afterwards.'

A selection committee was formed to pick the squad, the first
task being to select a captain, someone who would be acceptable
to both Indians and Englishmen. They decided on Maharaja
Bhupinder Singh of Patiala, a 'flamboyant' young man, according
to Prashant Kidambi, senior lecturer in historical studies at
Leicester University. First he played cricket, or at least he knew
which end of the bat to hold, but more importantly he was the ruler
of Patiala, 'a state the size of Yorkshire, who had been loyal allies
of the British in India ever since they had helped quell the great
uprising of 1857'.

The selection of Bhupinder Singh as captain was, says Kidambi,
'symptomatic of an era when it was taken for granted that the

Indian princes were natural leaders of men'. But in the rest of the team's selection, the committee showed uncommon courage. The final squad selected was a healthy mix of Hindu, Muslim and Parsi. There were even two 'untouchables' among the tourists – the great left-arm spinner Baloo Palwankar and his batsman younger brother Shivram.

The tourists arrived in England in May 1911, the Maharaja winning much praise in the British press for his 'gorgeous costume of rich-flowered silk'; he and his entourage stayed in a London mansion while the rest of the squad made do with the Imperial Hotel in Russell Square.

Not that the players minded. They were there to play cricket, and after a disastrous start, losing all their opening eleven matches, the Indians began to find their form. It may have helped that the Maharaja was no longer part of the squad. Having appeared in the first three matches, the prince spent the rest of the summer rubbing silk shoulders with members of the British aristocracy in an endless succession of balls, dinners and hunting parties.

It was the Palwankar brothers who spearheaded the Indians' renaissance in the second half of the tour. Victories against Leicestershire and Somerset were followed by wins in Scotland and Ireland.

In all the tourists won six and drew two of their twenty-three matches, with Baloo the undoubted star claiming seventy-five wickets at an average of 20.12.

The squad arrived back in Bombay to a sympathetic welcome. The results could have been better was the general feeling in the press, but what the tour had proved above all else was that a squad representative of Indian cricket could spend several weeks in each other's company. 'They have,' commented the *Hindi Punch*, 'established good fellowship all round. They have been on freedom's soil where caste is powerless.'

For the first time Indians understood that, on a cricket field at least, religion and caste were irrelevant, and the idea that a united India meant a stronger India became accepted.

Daily Telegraph

'Nine Tests provide a surfeit of cricket, and the contests are not a great attraction to the British public.'

That was the declaration in the *Daily Telegraph* in 1912 in the wake of the inaugural Triangular Tournament between England, South Africa and Australia. There were few dissenters, not even Abe Bailey, whose idea it had been to stage cricket's first international competition. The South African gold magnate, who, as we saw in chapter 30, also had the dubious distinction of proposing the ICC, came up with the idea of the Triangular Tournament following his nation's good showing against England in the 1907 Test series. South Africa had arrived as an international force, exclaimed Bailey, and the whole world would want to see them take on England and Australia in a series of Test matches. 'Inter-rivalry within the Empire cannot fail to draw together in closer friendly interest all those many thousands of our kinsmen who regard cricket as our national sport,' said Bailey, who proposed 1909 as the year for the first Triangular Tournament.

Owing to disagreement among the three protagonists, the tournament was postponed from 1909 until 1912, by which time anticipation among England's cricketing public was at fever pitch, despite the inevitable disruption caused to the county schedule. Having warmed up with a string of games against county sides, Australia and South Africa launched the tournament at Old Trafford on 27/28 May, and it soon became evident that the South Africans were not now the force of a few years earlier.

The Aussies won by an innings and 88 runs, a similar winning margin to that achieved by England when they faced South Africa at Lord's a fortnight later. The South Africans were all out for 58 in their first innings, extras top-scoring with 17, and England picked up a point to go level with Australia at the top of the Triangular Table.

The third match between England and Australia was billed as the 'event of the season', and more than 14,000 spectators flocked to Lord's on the first day. They saw just three hours of play because of the weather. Eight thousand turned up on day two and were rewarded with twenty minutes. Even the arrival of the Prince of Wales on the third day of the Test couldn't hold back the rain. As *Wisden* glumly noted, 'the weather ruined everything', and the match ended in a draw.

When the rain eased the tournament continued, though South Africa lurched from one defeat to the next, leaving England and Australia to try once again in the sixth match of the series at Manchester. Fat chance. 'The England and Australia match at Old Trafford proved an even greater disappointment than the meeting of the same sides at Lord's, rain spoiling everything,' grumbled *Wisden* again.

> **Even the arrival of the Prince of Wales couldn't hold back the rain**

When England did finally get to play Australia at the Oval in August, the hosts brushed aside the tourists with contemptuous ease. An opening century partnership between Hobbs and Wilfred Rhodes laid a platform from which England went on to crush their old enemy by 244 runs. But it was an enemy stripped of its stars, a winter row between the Australian Board and its players resulting in the squad sailing for England minus Victor Trumper, Warwick Armstrong, Tibby Cotter and Clem Hill.

The 45,000 fans who packed into the Oval during four rain-interrupted days of cricket deserved a better contest, but, as *Wisden* noted in its 1913 edition, from the start 'the fates fought against the Triangular Tournament'.

A divided Australia, a declining South Africa and the wettest summer in living memory (the three months June to August produced a record 410mm of rain) combined to make the Triangular Tournament a washout.

The ICC put on a brave face, meeting at Lord's in July 1912 and provisionally agreeing to stage a second tournament within the next five years. *Wisden* editor Sydney Pardon had his doubts. The inaugural tournament had been such an unmitigated disaster that in his opinion 'the experiment is not likely to be repeated for many years to come – perhaps not in this generation'.

Pardon's view sprang from his belief that the English summer was already chock-a-block with cricket, and the public couldn't be expected to fork out more money to watch nine Test matches on top of all the county matches.

Pardon's arguments were never borne out; it wasn't fixture congestion that killed off the Triangular Tournament, it was a world war of unimaginable scale.

When Harry Altham published his *History of Cricket* in 1926 he devoted a couple of pages to the sport's first international competition. 'It is probable that not even Sir Abe Bailey... can have claimed for it a great measure of success,' he concluded. 'Very possibly it was too ambitious a project, and, even under the most favourable conditions, there was not room for nine Test matches in our crowded domestic programme.'

A century after the short-lived Triangular Tournament, cricket still has no Test Championship. The ICC has for a number of years dithered over introducing such a competition, initially scheduling a Test match tournament for England in 2013. This was pushed back to 2017, and there is still no guarantee it will go ahead. Television doesn't much fancy the idea of broadcasting Test matches; it finds Twenty20 and fifty-over cricket far more to its taste.

Hostility from the *Telegraph* then in 1912, and from television in 2012 – it appears Test match tournaments just can't win.

'Your country needs you'

'Your country needs you,' cried Lord Kitchener in 1914, a rallying call that was reproduced on recruitment posters throughout the British Empire in those febrile August days of 1914.

The poster, our next object, had the required effect, prompting hundreds of thousands of young men to enlist in the war against Germany and the Austro-Hungarian Empire. Among their number were countless cricketers: British, Australian, South African, Indian, West Indian and New Zealander.

Cricket's martial lineage can be traced back to 1744 when Kent played England at the Artillery Ground in

front of the Prince of Wales and his brother, the Duke of Cumberland. Wellington, we've seen, was a fan; so too the Duke of Richmond. In the Crimean war of the 1850s the Scots Fusiliers Guards were fired upon during the Battle of Alma, a cannonball parting the ranks of the British. 'Duff, you are keeping wicket, you ought to have stopped that one,' cried Sir John Astley to George Duff, the regimental wicketkeeper. Duff, according to Astley, turned 'and smiling quietly said, "No, sir, it had a bit too much pace on. You are a long stop, sir, so I left it to you."'

That flippancy died in the First World War, a conflict that decimated the ranks of amateur cricket. A memorial in the Lord's pavilion lists the names of 330 MCC members who lost their lives, while in Melbourne the roll of honour commemorates 137 members, 12 per cent of the members who had answered Kitchener's call.

In an essay written for *Wisden* in December 1939, months after the start of the Second World War, Harry Altham recalled the outbreak of the first conflict (in which he served with great gallantry). 'For most of that August county cricket was played much as usual,' he said, '...until a dignified letter to *The Times* by "W. G." brought the first-class game to an end.'

'I think the time has arrived when the county cricket season should be closed, for it is not fitting at a time like this that able-bodied men should be playing cricket by day and pleasure-seekers look on,' wrote Grace. 'I should like to see all first-class cricketers of suitable age set a good example and come to the help of their country without delay in its hour of need.'

Grace's call was heeded. The County Championship closed down, and in May 1915 the president of the MCC, Lord Hawke, informed his members that 75 per cent of first-class cricketers in England had joined up. Lord's, meanwhile, 'accommodated various military units, whilst the staff that remained there spent part of their time in making thousands of hay-nets for horses'. At Old Trafford and Trent Bridge the pavilions were turned into hospitals, while a small-bore rifle range was installed at Leicester.

Even though cricket across the world had all but vanished, *Wisden* continued to print. The 1916 edition, slashed from 791 to 299 pages, carried few scores but many obituaries, including that of a young officer called Rupert Brooke, who had topped the Rugby School XI's bowling averages in 1906 with nineteen wickets at 14.05 apiece. Harry Altham received his copy of *Wisden* while serving in the trenches on the Western Front, recalling that he was more upset by the death of Victor Trumper from illness aged thirty-seven than those of any other of his former teammates killed in action. 'I can remember reading of them in France and feeling... an almost personal pain that Trumper's gallant spirit and matchless grace should have been called so early from the world it had enriched,' he wrote.

Gradually cricket returned to England, first in the northern leagues and then through a string of exhibition matches staged to boost the morale of the public and raise money for soldiers' associations. The MCC staged two matches at Lord's – the British Army playing their Australian counterparts, and a Navy & Army XI against a combined side from Australia and South Africa.

Soldiers at the front played where they could, the British in France, the South Africans in East Africa and the Australians in the Middle East.

First-class cricket recommenced in May 1919, just six months after the end of a war that had cost millions of lives. Initially a cricket Advisory Committee had been formed in December 1918 to explore the possibility of playing the following summer. They decided to stage two-day matches, fearful that this was all the public would want to see, but 'the fears were unjustified... cricket was as popular as ever'.

When Altham penned his essay for *Wisden* in the winter of 1939 he conceded that 'today the horizon is again dark', yet he urged readers – and particularly players – to keep cricket alive wherever and whenever they could. He ended by describing a recent visit of his to Lord's on a cold, dark December day. 'There were sandbags everywhere, and the Long Room was stripped and bare, with its treasures safely stored beneath ground,' he wrote. 'But the turf was a wondrous green, old Time on the Grand Stand was gazing serenely at the nearest balloon, and one felt that somehow it would take more than totalitarian war to put an end to cricket – *Merses profundo, pulchrior evenit.*'

You may bury it in the deep; it emerges more beautiful than ever.

> Cricket's martial lineage can be traced back to 1744

Catching cradle

The passing of the good Reverend Gilbert Harrison
Bartlett warranted only a few lines in the 1959 edition
of *Wisden*. Cricket's yellow bible announced that the
Norfolk vicar, who had died in a Norwich nursing
home aged seventy-six, was the inventor of 'the cradle
universally used for fielding practice'.

And that was about it from *Wisden*. It mentioned that
while at Cambridge Bartlett had represented Corpus
Christi at rowing and lawn tennis but didn't reveal how
a man of the cloth had come up with the idea for this
revolutionary coaching innovation.

But Bartlett was clearly a disciple of muscular
Christianity. A former pupil of Norwich Grammar, his first
parish was Thorpe St Andrew in 1905, and he combined
his Sunday sermons with running a boxing club from the
back of the Dove Inn public house.

Was it here in the back of a pub that Bartlett came up with the idea of a catching cradle? One would like to imagine it was while the reverend was preaching the importance to his boxing pupils of footwork and reflexes around a punchbag that it came to him in a vision. A curious contraption, shaped like a cradle, with curved wooden bars that at first glance seem innocuous enough. But hurl a cricket ball into the cradle and it spits out the other side with the speed and aggression of a striking king cobra.

By all accounts Bartlett didn't patent his invention, or if he did he preferred to preach from the pulpit till the end of his days rather than retire to Monte Carlo and live off the profits. By the time of his death in 1958 just about every cricket club in the world had a slip cradle, just as every club had numerous players nursing badly bruised or broken fingers from a ball that flew out of the contraption just a little too fast.

More than half a century after the death of the reverend, his brainwave isn't as popular as it once was. There may be the odd rickety one gathering dust in some quaint village pavilion, but professional teams are far too sophisticated to use wooden catching cradles. More's the pity,

Bartlett combined his sermons with running a boxing club in a public house

wrote former Hampshire captain turned cricket commentator Mark Nicholas in 2006. Having just watched England drop nine catches in a Test against Sri Lanka Nicholas lamented the demise of the catching cradle in an article for the *Daily Telegraph*. 'A lot of modern-day players go to ground when looking to catch, which suggests a lack of balance through poor footwork,' he wrote. 'Soft, giving hands should combine with flexible hips and knees that can turn and ride the pace of the ball...then it's a question of reaction time.'

But there is one modern-day player who bucks the trend of butter-fingered slip fielders. In December 2010 Rahul Dravid became the first player to take 200 catches in Test matches, achieving the feat in his 149th match for India. Now retired from the game, Dravid practised on cradles as a child but turned to the portable catching net, the modern adaptation of the cradle. Asked for the secret of his success in an interview shortly after he'd taken his 200th Test match catch, Dravid replied: 'There is no substitute to taking a lot of a catches as a youngster if you want to do slip catching. You've got to catch, catch, catch. And more than doing the normal stuff, you have to vary your catching – you've got to take some catches with the tennis ball, you got to take some closer, some further away.'

Which was the inspiration behind the Reverend Bartlett's invention all those years ago. After all, as every good coach will preach to his flock – catches win matches.

Bottle of whisky

He stood 6 feet 2 inches tall, weighed 20 stone and wore shoes that were 12^1/$_2$ inches long and 7 inches wide. In short, never did a man merit his nickname quite like Australia's Warwick Armstrong – the 'Big Ship', as he was called.

Neville Cardus once said of Armstrong that Australian cricket was 'incarnate in him', and during a first-class career that spanned nearly a quarter of a century his influence on the game Down Under was extraordinary. It wasn't just the 16,000 runs that he scored or the 800 wickets he took, it was his attitude and bearing that set the standard for future generations of Australian players.

Armstrong also liked a tipple now and again, whisky his liquor of choice – he even made his living as a whisky seller once his cricket career was over.

It was England who suffered most at the hands of Armstrong. In all he played in a record forty-two Tests against the old enemy, scoring 2,172 runs at an average 35.03, and taking seventy-four wickets at an average cost of 30.91. In ten of those Tests he captained Australia, never losing, and leading the boys in the baggy green caps to eight consecutive victories. It would have been more, but Armstrong was one of the six Australian players who refused to play in the 1912 Triangular Tournament (see chapter 32) because of a dispute with the Board.

The first of those victories came in the first Test of the 1920/21 series, the first to have Test status following the end of the First World War. Australia won by 377 runs (Armstrong scored 158), and they also claimed the second and third Tests. The fourth Test was at Melbourne where a bout of malaria led Armstrong to down a couple of whiskies before he went out to bat. He scored 123, and Australia won again. When they took the fifth and final Test the humiliation was complete – England were the first side to lose every match in a five-Test series. (The only other Ashes 'whitewash' was the 5–0 thrashing suffered by Andrew Flintoff's side in 2006/07.) It was, wrote Harry Altham five years later, 'a disaster unparalleled in the history of English cricket'.

Three months after the series win, Armstrong led his Australian side to England for another five-Test encounter with England. 'As the news came to hand of defeat after defeat people thought the Englishmen must be playing very badly,' commented *Wisden* in its 1922 issue. 'Not till the Australians came here in the summer and beat us three times in succession on our own grounds did we fully realise the strength of the combination that had set up such a record.'

Australia took the first three Tests, and in total won or drew thirty-six of their thirty-eight first-class matches. Altham pointed to the fast bowling of Jack Gregory and Ted McDonald as crucial to the Australian success, allied to the batting of Charlie Macartney and Warren Bardsley. Harry Altham compared Macartney – dubbed 'The Governor-General' – to Victor Trumper, writing that their 'methods were unorthodox and unique'. In scoring 2,317 runs on the tour at an average of 59.41, Macartney 'reduced our best bowlers to impotence'.

> A bout of malaria led Armstrong to down a couple of whiskies before he went out to bat

By the fifth Test the series was won, and though England were finally showing some resistance, Armstrong appeared tired of so many one-sided encounters. He was also irritated that England hadn't agreed to his proposal to play the Test to a finish, as was the habit in Australia. With the match petering out to a draw on the final day Armstrong 'lost interest in proceedings'. According to David Mortimer, author of *The Oval: Test Match Cricket Since 1880*: 'He wandered off to long leg, leaving instructions for his batsmen to have a bowl and set their own fields. Bill Hitch [the England batsman] took advantage, scoring the second-fastest fifty (35 minutes) in Ashes history, and Armstrong trapped a copy of *The Times* as it blew past "to see who we were playing", as he said later.'

That Test at the Oval was Armstrong's last for Australia. He retired from the game in 1922 and enjoyed a successful post-cricket career as a whisky merchant. Yet his legacy lives on. As recently as 2001 the Australian cricket writer Gideon Haigh wrote an article for the *Guardian* about Steve Waugh's all-conquering Australia team. Under the headline 'Why art of Waugh owes much to Armstrong', Haigh added: 'Armstrong's team created the formula by which later Australian XIs have lived... Australia was led by a rugged veteran cricketer whose captaincy culminated a distinguished career: Warwick Armstrong in 1920–21, Steve Waugh today.'

Pen

Cricket has produced fine writers, as skilled with their pen and as bold with their strokes as the most graceful batsmen upon whom their gaze has fallen.

A writers' XI would most likely include such luminaries as Neville Cardus, A.A. Thomson, John Woodcock, Matthew Engel, John Arlott, Alan Ross, David Foot and E.W. Swanton. Perhaps too Harold Pinter, whose musings on the game he so loved were few but memorable. 'I tend to think that cricket is the greatest thing that God created on earth,' Pinter once said, 'certainly greater than sex, although sex isn't too bad either.'

No sport has generated such a library as cricket boasts. When John Arlott wrote about the genre of cricket writing for the 1964 edition of *Wisden* he noted that there were some 8,000 books about the sport. Half a century later and the number must be nearer 20,000. Players' autobiographies have flourished, so too 'tour diaries' and photo-heavy books celebrating one tournament or another. Fewer are the more thoughtful books, considered reflections on the game we love so much.

But then again, fewer are the maudlin books when village greens were lush, evenings golden and the caress of leather on willow was a balm to all our hearts, etc. As Stephen Moss, literary editor of the *Guardian* in the 1990s, pointed out in an essay for the 2000 edition of *Wisden*, much of the early cricket writing was characterised by 'the pastoralism; the belief in the rootedness and essential Englishness of the game'. He cited the example of Sydney

Goodman's 1898 work, *The Light Side of Cricket*:

> *Under the blue sky, field after field stretches far away to the wooded hills, while from hedge and copse alike comes the music of birds and streams, and the mingled fragrance of summer flowers. This primeval grace and rural poetry of the game is in great measure lost in routine-like dullness in vast and crowded amphitheatres surrounded by ugly pavilions, smoky houses and evil-smelling gasometers. Cricket on the village green... is more like the cricket in the days of those heroes of renown, Alfred Mynn and Caesar, Felix and Fuller Pilch, and round it still lingers that halo of glory which many minds love to associate with a far-off and forgotten time.*

This obsession with cricket as representative of rural England, pure England, an England before steam engines, factories and 'evil-smelling gasometers' defined cricket writing up until the First World War. But idealism died in the trenches, and the 1920s brought a fresh approach to the genre: less elegiac and more erudite.

In the vanguard of this new style was Neville Cardus, who, in 1922, published *A Cricketer's Book*. Cardus was an intellectual, a journalist on the *Manchester Guardian* with early aspirations to become the next Walter Pater, the celebrated essayist and art critic of the nineteenth century.

The primeval grace and rural poetry of the game is in great measure lost

Cardus searched for metaphors in every place, attending concerts, recitals and readings with the aim of unearthing the 'theory of laughter' or drawing some Rabelaisian parallel. He came to hate the world, and so sought solace elsewhere. 'Cricket took me into a different element,' he would later write. 'I met unlettered people with no pretence, good craftsmen with bat and ball on the field of play, and for an audience they had crowds that expressed themselves honestly.'

Cardus moved to London and began writing regularly on the game, becoming the first – and arguably greatest – writer on cricket, deftly portraying the players not just as cricketers but as men, with strengths, weaknesses and idiosyncrasies. Often at the end of a day's play at Lord's Cardus spent the evening at the Covent Garden opera or listening to a concert at the Queen's Hall.

Cardus searched for metaphors in every place

'As I have changed from one place to another, I have felt an acute lowering not only of standards of skill but of genuine English character; for taking them as a whole, concerts and opera audiences in London do not ring true, with their absurd "fashions", their whoopings and screamings in the corridors at the intervals: "Marvellous, my dear!", "Actually, you know, I prefer Toscanini's Ninth!".'

This love for the game shone through his prose. 'Before him, cricket was reported,' John Arlott wrote, 'with him it was for the first time appreciated, felt, and imaginatively described.'

When Cardus died in 1975 (by then a knight of the realm) aged eighty-six, more than 700 people filed into St Paul's Church in Covent Garden for a memorial service. The Royal Philharmonic Orchestra offered Elgar and Mozart in tribute to his standing as one of England's finest music critics before the writer and broadcaster Alan Gibson addressed the congregation on the subject of cricket. 'All cricket writers of the last half-century have been influenced by Cardus, whether they admit it or not, whether they have wished to be or not, whether they have tried to copy him or tried to avoid copying him,' he said. 'He was not a model, any more than Macaulay, say, was a model for the aspiring historian. But just as Macaulay changed the course of the writing of history, Cardus changed the course of the writing of cricket. He showed what could be done. He dignified and illuminated the craft.'

Yorkshire rose

You'll remember we left English cricket in 1919 just as it started its rise from the ruins of war – *Merses profundo, pulchrior evenit.* **What emerged from the wreckage was certainly more stunning that anything the county game had seen before.**

The 1919 County Championship was won by Yorkshire, and the 1920 campaign was a thrilling race with any one of five sides in the hunt until finally Middlesex prevailed on the last evening of the season in front of the largest crowd ever seen at Lord's for a county match. It was a win for the sentimentalists, coming as it did in the last match of Plum Warner's career.

Middlesex retained the title the following season, but then Yorkshire embarked on a period of dominance that – with the exception of a blip in the late 1920s – continued until 1939.

This remarkable streak was sustained by two distinct sides – the Yorkshire XI that won four consecutive titles from 1922 to 1925 and the team that won seven of the ten championships of the 1930s. Which of the two sides was the greater remains up for debate.

The Yorkshire side of the 1920s were ruthlessly efficient, winning eighty-six and losing just seven of the 141 matches played in those four title-winning seasons. There was strength all round with five batsmen in the 1922 season scoring more than 1,000 runs – Edgar Oldroyd, Herbert Sutcliffe, Wilfred Rhodes, Percy Holmes and Roy Kilner. But it was their bowling attack that terrorised opponents. 'For every variety of condition Yorkshire had the corresponding bowler,' wrote Harry Altham in 1926. Spinners Rhodes and Kilner were as effective with the ball as with the bat, while in George Macaulay and Emmott Robinson the White Rose County had two of the finest fast bowlers of their time. Robinson, said Altham, was so dangerous simply because he adhered to the two guiding principles of fast bowling: 'He pitched it right up and made the batsmen go on playing by bowling it straight.' As for Macaulay, he reached his peak in 1925, taking 200 wickets as Yorkshire vanquished all before them, winning twenty-one times and losing not once.

The late 1920s was a time of transition for Yorkshire. Holmes, Oldroyd and Robinson were by now past their peak, Kilner died of enteric fever on his way back from India and even the indefatigable Rhodes yielded to Old Father Time. Not, however, before he 'had spent one valuable summer introducing Verity to the arts of length and deception'.

Verity was Hedley Verity, who by the time of his death in action in 1943 had become one of the greatest slow left-arm bowlers of any age. He announced himself to the world by taking all ten Warwickshire wickets for just 36 runs in a 1931 county match, a feat he repeated the following year against Nottinghamshire. This time Verity's figures were ten wickets for 10 runs in 19.4 overs, and they included a hat-trick. Neville Cardus once wrote of Verity that his approach to the wicket 'so loose and effortless was feline in its suggestion of silkiness hiding its claws'.

The Yorkshire side of the 1920s were ruthlessly efficient

Verity wasn't alone in savaging Yorkshire's opponents; Herbert Sutcliffe reached his zenith in the 1930s. In 1931, when they regained the championship title after a break of five years, the England opener scored over 2,000 runs at an average of 97.57.

The third member of the triumvirate was the 6-foot-4-inch Bill Bowes, a fast-medium bowler of rare guile who could change from an in-swinger to an away-swinger with barely a change of action.

In 372 first-class matches Bowes took 1,639 wickets at 16.76, the majority of them during Yorkshire's dominance of the 1930s.

County champions in 1931, they retained the title the following two years before Lancashire stole their crown in 1934. Yorkshire seized it back the next season, and though Derbyshire took the title in 1936, the last three seasons of the decade were all Yorkshire's. 'There have been many essays from time to time on the "Golden Age of Cricket",' mused Gordon Ross in his 1972 book *A History of Cricket*. 'But who is competent to judge a golden age? Does distance lend enchantment? Were the days of one's youth as enchanting as they seem in retrospect?... Yorkshiremen though (and who better to judge their own players) will tell you that the 'thirties was a golden age of Yorkshire cricket.'

An adding machine

He's had a plane named after him, several roads, a plant, a gate, a stand and a stadium. His face has appeared on stamps and on coins, songs have been sung about him, portraits painted of him and over twenty biographies have been written. There's a museum dedicated to him, a website and he even has his own foundation. No doubt about it, Donald Bradman will always be the world's most famous – and greatest – cricketer.

Born in Cootamundra in New South Wales in 1908, Bradman moved with his family to Bowral when he was two, and it was there with a stump and a golf ball that he developed the skills to become the world's best. 'I threw the golf ball at the brick tankstand with one hand and then held the stump with the other hand,' he later recalled, 'and as the ball rebounded I gripped the stump in two hands and tried to play a shot.'

Affectionate anecdotes about Bradman were as rare as a loose stroke from his bat

He was a solitary child, more interested in cricket than people, and as a player his joy at the crease came from accumulation not entertainment. As R.C. Robertson-Glasgow wrote of Bradman in 1948 following his retirement, he was 'a business cricketer... If there was to be any charm, that was for the spectator to find or miss. It was not Bradman's concern.'

Bradman's concern was making runs and not winning friends. Affectionate anecdotes about Bradman were as rare in his career as a loose stroke from his bat. 'No one ever laughed about Bradman,' said Robertson-Glasgow. 'He was no laughing matter.'

The last of his fifty-two Tests was against England at the Oval in 1948. Bradman came to the crease needing four to take his Test average into three figures. He was bowled for a duck by Eric Hollies. It was said later that Bradman had failed to spot Hollies' googly because he was so overcome by emotion at the standing ovation he'd received from the crowd. Never the romantic, Bradman dismissed the idea. 'To suggest I got out, as some people said, with tears in my eyes is to belittle the bowler and is quite untrue,' said Bradman. 'Eric Hollies deceived me and deserves full credit.'

So Bradman finished his career with 6,996 Test runs at an average of 99.94, a staggering statistic that amazed even King George VI. Introduced to Henry Ferguson, cricket's pre-eminent scorer during Australia's 1948 tour to England, The King enquired: 'Mr. Ferguson, do you use an adding-machine when the Don is in?'

Cocoa bean

Learie Constantine isn't the greatest cricketer to hail from the West Indies, not even from his native Trinidad, but no man has done more for Caribbean cricket than the player who grew up among the beans on his father's cocoa estate.

Constantine was born in 1902, to Lebrun, a grandson of slaves, and Anaise Pascall, the daughter of slaves. Lebrun lifted himself out of servitude and oversaw a cocoa estate close to Diego Martin in Trinidad.

There on the estate father and son played cricket, and Lebrun would thrill young Learie with stories of the time he toured England with the West Indian cricket team in 1900 and 1906. Cricket, as elsewhere in the British Empire, had been introduced to the Caribbean by British soldiers in the early nineteenth century; the Trinidad Club were one of the first West Indian sides, playing the 59th Foot Regiment in 1842, though the first intercolonial match was between Barbados and British Guiana in 1865.

It was Lebrun's generation, however, who in 1900 toured England for the first time, five years after Robert Lucas had led the first English side to the West Indies. In 1906 they toured again, though no one paid them much attention. *Wisden* failed to mention them in its review of the 1906 season, instead concentrating on the 'north-east wind of a peculiarly searching character' that blighted much of county cricket that summer.

The West Indies didn't return to England for another seventeen years, by which time the Constantine on the team sheet was Learie and not Lebrun (father and son actually played for Trinidad that year in a match against British Guiana, a rare case of a filial ties in a first-class match).

Constantine was still learning his trade when he arrived in England in 1923 in a side led by Harold Austin; the cricketer who caught the eye of the English was George Challenor. He scored 1,556 runs – more than twice as many as anyone else in the touring party – at an average of 51.86. The MCC was so impressed they elected Challenor a member 'as a special compliment'.

The West Indies didn't return to England for another 17 years

But that 1923 tour opened Constantine's eyes to the world. He stayed in fancy hotels, visited theatres and ate in good restaurants, opportunities that would otherwise have been denied him were he not on a cricket tour.

Five years later Constantine was back in England, by which time the West Indies had been granted Test status. The tourists began the tour well, beating Derbyshire and Cambridge University and winning a Minor Counties match against Northumberland. Then came a visit to Lord's to play Middlesex. The home side batted first, Nigel Haig and Patsy Hendren hitting hundreds, as they declared on 352 for six. West Indies' reply was abysmal, and Constantine walked out to bat with his side 79 for five. What followed was a new kind of cricket, unknown to Englishmen, Australians, South Africans and Indians. As Constantine destroyed the Middlesex attack Neville Cardus watched in disbelief from the press box, marvelling, in prose that to the modern eye appears to have an undertone of racial stereotyping, 'on this fury of primitive onslaught, beautiful if savage and violently destructive'. Constantine smashed 86 runs out of the 107 West Indies made while he was at the wicket. It was enough to bring the tourists back into contention, though they still trailed Middlesex by 122. But Constantine had only just started. With the ball he tore through the opposition batting order, finishing with seven wickets for 57 runs. 'Constantine's bowling,' wrote Cardus, 'the line and direction of it, always strikes me as a visible flashing current of the man's life-force.'

Now the West Indies were chasing 259 to win, but once more their top batsmen flopped. Constantine came out to bat with the tourists 121 for five but 'again Constantine's genius shot out lovely streaked lightning, swift cuts, punctuated by the thunder of his drives'. One drive broke the fingers of Jack Hearne, another cleared the boundary ropes by an astonishing margin. When it was all over Constantine had scored 103 and the West Indies had won by three wickets.

Though Constantine wasn't able to scale such heights in the three-match Test series, he ended the tour with 1,381 runs, 107 wickets and 33 catches.

Two years later, in February 1930, Constantine did come good in a Test, taking nine English wickets at Georgetown as the West Indies destroyed England by 289 runs for their first Test victory.

Constantine continued playing Test cricket until 1939, but his greatest devotion throughout the 1930s was to the Nelson Club in the Lancashire League. In his ten seasons with the club he inspired them to eight championship titles, and his presence regularly drew crowds of several thousands. 'Connie', as he was called, also changed people's perceptions about Afro-Caribbeans. As *Wisden* noted in Constantine's 1971 obituary, he and his wife arrived in Lancashire at a time when most people 'had never seen a black man before'. It didn't take them long to realise there was no difference between a white man and a black man – except one: Constantine could play cricket better than any of them. In 1963 the Freedom of the Borough of Nelson was bestowed upon Constantine, a year after he had been knighted by the Queen.

> Constantine changed people's perceptions of Afro-Caribbeans

Reflecting on the legacy of Constantine, Neville Cardus wrote that he 'has at the same time told the tale of his people'. Cardus recalled his performance at Lord's against Middlesex in 1928, and the handful of West Indian supporters he observed at the Nursery

End from his place in the press box. 'While Constantine was batting, a number of his compatriots wept for joy and shook hands in brotherly union. Constantine was their prophet; they saw in his genius some power all their own, a power ageless, never to be put down, and free and splendid.'

HMS *Beagle*

New Zealand was conquered by cricket as easily as the rest of the Dominions, and though the Land of the Long White Cloud is now the world's pre-eminent rugby power there was a period when the little red ball was far more popular than the oval white one.

In December 1835 HMS *Beagle* arrived in New Zealand's Bay of Islands and a young naturalist called Charles Darwin stepped ashore. He spent a few days collecting specimens but wasn't much impressed by what he saw, noting in his journal that 'I am disappointed in New Zealand, both in the country & in its inhabitants'. His mood brightened on Christmas Eve when he accepted an invitation to visit the missionary station at Waimate, 15 miles inland from where the *Beagle* was anchored. Here he found a cricket match in progress and tea for refreshment. 'It was not merely that England was brought vividly before my mind,' wrote Darwin. 'The domestic sounds, the fields of corn, the distant undulating country with its trees might well have been mistaken for our fatherland...'

According to an article in the 1949 edition of *Wisden* entitled 'Growth of New Zealand Cricket', the game was 'first mentioned in a newspaper in 1841, and the first match fully recorded was played at Nelson in March 1844'. Twenty years later George Parr led an England XI to New Zealand, the first touring side to visit the island, and up until the First World War Australian and English sides stopped by to play matches whenever they could.

But unlike Australia, where cricket became established as the nation's favourite sport, in New Zealand rugby was king. Once the first official match was staged – in 1870 – rugby held sway over the country's indigenous Maoris, and many of the Scots who settled in New Zealand preferred the ruggedness of rugby to the gentility of cricket. While Australia and England played their first Test match in 1877 it wasn't until 1930 that New Zealand were granted Test status, the fifth nation to be accorded the honour. By that time the All Blacks had already beaten England twice at rugby.

In the winter of 1929/30 Harold Gilligan led an England side to New Zealand for a four-Test tour, and though the first Test in Christchurch was a one-sided contest, England winning by eight wickets, the other three matches were drawn and the tourists returned home full of admiration both for their opponents and their environs. 'There are no Australia shirt-front [i.e. flat, lifeless] wickets and the main grounds might be English county grounds,' wrote Gilligan. 'Who can ever forget the lovely surroundings of the Nelson ground or the natural arena at New Plymouth?'

The following year, 1931, New Zealand toured England and were beaten 1–0 in a three-Test series. It was a creditable display, considering they were up against the likes of Wally Hammond, Herbert Sutcliffe and Bill Voce. Creaking under the weight of its condescension,

> Creaking under the weight of its condescension, *Wisden* praised the New Zealanders

the 1932 edition of *Wisden* praised the tourists, saying that as 'representatives of one of our great Dominions beyond the seas, the New Zealanders looked upon the tour perhaps from a bigger point of view than the mere playing of cricket... they were still very young in the history of cricket and primarily were here to learn and thereby lay the foundations for stronger sides to come later on to England.'

The strongest New Zealand side to tour England was the 1986

vintage, the first to win a series in the cradle of the sport. Theirs was a squad containing some of the greatest names ever to wear the silver fern – Richard Hadlee, Martin Crowe and John Wright – and they defeated an England equally blessed with once-in-a-generation talent, players such as Botham, Gooch and Gower.

The victory wasn't well received in some quarters. 'New Zealand were a solid side, with two outstanding players in Hadlee and Martin Crowe,' muttered *Wisden* in its 1987 editorial. 'But I do not think that any England team, possessing pride and spirit, would have allowed themselves to be beaten by them.'

Ouch! Bitterness from cricket's yellow bible.

Martini glass

'Bodyline'. Even now, eighty years on, it's the most emotive word in the history of cricket, guaranteed to anger Australians and embarrass Englishmen.

Bodyline bowling is how England regained the Ashes in the 1932/33 series Down Under, having lost them to Australia two years earlier. In that series Don Bradman had touched greatness, scoring 974 runs in seven innings (including a then record individual score of 334) at an average of 139. Put simply, he had been too good for the English.

A plan was needed, and a plan was found, one that would cut Bradman's average in half and prompt former Australian captain Warwick Armstrong to describe him as 'no more than a cocktail cricketer'. The plan was hatched at the Piccadilly Hotel in the summer of 1932, when England captain Douglas Jardine sat down with Nottinghamshire fast bowlers Harold Larwood and Bill Voce to discuss the best way to neutralise Bradman. It was agreed that the only weakness of his that they could detect was a dislike of the short ball, a belief that stemmed from a passage of play in the 1930 Test at the Oval when, after a heavy shower, the wicket was unpredictable and Bradman appeared uncomfortable against the England pacemen.

So the plan was agreed: once in Australia, Larwood, Voce and the other England fast bowlers would bowl short at the Australians, while packing the leg side with fielders waiting for a catch as the batsmen fended off the rising deliveries.

Jardine was sure he'd got the measure of Bradman; he was surer still when the first Test began in Sydney – Bradman was nowhere to be seen. Sick, said the Australians, but Jardine was convinced his nemesis was too scared to face the England bowlers. The tourists won the first Test by ten wickets; Larwood terrorised the Australian batsmen and took ten of their wickets. Only Stan McCabe stood tall, striking a stirringly defiant 187.

Bradman was back for the second Test in Melbourne, part of an Australian team that refused to retaliate with its own theory of short-pitched bowling. By now the local press had stopped calling it 'Leg-Theory' and were using the term 'Bodyline'. Jardine didn't care what it was called, just as long as it won him the series. But Australia fought back in the second Test, and Bradman, out for a duck in the first innings (to a normal delivery), scored a century in the second innings.

Australia had levelled the series, and Jardine was dumbstruck. Australians were, in his informed opinion, 'uneducated and an unruly mob', and he would not countenance defeat. England's bowling in the third Test at Adelaide was as ferocious as anything ever seen on a cricket ground. Bill Woodfull was hit under his heart by a vicious delivery from Larwood. The Australian staggered around the crease, supporting himself

The plan was hatched at the Piccadilly Hotel in the summer of 1932

on his bat. The crowd became agitated, police readied themselves for a riot and Jardine turned to Larwood and said coolly: 'Well bowled, Harold.'

Woodfull was hit again, and again, but he remained at the crease for an hour and a half before being bowled by Gubby Allen, ironically the only member of the English pace attack who refused to fall into line with Jardine's tactics. Back in the dressing room, as Woodfull tended to his bruises, he received a visit from Pelham Warner, manager of the England team. Woodfull sent him away with what would become the most famous line of Bodyline: 'I don't want to see you, Mr Warner. There are two teams out there, one is playing cricket. The other is making no attempt to do so.'

The day after Woodfull was hit, wicketkeeper Bert Oldfield had his skull fractured when he miscued a hook shot off Larwood. It wasn't a Bodyline ball, but few Australians were in any doubt that Oldfield had been unsettled into playing such a shot. Woodfull rushed out to the pitch to help his blooded teammate, screaming, 'This isn't cricket, it's war!'

Jardine was sure he'd got the measure of Bradman

As the press dubbed Larwood 'The Killer', the Australian Board cabled the MCC to tell them that 'Body-line bowling assumed such proportions as to menace best interests of game... causing intensely bitter feeling between players as well as injury. In our opinion is unsportsmanlike. Unless stopped at once likely to upset friendly relations existing between Australia and England.'

The MCC was outraged, replying that 'we the Marylebone Club deplore your cable message and deprecate the opinion that there has been unsportsmanlike play'.

Larwood also received a couple of telegrams from the MCC. One read 'Bravo!', the other 'Well bowled, congratulations'.

Backed by the MCC, Jardine ignored Australian protests and continued with Bodyline for the rest of the series, a series that England won by four Tests to one. Jardine rejoiced in diminishing Bradman, who still topped the Australian averages with 396 aggregate runs at an average of 56.57, excellent for most batsmen but mediocre for him. Larwood, who finished the series with thirty-three wickets, dismissed Bradman four times, prompting Warwick Armstrong's jibe.

Bradman chose not to respond to the taunts, but Larwood did so on his rival's behalf, writing: 'That fellow is a very long way from being the "cocktail" cricketer which Warwick Armstrong in a rather uncouth sneer styled him last season... to him, leg-side bumpers would be mere gifts for four as often as any bowler was fool enough, and incompetent enough, to serve them up.'

England returned with the Ashes, but at what price to cricket? It took many years for Australia to entirely forgive the English for what they had done to the good name of the sport, and as a direct consequence of the series a new law was introduced in 1935 permitting umpires to intervene if they believed a bowler was deliberately trying to an injure a batsman. Ultimately, however, it was the cricketers themselves who killed Bodyline by realising it could spell the ruin of cricket. Winning wasn't that important – unless your name was Jardine.

The Ranji Trophy

The Ranji Trophy, first contested in 1934/35, was so christened in honour of Kumar Shri Ranjitsinhji, one of the finest and most flamboyant cricketers the game has ever seen.

Born in 1872, Ranji learned his cricket at Rajkumar College in Kathiawar and perfected it at Cambridge University. He made his first-class debut for the university in 1893, played his first game for Sussex in 1895 and the following season won his first cap for England. On that occasion, at Old Trafford, Ranji scored 62 and 154 not out against the Australians, rendering *Wisden* practically breathless with admiration. 'The famous young Indian fairly rose to the occasion, playing an innings that could, without exaggeration, be fairly described as marvellous,' gushed the Almanack.

In total Ranji played fifteen Tests for England, scoring 989 runs at an average of 44.95. He also bowled, wrote (his 1897 book, *The Jubilee Book of Cricket*, is a classic) and generally bedazzled the English. 'The magical opulence of "Ranji" was entirely in accordance with the India of the rajahs and principalities,' wrote Neville Cardus. 'He played many a Koh-i-Noor of an innings; his cricket was scintillating and of the East. He seemed to wear flannels that were more easily and beautifully rippled by the wind than the wear of other players.'

But Ranji didn't consider himself 'of the East', certainly not in a cricketing sense. In 1907 he succeeded his father as Jam Saheb of Nawanagar, and four years later, when

India toured England (see chapter 31), he was invited to captain
the party, an offer he rejected because he didn't regard himself as
an Indian cricketer.

Nonetheless, Ranji contributed much to India's standing in
world politics before his untimely death in 1933. The following year
the Indian Board, spurred on by the burgeoning popularity of the
game in the country following England's 1933/34 tour, decided the
time had come to set up a national championship, similar in style
to Australia's Sheffield Shield competition.

In July 1934 the Indian Board met at Simla, at a hill station
built during the Raj, to finalise the details of the championship.
Anthony De Mello, one of the founders of the Board, was explaining
to delegates how he
envisaged the tournament's
structure when Patiala
leapt to his feet. De Mello
left an account of what
happened next: 'The pine-
scented air appeared to be
immediately electrified. In deep tones charged with emotion, His
Highness claimed the honour and the privilege of perpetuating the
name of the great Ranji, who had prematurely departed this life
the year before. He offered straightaway to present a gold cup of
the magnificent design submitted by me and valued at £500 to be
called the Ranji Trophy.'

**Kumar Shri Ranjitsinhji, one
of the finest cricketers
the game has
ever seen**

Initially the announcement was well received by the Board, but
then Vijayananda Gajapathi Raju, better known as 'Vizzy', began
to suggest discreetly that Ranji might not be an appropriate name:
after all, didn't he consider himself an English cricketer?

In fact the real reason Vizzy subtly questioned the suitability
of having Ranji's name on the cup was that he wanted the glory of
donating the new tournament's trophy, which would be named in
in tribute to Lord Willingdon, the viceroy of India.

Vizzy even went so far as to have a cup made, in England, of
chiselled gold, and in October 1934 he duly presented it to the

Indian Board. The *Times of India* approved, carrying a photo of the glittering prize in a November edition and calling it 'The Willingdon Trophy for the Cricket Championship of India'.

By now the championship had been launched, Madras beating Mysore on 4 November in the first match, and the longer the tournament ran the more resistant newspapers turned towards the idea of playing for the Willingdon Trophy. Ranji may have played cricket for England, but he was still an Indian.

Bombay beat North India in the inaugural final of the Indian championship, though it was another week before they received the trophy, and only after they had travelled to Delhi to play a festival match against the Cricket Club of India. The man who presented the trophy to Bombay was none other than the viceroy himself; but it wasn't *his* trophy he handed over, it was the Ranji Trophy. The fate of Vizzy's cup remains a mystery.

Though the format has been radically altered in the eighty years since its inception, the Ranji Trophy still exerts a hold over Indian cricket. Successive generations of cricket fans have come to acknowledge the debt they owe to one of the great men of the game, regardless for whom he played.

A red ribbon

The date was July 1745, the venue Gosden Common and the *Reading Mercury* reported the event in its edition of 26 July.

'The Bramley maids had blue ribbons and the Hambledon maids red ribbons on their heads,' noted the paper. 'The Bramley girls got 119 notches and the Hambledon girls 127. The girls bowled, batted, ran and catches [*sic*] as

well as most men could do in that game.' Gosden Common had witnessed the first game of women's cricket.

Two years later a women's match was staged on the famous Artillery Ground, where three years earlier Frederick Louis, Prince of Wales, had looked on as Kent beat an All-England XI in what was called 'the greatest cricket match ever known'.

Women's cricket carried a cachet at the start of the nineteenth century, the first county match reputed to be the one between Surrey and Hampshire in 1811. Thomas Rowlandson drew a famous caricature of the game entitled 'Rural Sports'. There was a lot riding on it, according to contemporary sources, with Hampshire pocketing 500 guineas after their three-day victory.

Thereafter the women's game appears to have fallen into abeyance, presumably because the Victorians deemed the weaker sex too fragile to play cricket. Women in the second half of the nineteenth century were supposed to swoon not sweep, and it wasn't until the early twentieth century that women's cricket underwent a resurgence.

In October 1926 the Women's Cricket Association (WCA) was formed, and the following summer saw the first organised matches. Instrumental in establishing the Association was Marjorie Pollard, one of England's leading hockey players of the era. When the MCC celebrated its 150th anniversary in 1937 Pollard was invited to contribute an essay on women's cricket to a commemorative book. She began by explaining the role of the WCA, how it 'gave an incentive to something that already existed, and set out to make the game possible for any woman or girl who felt inclined to play'.

> **Perhaps the Victorians deemed the weaker sex too fragile to play cricket**

Then Pollard described the evolution of the women's game in the eleven years since the formation of the WCA. The first representative game to be played under its auspices was the 1929 fixture at Beckenham between London and District versus The Rest of England. County associations were established in 1933.

First England played The Rest at Old Trafford, and then a fifteen-strong England squad sailed to Australia and New Zealand, where women's cricket had been thriving for the best part of fifty years.

The tourists returned unbeaten from their fourteen-match tour and, according to Marjorie Pollard, 'this tour stirred the imagination and whetted the keenness of many women and girls in England, and seasons 1935 and 1936 reaped the benefit'.

But just as the impetus began to grow, the world went to war, and women's cricket took decades to re-establish itself. Nevertheless, the inaugural women's World Cup was staged in 1973, two years before the men got round to organising such an event. England lifted the trophy, defeating Australia by 118 runs at Edgbaston, but the Aussies dominated the next three tournaments; and it wasn't until the 1993 World Cup that England wrested back the trophy.

Watching that year was a young Claire Taylor, who would go on to become one of the world's great batsmen and in 2009 became the first woman to be selected as one of *Wisden*'s Cricketers of the Year. 'There is no element of political correctness or publicity-seeking about her selection,' explained editor Scyld Berry. 'The best cricketers in the country should be recognised, irrespective of gender. Taylor has been chosen on merit, for being pre-eminent in her form of the game.'

In the 2012 edition of *Wisden*, the recently retired Taylor reflected on the journey made by women's cricket. 'The game I finally left last year felt like a different world from the one I watched at Lord's 18 years earlier,' wrote Taylor. 'The 1993 squad was, on average, three years older, and had jobs outside cricket. Players wore white culottes [trousers replaced culottes in 1997] and long socks – not quite the blue and red ribbons used to distinguish the "11 maids" of Bramley and Hambledon who earned a mention in the *Reading Mercury* in 1745, but not exactly the attire you might associate with an athletic game.'

Taylor explained that in 2012 players are young, fitter and semi-professional, their skills honed by an array of specialist coaches.

The rise of India and the emergence of Pakistan would only further enhance the women's game, hoped Taylor, while the fact that the ICC had taken over the running of the women's game in 2005 'can only improve the state of the sport at the highest level'.

Passenger liner

Ship Ahoy! Which is what the England tourists must have cried in March 1939 as they just about made it to Cape Town in time to catch the boat back to Blighty.

But before we come to the ship and why it merits a place in our list, let's go back a year to the publication of *Wisden*. Reviewing the 1937 season, the editor of cricket's bible, Wilfrid Brookes, warned that there 'exists a danger of the Test Match drifting into a dull, monotonous exhibition'. It noted that the Cricket Commission appointed in 1937 had reported that the matter needed to be addressed otherwise it could have far-reaching and damaging consequences for county cricket. To this end *Wisden* was pleased that moves were afoot to limit Test matches to a maximum of thirty hours, in other words five days' duration, as this would increase the 'chance of a definite result'. The onus was on the Australian Board of Control, as so-called Timeless Tests had been played there from 1883, while in England only a handful of such matches had been played, the first the fifth and final Test against the 1926 touring Australians.

Yet, noted Brookes in his editorial, even as he was writing these words, England's first two Test matches in South Africa had ended in dull draws. Brookes laid the blame for the situation not so much on the batsmen, though he suggested they could try and be more positive in their stroke-play, but in the 'artificially prepared wickets' that made for an unequal contest between bat and ball. 'It is obvious that the groundmen [*sic*] in the Union

[South Africa] are becoming as proficient as those in England and Australia in the preparation of a perfect wicket,' he wrote. 'One may logically assume that unless the work of the groundman is to be controlled the aim to bring about more results by extending the number of days allotted to a Test match will once more be defeated.'

Little did Brookes know that within a matter of weeks all his concerns would be crystallised in a match of mind-numbing longevity.

England went into the fifth and final Test at Durban leading South Africa by 1–0 in the series. After the first two drawn matches alluded to by Brookes in his editorial, England had won the third Test by an innings and 13 runs, thanks to a double century from Eddie Paynter and a seven-wicket haul from Ken Farnes.

With the series still in the balance, therefore, it was decided that the fifth Test would be played to the finish. Big mistake. South Africa batted first and were all out for 530 on the afternoon of the third day. England made 316 in reply, though it took them 117 overs to do so.

South Africa batted again, making 481, therefore leaving England to chase 696 for victory. Len Hutton and Paul Gibb came out to bat but only one ball was possible before bad light brought an end to the sixth day of play.

Day ten began with England in a race against time to catch their ship home

Day seven saw England finish on 253 for the loss of just Hutton. Gibb had poked and prodded his way to a painstaking 78 while Bill Edrich had reached his maiden Test century. Day eight brought rain, and the players sat in their dressing room. One thousand miles south-west in Cape Town the crew of the *Athlone Castle* started making final preparations for the passage to England.

Play resumed on day nine, and Gibb's nine-hour stay at the crease ended when he was bowled by Dalton for 120. Edrich was finally dismissed for 219, but England finished on 493 for three.

Day ten, a Tuesday, began with England in a race against time. If they wished to make the *Athlone Castle* they would have to catch the 8.05 p.m. train from Durban to Cape Town. The batsmen forced the pace, Hammond hitting another century and Paynter contributing 75. But at tea it began raining. The captains consulted, reported *Wisden*, and there was speculation the game could go into a twelfth day. 'There was even talk that the squad could go on and leave the two not-out batsmen and the four yet to bat behind to play on, or even that a plane could be chartered to replace the train.'

But in truth, after ten days and forty-six hours of cricket, the players no longer had the will to go on. 'What all of us felt,' wrote Bill Edrich, in his autobiography, 'was that it was an absurdity for any cricket match to go on through ten playing days and two Sundays.'

So the match was abandoned, and the England players hurriedly packed their kit bags and dashed to the train station. They caught the boat in time, and it's probably fair to assume that after those ten days in Durban, the players' only exercise during the voyage back home was the stroll to the ship's bar.

Six months later many of the players would swap cricket whites for military uniform as the Second World War erupted. When Test cricket resumed in 1946 Test matches had been capped to five days.

Pataudi Palace

We left Indian cricket enjoying the delights of the
country's first national championship, named after
the legendary Ranjitsinhji. This next object honours
another hugely influential Indian cricketer who – like
Ranji – was revered in both England and India.

Born Iftikhar Ali at Pataudi House in the Punjab in 1910,
he became the 8th Nawab following the death of his father
in 1917, and in 1926 arrived in England to study at Oxford.
Within six years he was named as one of *Wisden*'s Five
Cricketers of the Year, his citation describing his form
during the damp summer of 1931. 'Despite the wet wickets
so generally prevalent, he actually scored 1,307 runs in
sixteen innings and came out at the head of the Oxford
batting with an average of over 93. His form, to say the
least, was amazing.'

In 1932 the Nawab was selected to tour Australia with Douglas Jardine's England team. It was the infamous Bodyline tour, and Jardine's tactics didn't sit well with a man of the Nawab's class. 'I see His Highness is a conscientious objector,' sneered Jardine when the Nawab of Pataudi refused to field in the leg cordon set for Harold Larwood's bowling. Pataudi's stance cost him his place in the side, and he returned home early from the tour.

He played a third and final Test for England in 1934, and two years later was appointed captain of India on their upcoming tour of England. A couple of months before the Indian team departed, however, Pataudi withdrew saying he was not fully fit. It would subsequently emerge, however, that he had pulled out because of the pressure on him to please 'each community, each province and association, and the rich patrons of the game'.

Ten years would pass before he would finally lead India to England, during which time the world had come through another cataclysmic world war. India, which had played such a prominent part in defeating both Germany and Japan, was on the brink of becoming an independent nation; it was against this turbulent backdrop that India accepted an invitation to tour England and recommence Test cricket.

'I see His Highness is a conscientious objector' sneered Jardine

But there was plenty of strife within Indian cricket in the lead-up to the tour. Many wanted Vijay Merchant to captain the team, believing him more representative of India than Pataudi, who, after all, had won three caps for England. In the end the two men went head to head in a vote among the Indian Board, Pataudi winning the captaincy by ten votes to eight. There were accusations afterwards of skulduggery and of Pataudi winning the vote by underhand methods. 'It will do no harm if a lot of dirty linen is washed in public,' said Pataudi, in response to the claims. 'At least it will enable us to go to England in clean shirts.'

The sixteen tourists who arrived in England in 1946 found a country still reeling from war. Large swathes of British cities had been destroyed by the Luftwaffe, rationing was still in full force (the vegetarians among the Indian squad suffered particularly, and an appeal was issued asking for donations from the British public) and, to cap it all, it rained for much of the summer. Nonetheless, the tourists were royally received wherever they went. The English public, starved of Test cricket for seven years, turned up in huge numbers to watch the tourists, who won eleven and drew fourteen of their twenty-nine first-class matches. One of India's defeats came in the first of the three Tests they played against England, the other two being drawn, a series in which Pataudi failed to live up to his reputation. He managed only 55 runs in his five Test innings, prompting *Wisden* to lament that he was 'but a shadow of the Pataudi England knew so well'.

> The cricketers had been more effective than any official ambassador

Nonetheless, said *Wisden* in its review of the tour, who cared about the form of Pataudi compared with what the visit had achieved elsewhere? The Indian tour had demonstrated to the world that they 'could put aside differences of race and creed and join together on and off the field as a single unit, working as one for the same cause'. In short, the cricketers had been more effective than any official ambassador, endearing themselves and their country to the English public.

The following year India gained its independence, though sadly Pataudi didn't live to enjoy the new-found freedom for long. He died of a heart attack playing polo in 1952, on the day of his son's eleventh birthday. His son, the 9th Nawab of Pataudi, would within ten years score a century for India in their first series defeat of England playing as Mansur Ali Khan – or, as he was nicknamed, 'Tiger'.

An old English coin (pre-decimal)

In the English summer of 1948 the coin toss was the only thing the Aussies lost as they thrashed England in a series of ruthlessly magnificent performances.

Only once in the five Tests did captain Don Bradman guess right when asked to call heads or tails. No matter, for his boys won the cricket. And handsomely, earning the sobriquet 'The Invincibles', and prompting John Arlott to reminisce more than thirty years later that they were so 'brilliant and so full of character as to compel respect from the losers, and admiration from even their most devoted supporters'.

England knew they were in trouble even before the Aussies had set foot in the Old Country. When England batsman Bill Edrich wrote his autobiography in the winter of 1947/48, he cast an eye towards the impending Ashes series with Australia, the first in England since 1939. 'They are indisputably the strongest cricketing nation at the moment,' wrote Edrich, who then listed their names. Some had been to England before, men such as Bradman, Bill Brown, Lindsay Hassett and Sid Barnes, but most were unknown to the English other than what they read in the papers. Were Bill Johnston, Ray Lindwall and Keith Miller really as quick and as dangerous as they said with the new ball?

Just how good a batsman was the nineteen-year-old Neil Harvey,
bearing in mind that against India at the start of the year he'd
become Australia's youngest Test centurion? And was Arthur
Morris almost as prolific a run-getter as Bradman?

'Many of these names will go on from strength to strength for
many seasons yet,' predicted Edrich, who then finished with a
word about Bradman. 'He is the greatest batsman the game has
produced up to now... I am sure
he will end his cricket career in
a blaze of glory.'

Colin McCool's googlies
did the damage
with the ball

But not even Edrich could
have guessed how fiercely
the blaze would burn. The
Australians opened their
tour at Worcester on 28 April; they won by an innings and 17
runs. Bradman and Morris scored tons, and the googlies of the
beautifully named Colin McCool did the damage with the ball.

Next up were Leicestershire, demolished by an innings and
171 runs. Keith Miller helped himself to a double century, and Ian
Johnson's right-arm off-breaks skittled out the hosts.

Yorkshire's turn came a few days later. Mighty Yorkshire,
winners of four of the last five County Championship titles. They
were all out for 71 in their first innings and all out for 89 in their
second.

And so the carnage continued for the rest of the summer. In
all, the tourists won half their thirty-four matches with an innings
to spare. Eleven Australians hit fifty centuries and seven of their
batsmen scored more than 1,000 runs on the tour. In twenty-four of
their innings they made 350 or more, and the highest score against
them by a county side was Nottinghamshire's 299 for eight.

As for the national side, England's finest fared little better than
their county colleagues. They lost the first Test at Trent Bridge by
eight wickets; the second at Lord's – where Bradman won his one
and only toss – by 409 runs; the fourth by seven wickets and the
fifth by an innings and 149 runs. Only the rain-affected third Test at

Old Trafford prevented Bradman's side from attempting to emulate Warwick Armstrong's 1921 feat of a 5–0 Ashes whitewash.

But Bradman's side achieved something that not even Armstrong had managed. In the fourth Test at Leeds England put up a hell of fight and set the tourists 404 to win the match. No side in history had ever scored more than 400 in the fourth innings of a Test to seal victory. Australia did it with seven wickets to spare, on a wicket taking spin, thanks to a stand of 301 between Bradman and Morris.

The match was one of the greatest – if not the greatest – ever seen in England, and a record 158,000 had squeezed into Headingley over the course of the five days. The aggregate of 1,723 runs that they saw was highest for any match in England, and, as *Wisden* said, it was 'the most remarkable performance by any touring side'.

In an unprecedented move *Wisden* selected all of its Five Cricketers of the Year for 1948 from the tour party (Morris, Johnston, Hassett, Lindwall and Tallon), but the biggest honour was bestowed on Australia's captain.

The coin toss was the only thing the Aussies lost

Bradman scored 508 runs in the Test series at an average of 72.57, and overall he scored more centuries that summer in England than any other batsman – and this in his fortieth year. It was an imperious way in which to bow out of the game he'd graced for twenty years, and his reward came in the New Year's Honours list of 1949 when he was knighted by King George VI for services to cricket.

'There was no thought of reward,' wrote Bradman, reflecting upon his knighthood. 'However, it was clear that I was the medium through which was to be expressed England's appreciation of what Australian cricket has meant to the British Empire. In that it was a compliment to Australia and to the game of cricket.'

Pot of Brylcreem

Frankly, any number of objects could have been chosen to represent our next subject.

A bottle of champagne, a deck of cards, a betting slip, a dinner jacket... the list is endless, just like his run-getting in the golden summer of 1947 when Denis Compton became the most famous batsman in the world. More famous even than Don Bradman, a cricketer who played the puritan to Compton's playboy.

We've settled on a pot of Brylcreem because this little object led to something rather big – celebrity endorsements. Compton was a pioneer in putting his face to a product in return for piles of cash. But Compton being Compton he wasn't really interested in the money. Fun was the driving force of his life; fun and runs. He got plenty of both.

Born in north London in 1918, young Denis was a dab hand at cricket and football. Middlesex signed him for the summer, Arsenal for the winter, and he made his debut for both teams while still a teenager. Compton was better at cricket, just, scoring 65 on his debut for England against New Zealand in 1937. Two years later war put his sporting career on hold, though Compton still found time to play on the wing in several wartime internationals for England while serving in the army.

It was after the war that Compton became Britain's Brylcreem Boy. The nation cried out for a hero, and Compton responded. Neville Cardus recalled how in 1947 'the crowd sat in the sun, liberated from anxiety and privation. The strain of long years of affliction fell from all shoulders as Compton... danced forward or danced backwards, his hair tousled beyond the pacifying power of any cream or unguent whatsoever.'

In the summer of 1947 Compton scored 3,816 runs at an average of 90.85, including eighteen centuries. It was a record no one has ever got close to surpassing. Four of the tons came against the touring South Africans, and in the second Test at Lord's Compton and his Middlesex teammate Bill Edrich put on 370 for the third wicket. Writing a few months later Edrich reflected: 'Denis Compton, no less than Don Bradman, is an example of cricket genius. And whenever you hear or read of Cricket's Golden Age, and that the art of batting went out with "Ranji" and Trumper, I would like you to recall these two names. There is no need to apologize to the Immortals for our own cricketing generation.'

By early 1948 Compton was being bombarded with pleas for product endorsements from companies. He didn't have time to sift through them so he stuffed all the correspondence into a suitcase and took it on tour when England toured South Africa in the winter of 1948.

Reg Hayter, the Press Association's cricket correspondent, saw the suitcase and asked what was inside. Compton showed him. Hayter was staggered. There was one from the *News of the World*, pleading with Compton to write a weekly column in return for £2,000, another from Bryclreem beseeching him to give serious thought to their offer of a £300-a-year contract.

Hayter persuaded Compton to let him represent his commercial interests. On their return from the tour he brought on board Bagenal Harvey, a skilled advertiser. They got Compton his newspaper column and they trebled Brylcreem's offer to £1,000. The England batsman was on his way to becoming the first sportsman to be used as a marketing tool, his face appearing in magazines, on billboards and, before long, on television screens.

To his credit Compton's immaculately coiffured head was never turned by his commercial success. He kept scoring runs for Middlesex and England, and in 1950 he helped Arsenal beat

Liverpool 2–0 in the final of the FA Cup. Legend has it that at half-time one of the back-room staff slipped him a large brandy; down the hatch it went and out trotted Compton to tee up Reg Lewis for the Gunners' second goal.

In the end it was an old football injury that brought down the curtain on Compton's sporting career, a collision with Charlton goalkeeper Sid Hobbins in 1938 that ultimately required the great man to have a kneecap removed in 1955. Hobbins wrote to apologise for the accident; the surgeon who removed the kneecap put it on display in his office. Such was the pull of Denis Compton, who, when he finally sheathed his bat, had scored 38,942 runs at an average of 51.85 and played in seventy-eight Tests for his country.

In the days after his death in 1997 friends, former teammates and journalists competed to see who could come up with the anecdote that best captured the essence of Compton. *Daily Mirror* cricket correspondent Colin Price recalled how Compton 'would often turn up late for the start of play, still wearing his dinner jacket from dancing the night away, stretch out on a settee and fall asleep until it was his turn to bat'.

Former England teammate Colin Cowdrey recalled Compton arriving for the Old Trafford Test against South Africa 1955 having forgotten his kit bag. He strolled into the museum, borrowed an antique bat from a display case and scored 158 out of an England total of 284.

Brylcreem made Compton famous and wealthy, though not wealthy by the standards of today's overpaid sports stars. Asked shortly before his death if he regretted missing out on the vast sums of money now on offer, Compton replied: 'We didn't do it for the money. Did it for the fun. I remember I went to Highbury in 1950 to pick up my wages. We'd beaten Liverpool in the Cup and the following Wednesday we defeated the League champions Portsmouth, 4–1. Last game I ever played. My week's wages and bonuses for both games came to 50 quid. I walked out thinking I was a millionaire. Still wouldn't change a bit of it.'

The calypso record by Lord Beginner celebrating Ramadhin and Valentine

The men responsible for our next object arrived in England in the summer of 1948 – just as Don Bradman's 'Invincibles' were running riot in the Old Country – aboard the SS *Empire Windrush*.

Egbert Moore and his friend Aldwyn Roberts had each paid £28 for their passage from the Caribbean to Tilbury docks; they arrived with little else than a desire to see this great city called London and introduce the natives to the joys of calypso music.

The pair of Trinidadians were better known as Lord Beginner (Moore) and Lord Kitchener (Roberts), and for the first couple of years they played their music in small clubs and dance halls until calypso began to grow, helped in part by the success of the West Indies cricket team in 1950.

It was during that decade that the West Indies began to assert a new-found confidence in both culture and cricket.

As we saw in chapter 39, the West Indies had beaten England twenty years earlier in Georgetown and again in the 1947/48 series. But they were defeats in the Caribbean, on pitches and in stadiums that were not considered up to standard. In England, so the thinking went, the West Indies would be murdered.

But the 1950 West Indian tourists were to shatter the smug superiority of the hosts and prove to the world that a black side could be the equal of a white side no matter where the match. As the Trinidadian historian C.L.R. James noted in his book *Beyond a Boundary*, 'true West Indian independence and the national consciousness it required would be impossible until the West Indies had taken on the colonisers at their sacred game and mastered it sufficiently to defeat them at home'.

When the 1950 side arrived all attention was focused on the three Ws: Everton Weekes, Clyde Walcott and Frank Worrell. Here was a trio of master batsmen to take on the English bowling attack, but what about the West Indian bowlers? How would Johnson, Jones and Pierre fare on the slow, green English wickets?

The West Indian tourists shattered the hosts' smug superiority

Not well was the answer. Between them they took just ninety-one wickets in thirty-one first-class matches. But no matter because 258 wickets were shared between the West Indies two twenty-year-old slow bowlers – Sonny Ramadhin and Alf Valentine.

To look at either Sonny or Alf, one wouldn't have thought they were capable of reducing an England side containing Len Hutton, Bill Edrich, Cyril Washbrook and Denis Compton to a gibbering wreck, but they did. 'Valentine was toothy, bespectacled, crinkly-haired and kept his left index finger in order by constant applications of surgical spirit,' wrote David Frith in *The Slow Men*. Ramadhin, on the other hand, was 5 feet 4 inches and 9 stone (and immaculately attired). Yet he was capable of bowling leg-breaks, off-breaks and straight balls without any discernible change of action.

In the first Test at Old Trafford Valentine took eleven wickets, bowling with the 'briefest of run-ups, the ball cradled in a curled wrist... [and] an energetic full sweep of the arm'. Yet the West Indies still lost thanks to two poor displays with the bat. But the batting improved in the second Test at Lord's, while Ramadhin

joined Valentine in cutting a swathe through the English order.
Between them they took eighteen of the twenty wickets, eleven of
them going to Ramadhin, as the West Indies claimed their first Test
match victory in England by the massive margin of 326 runs. 'Such
a sight has never been seen before at Lord's,' said BBC commentator
Rex Alton, talking not about the cricket but the pitch invasion
with Lord Kitchener at its head. Wearing a bright-blue shirt and
strumming his guitar, His
Lordship led around forty
West Indian fans on to the
pitch. 'I took my guitar and I
call a few West Indians, and I
went around the cricket field
singing,' he reflected years
later. 'And I had an answering chorus behind me and we went
around the field singing and dancing. So, while we're dancing, up
come a policeman and arrested me. And while he was taking me
out of the field, the English people boo him. They said, "Leave him
alone! Let him enjoy himself. They won the match, let him enjoy
himself." And he had to let me loose, because he was embarrassed.'

> **Lord Kitchener led the pitch
> invasion as the West
> Indies won at
> Lord's**

Kitchener led the crowd, singing and dancing, 'from Lord's into
Piccadilly in the heart of London. And while we're singing and
dancing going into Piccadilly, the people opened their windows
wondering what's happening.'

The English batsmen were just as bemused for the rest of the
series. Humiliation at Lord's was followed by defeat at Trent Bridge
and the Oval, the latter by a thumping innings and 56 runs. By this
stage of the tour, sighed *Wisden*, Valentine was 'almost unplayable'.
He ended the series with thirty-three wickets and Ramadhin
with twenty-six. No other West Indian bowler took more than six
wickets in the series.

Though they never would scale such giddy heights again
(England in 1957 resorted to padding away Ramadhin to such
effect that calls began to grow for an adjustment to the lbw law),
Ramadhin and Valentine achieved cricketing greatness on that

tour. They also helped Lord Beginner achieve calypso greatness, when he released a song written by Lord Kitchener, the chorus of which went: 'With those two little pals of mine, Ramadhin and Valentine'.

West Indian cricket had finally arrived in Britain, and so had Caribbean culture.

According to a 2009 article in the magazine *Caribbean Beat*, when the tourists sailed home in September 1950 they left behind an England different to the one they had found five months earlier. 'Almost imperceptibly, England had changed. Immigrants had found their voice, a sporting triumph had given them a vehicle to express themselves, "without fear", and that voice was not about to be silenced.'

A school cap

**In July 1956 a ten-year-old schoolboy named Richard
Stokes was taken by his father to watch Australia play
England at Old Trafford.**

The five-Test series was one apiece when Stokes junior –
no doubt wearing his regulation school cap – and Stokes
senior arrived in Manchester for the fourth Test. England
batted first and made 459. Australia began their innings
well, reaching 48 without loss. Then on came Jim Laker.
Laker and the Aussies had previous; playing for Surrey
against the tourists earlier in the season the off-break
bowler had taken all ten of their wickets for just 88 runs.

First down at Old Trafford was Colin McDonald, caught
Lock, bowled Laker. Neil Harvey went next, bowled second
ball by an absolute snorter. Laker claimed it was the 'ball
that won the Test series'.

At that point Laker's spinning twin had a say,
Tony Lock having Jimmy Burke caught for 22. But the
remaining seven Aussie wickets all went to Laker for
just 37 runs. 'Naturally I was proud of my return of nine
wickets, but it would never have been as profitable if
there had been much sanity in the Australian display,'
commented Laker, who was as surprised as anyone by the
tourists' crazy batting performance.

The Aussies sat stunned in their dressing room. No one
much fancied going out again to face Laker on a pitch that
was dry, white and dusty, and taking spin to a terrifying
degree. 'Our mental attitude was not very good,' admitted
Ian Craig, one of the Australian batsmen, on the fiftieth

anniversary of the match. 'We had lost some of our resolve.'

But out they went into the arena, brave gladiators being fed to Laker. Soon, though, rain intervened, and when young Richard Stokes turned up at Old Trafford for the final day's play Australia were 84 for two with Laker having claimed both second-innings wickets. 'It was cold, maybe wet, and there were lots of people in the ground,' recalled Stokes.

Australia needed to bat all day if they were to save the match and stand any chance of reclaiming the Ashes in the final Test at the Oval. Colin McDonald and Ian Craig began the day in pugnacious mood, the pair finding that the damp conditions made batting easier. 'When the wicket was wet it wasn't as difficult, the ball wasn't gripping,' reminisced Craig. 'It was only when it was dry that they were able to get the turn and bounce that they did.'

After lunch the sun came out and the Aussies caved in. As the pitch embraced spin so the wickets tumbled. Craig out for 38. Mackay, Miller and Archer, a trio of ducks, then McDonald, finally winkled out for 89. The rest were mopped up without too much trouble. Australia were all out for 205, and Laker had taken all ten wickets. It was an unprecedented feat in Test cricket, yet Laker took it all in his stride. Neil Harvey shook hands with his adversary and congratulated his historic achievement. 'Well done, Jimmy,' said the Australian. 'You've done a great job.' 'Well,' replied Laker, 'you've got to get them when you can, don't you?'

No one fancied facing Laker on a dry, white and dusty pitch

On the way back home to his wife, Laker stopped at a Lichfield pub, had a sandwich and a bottle of beer and, unrecognised, listened to other customers as they described the events at Old Trafford.

It was a day to remember for young Richard Stokes. A piece of cricket history and the retention of the Ashes. His love of cricket never left him, and forty-three years later, when he found himself in Delhi in February 1999 on a business trip, he decided to celebrate his fifty-third birthday by watching a day's play between

India and Pakistan at the Feroz Shah Kotla. 'When I planned my trip to India, I knew I could not return without watching the Indo-Pak rivalry on the cricket field,' the financial consultant told an Indian newspaper. Stokes arrived at the ground just after lunch when Pakistan had just passed 100 for the loss of two wickets. Almost immediately the Indian spinner Anil Kumble dismissed Inzamam-ul-Haq and Yousuf Youhana. 'I told a friend of mine that I have brought luck to Kumble and India,' recalled Stokes. 'When he had taken six wickets, I told him about my having watched Laker's feat, and he just said that history was about to be repeated. I merely laughed.'

Laughter turned to disbelief when Kumble took the last four Pakistan wickets to finish with figures of ten for 74. For only the second time in Test match history a bowler had claimed all ten wickets in an innings. 'My first reaction is that we have won,' said Kumble afterwards. 'No one dreams of taking ten wickets in an innings, because you can't.'

But Laker had, and now Kumble, both spinning their way into cricket immortality, both watched by Richard Stokes. 'My God! What luck!' he told Indian reporters. 'If Kumble himself couldn't believe it, then how can I?'

Radio mic

The names roll off the tongue like runs from the bat of Alastair Cook. Rex Alston, John Arlott, Brian Johnston, Henry Blofeld, Jonathan Agnew, great commentators all, and men who at one time or other have sat behind out next object – a radio mic.

Fifty-six years after its first broadcast, BBC Radio's *Test Match Special* is still going strong, the Corporation guaranteed exclusive rights to England matches up to 2019. A new deal was agreed with the England and Wales Cricket Board in 2012 in the same week that Sky Sports signed a four-year deal with the ECB for similar live television rights. Sky are believed to have paid £260 million for the rights, money that the ECB will plough back into the game for the benefit of the cash-strapped counties as well as the Team England programme.

The BBC didn't bother to submit a bid for television rights. What was the point? They not only lack Sky's muscle but scheduling issues precluded a bid. Old 'Auntie's' stranglehold on televised Test cricket was broken in 1999 when a joint bid of £102 million from Sky and Channel 4 surpassed anything the BBC could muster. So ended an era, one that had begun sixty years earlier when the Corporation paid the MCC thirty guineas to cover the 1938 Lord's Test against Don Bradman's Australia using three Marconi Emitron cameras.

Though the BBC had broadcast the odd snippet of radio commentary in the late 1920s it was the splendidly named Seymour Joly de Lotbiniere ('Lobby' to his friends) who in his capacity as the BBC's Director of Outside Broadcasting understood the potential of televised cricket coverage.

The MCC were open to the suggestion, though they expected payment for the inconvenience of admitting the three cameras and other fancy equipment. The BBC agreed to pay the MCC 100 guineas – seventy for radio and thirty for television – and for that first Test at Lord's the BBC installed its cameras on the Mound Stand and the Grandstand and transmitted a maximum of three hours' play each day.

The coverage was a hit with the public. Everybody enjoyed seeing England's Len Hutton scoring runs, and the sight of Bradman making hay was also a joy to watch, whatever one's allegiance. In 1939 the BBC proposed covering twenty-four matches on the wireless and televising the Lord's and the Oval Tests as well as the Eton vs Harrow match. Colonel Rowan Rait-Kerr, secretary of the MCC, listened to what the BBC had to say and replied: 'In 1938 television of sport was experimental. The situation has now changed. The number of sets in use has increased enormously, and it is thought that the fee for televising the Test Match should not be less than 50 guineas, and for Eton v Harrow 20 guineas.'

What could the BBC do, other than cave in to the MCC's new evaluation (though they dropped the Eton match to save costs)?

When cricket resumed after the war, the BBC once more danced to the MCC's tune, paying 125 guineas for three days of the 1946 Lord's Test against India and agreeing 'not to transmit any footage before 3:00 p.m. thereby off-setting any possibility of dissuading fans from going to cricket'.

In the decade that followed the balance of power tilted further in favour of the MCC, as for the first time the BBC faced competition. The 1954 Television Act established the first commercial television franchises in Britain, and soon cricket's governing body was being courted by the likes of ATV (Associated Television), who in 1956 'offered £500 a day for coverage of the Australians in their warm-up matches against the counties'. This offer subsequently collapsed, and the MCC took note. The BBC might not have had the same purchasing power as some of the commercial stations but at least they were financially reliable. So when Sir William Becher of Associated Rediffusion offered to pay the extraordinary sum of £1,500 per day for exclusive rights to all five England Tests against the Australians (a total of £37,500), the MCC instead accepted the BBC's bid of £30,000 because it considered it had a 'duty to viewers to ensure that during the times when the television of a Test Match was taking place a nation-wide coverage would be effected'. As Richard Haynes of the Stirling Media Research Institute wrote in his 2009 essay 'The Early Courtship of Television and Sport', 'the lack of professionalism and the fractured nature of the ITV franchises [...] enabled the BBC to gain its predominant position in the coverage of the sport from 1956 on. It was a process that ultimately made BBC Television synonymous with cricket for more than forty years until the shackles of regulation were released once more in the 1990s.'

A year after the 1956 deal between the MCC and the BBC, *Test Match Special* was launched on the radio in time for England's series against the touring West Indies.

Rex Alston, John Arlott and E.W. Swanton were the commentators for the inaugural occasion, and it was Arlott's Hampshire burr which became the voice of cricket on the radio until his retirement in 1980. 'A sound like Uncle Tom Cobleigh reading Neville Cardus to faraway natives,' as Dylan Thomas once said.

Brian Johnston was the main man behind the mic once Arlott had stepped down, and following his death in 1994 the fine tradition of radio cricket commentary has been carried on by the likes of Henry Blofeld, Jonathan Agnew and Christopher Martin-Jenkins, whose death in early 2013 has left an unfillable hole in the commentary box. Part of TMS's continued appeal is its streak of English eccentricity in an age where television has become obsessed with being brash, sexy and high-tech. Tuning into TMS is to be transported back to a gentler age where as much pleasure can be derived from a good chocolate cake as from a good cover drive.

A sitar

Hanif Mohammad was born and brought up in Junagadh, north of Bombay. That's where, with his four brothers, he first played cricket, until in 1947 the family left India for the newly founded nation of Pakistan.

The Mohammads set up home in a disused Hindu temple in Karachi, and the boys continued to play cricket (four of them would be capped by Pakistan). 'A small, low wall separated the garden from the road on the legside,' Hanif recalled later. 'If we lifted the tennis ball over it we were out. We seldom did. That was our secret.'

Five years after the formation of Pakistan Hanif was playing cricket for them aged just seventeen. Two years

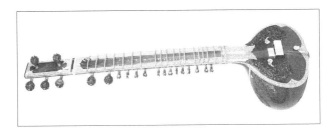

earlier he'd announced himself to the world as a 'Boy Wonder', scoring a century for Karachi Muslims against Punjab.

Now, on his Test debut for Pakistan, he again showed his class, scoring 51 out of a total of 150. The 'Boy Wonder' had graduated to the 'Little Master', and for the next two decades Hanif Mohammad broke cricket records at will.

No other cricketer had ever shown such concentration as Hanif did match after match, and because of it he did more than anyone to establish Pakistan as a force in international cricket.

In 1954 Pakistan made their first tour to England led by Abdul Hafeez, who eight years earlier had been a member of the Indian party skippered by the Nawab of Pataudi (see chapter 45). The Indians had failed to win any Tests; but Pakistan won their fourth match of the series, beating England by 24 runs at the Oval, the only side to win a Test match on a first visit to England. In its account of the tour *Wisden* described Hanif as 'by far the best batsman in the party. At first almost purely defensive, he later blossomed into a most attractive opening batsman, bringing off delightful all-round strokes with a power his slight build belied.'

Hanif continued to plunder runs against the best in the world, racking up centuries against India, New Zealand and the West Indies. But it was what happened at Bridgetown, Barbados, against the West Indies in January 1958 that elevated Hanif to a higher plane.

West Indies batted first and made a daunting 579. Then they skittled out Pakistan for 106 with paceman Roy Gilchrist taking four for 32. Pakistan went out to bat again requiring 473 to avoid an innings defeat. The helmetless Hanif, all 5 feet 4 inches of him, ducked under a bouncer for his very first ball, and then turned to watch as the ball kept on rising and rising, over the head of the wicketkeeper and into the sightscreen. For a Pakistani batsman, playing in his country's first Test against the West Indies, it was a knee-trembling introduction to Caribbean cricket.

Hanif saw off Gilchrist, and then the fast-medium swing bowling of Denis Atkinson. Each hour he called for a drink, wrung out his neckerchief, and refocused his mind. Colin Smith came on with his off-breaks but failed to dislodge Hanif. Nor did the left-arm spin of Alf Valentine, nor even the trickery of Garry Sobers.

At the end of the day Hanif had reached an unbeaten 161, but Pakistan were still 200 shy of the West Indies' total with two days to play. That night teammate Abdul Kardar, who had played for India under the name Abdul Hafeez, pushed a note under the door of Hanif's hotel room: 'Little One,' ran the note. 'You can still save us. Understand that they just cannot get you out. It is them that are becoming desperate now.'

The next day Gilchrist tried again to dislodge Hanif, but again he wouldn't budge. By now the sun had burned three layers of skin from his face, but his mind remained intact. The penultimate day ended with Pakistan 525 for three (a lead of 52) with Hanif still there on 270. He was finally out the next day for 337, second only to Len Hutton's 364 in the annals of Test-match batting. The sixteen hours and thirty-nine minutes that he batted was a new record – one that will probably never be broken.

But that wasn't what mattered to Hanif. The match had been saved, and Pakistan had shown once again that they were a match for any team in Test cricket.

A year later Hanif set another record, batting for Karachi against Bahawalpur, when he was run out for 499 while attempting to reach the magical 500. This feat would stand until Brian Lara's 501 for Warwickshire against Durham in 1994.

Each hour he called for a drink, wrung out his handkerchief, and refocused his mind

The last of Hanif's magnificently obdurate innings was at Lord's in 1967. Remembering it, the *Independent* wrote in 1992 that Hanif 'clung to the crease like a leech until he ran out of partners at 3.24pm on the Monday'. But once more he had done enough to save Pakistan, his unbeaten 187 dragging his side from 99 for six to the safety of 354. It hadn't been pretty; in fact it had been characteristically dour, with Hanif taking nine hours and 556 balls to compile his runs. Yet Pakistan's honour was intact and Hanif could rest easy that night. 'Indifferent to the ensuing trickle of adulation as he was to the torrent of criticism,' commented the *Independent*, 'the reluctant entertainer returned to his hotel room and lost himself in a soothing recording of his beloved sitar music.'

Cricket boot

It was a toss-up for our next object between a cricket boot and a pair of spectacles. In the end we plumped for the boot. Oh, didn't we mention? The spectacles would have to have been rose tinted, so we could all look back to an age when cricket was golden and players good sports.

Because, according to legend, back in the good old days batsmen did more walking than ramblers. Really? Try telling that to W.G. Grace, one of the game's biggest cheats, or Gubby Allen, the arch opponent of Bodyline, who once commented 'between the wars, few batsmen ever walked unless given out'.

Then there was Bradman, the legendary Bradman, who upon retiring reflected: 'I have the abiding conviction that I played the game as it should have been played.'

In which case, a bit like the umpire in question, let's give the Don the benefit of the doubt and say that what occurred in the first Ashes Test at Brisbane in November 1946 must have slipped his mind. Having made a scratchy 28 in the first innings against England, Bradman edged a ball from Bill Voce. Bill Edrich, fielding near by, wrote in his memoirs the following year: 'We heard and saw it hit the upper edge of an almost horizontal bat and go at a tremendous pace towards [Jack] Ikin, who caught it shoulder high at second slip. Time stood still for a momentous half-second of silence while we waited for Bradman to leave, but he stared down on the ground with a black frown... I can only suppose he must have thought that the ball hit the ground after leaving the bat; but every English player thought that it never went within nine inches of the grass.'

A dumbstruck Ikin appealed to the umpire, an Australian, who took the side of Bradman. The Don went on to amass 187 out of 645, leaving Edrich to suggest, 'had Bradman gone then, I firmly believe the Tests [Australia won the series] would have run a quite different course'.

Walking has often come down to a personal choice, a matter of conscience. Colin Cowdrey had a reputation for walking; so too Peter May, one of England's great captains of the last fifty years. One of his predecessors, David Sheppard, admitted in an interview with the *Independent* in 1997 that he had been a non-walker when he first played for England in the early 1950s. Then he began opening the batting for Sussex with John Langridge. 'I never saw John fail to walk when he knew he had nicked the ball and it was his example that made me say, "That's what I'll do",' reflected Sheppard.

Playing against Victoria during England's tour of Australia in the winter of 1962/63, Sheppard walked when he got the lightest of edges on a ball going down the leg side. After the game Sheppard was approached by Jack Fingleton, the former Australia Test batsman turned writer. 'You made the umpire look silly,' he told Sheppard. 'There he was shaking his head and you were walking off.' Sheppard replied: 'Then he was a stupid umpire. He should have watched what I was doing.'

Let us look back to an age when criket was golden and players good sports

Sheppard, who later became the Bishop of Liverpool, claimed erroneously in that 1997 interview that 'Australians never walk'. Most don't, but some have; notably wicketkeeper/batsman Adam Gilchrist, capped ninety-six times between 1999 and 2008. Gilchrist walked during the semifinal of the 2003 World Cup, later explaining in his book *Walking the Walk* that 'I felt it was time that players made a stand to take back responsibility for the game'.

Gilchrist's laudable stance perhaps stemmed from the ruthless approach to the game encouraged by Steve Waugh, the most successful captain in the history of Test cricket with forty-one wins in fifty-seven Tests. The year before Gilchrist's action, Waugh had stood his ground at Melbourne after edging a ball from England's Steve Harmison to wicketkeeper James Foster. Waugh survived and used a motoring metaphor to excuse his behaviour. 'If you're driving a car over 70 kilometres an hour in a 70 kilometre zone are you going to report yourself to the police station to say you were speeding?' he retorted to reporters. Then he added: 'People… as long as I've played, they've never walked. There have been plenty of instances of that in this match and throughout the series. Players accept that. Umpires are there to make a decision and that's where I think it should be left.'

Walking has ten come down to a personal choice

England captain Nasser Hussain was later described as 'spewing' at Waugh's escape, while the English press rushed to occupy the moral high ground. In their stampede to reach the summit of sportsmanship they overlooked the actions of Michael Vaughan the previous month. The England batsmen had reached 19 when he was involved in a disputed catch at cover point. The Australians felt they'd caught him, Vaughan disagreed, though television replays suggested the Aussies were right.

Vaughan went on to make 177, and when he finally returned to the pavilion he was asked about the catch that never was. 'There are times as a batsman when you are given out and you aren't,' he replied. 'It's a tough game.'

Tough as old boots. With or without the walking.

A duck's egg

While rugby has its 'scissors' and 'garryowens', golf its 'birdies' and 'bogies' and football its 'nutmegs', no sport can match cricket when it comes to colourful terms. Only in cricket can you see a 'ferret' facing a 'pie chucker', or a 'nightwatchman' 'fishing' in the 'corridor of uncertainty'. And what other sport can offer you a 'maiden over' containing a 'flipper', a 'googly' and a 'jaffa'?

Then there are the 'dollies', the 'doosras' and the 'daisy-cutters', and of course probably the most famous cricketing expression of all – the 'duck', sometimes 'golden', occasionally 'diamond', always unwanted.

   A duck is what a batsman who is dismissed without scoring gets. On Australian television the luckless batsman traipses back to the 'hutch' (pavilion) followed by an on-screen duck, though the origin of the term actually derives from a duck's egg, similar to the shape of a 0 in the scorer's scorebook. A duck is golden when the batsman is out first ball, and it's a diamond duck when the player is run out without facing a ball.

A bowler's arsenal includes 'dollies', doosras' and 'daisy-cutters'

   Duck is one of cricket's oldest terms, as is googly, a leg-break that is bowled out of the back of the hand so that it spins from left to right instead of the customary right to left. According to Simon Hughes, the former Middlesex player turned cricket technician, the googly got its name 'because when it was first seen in the 1890s, it made the batsman "goggle" with surprise'. As for a jaffa , Hughes defines it as a delivery that 'deviates or spins alarmingly off the pitch. The origin could be related to the delivery being "juicy".'

Then there's the 'yorker', another term that's been around since time immemorial, used to describe a (usually fast) ball that is pitched very close to the batsman's feet with the aim of going under the bat and on to the wicket. According to Hughes, the word yorker derives from an old phrase to 'york' or 'put yorkshire on' someone – common parlance for hoodwinking.

Caught at cow corner off a pie chucker

Some terms have entered cricket's vocabulary more recently. Former England batsman and professional Yorkshireman Geoff Boycott is credited with giving the game 'the corridor of uncertainty' in his capacity as an analyst for BBC radio's *Test Match Special*. The corridor is the imaginary area just outside the batsman's off stump, which, when the ball travels down it, leaves him uncertain whether to leave it or play it.

The 'doosra' is another latecomer to the lexicon of cricket. The off-spinner's equivalent of a googly, the doosra spins the wrong way and was mastered by Pakistan's Saqlain Mushtaq and Muttiah Muralitharan of Sri Lanka, though it's said Pakistani wicketkeeper Moin Khan coined the word doosra, which means 'other' in Hindi and Urdu.

Most of cricket's jargon is colourful, but one or two terms are controversial. The term 'whitewash' – to describe a side winning every match of a Test series – furrowed the odd politically correct brow in years gone by, but it's the 'chinaman' which has really raised the hackles of the right-on. As recently as 2012 a complaint was made in South Africa about a TV commercial featuring a cartoon picture of a Chinese man. The Advertising Standards Authority dismissed the complaint, saying 'the term "Chinaman" was a legitimate name for a legitimate bowling delivery in cricket, being a left-arm, unorthodox spin'. It added that the cartoon used in the commercial 'was neither in bad taste, nor intended to negatively stereotype Chinese people'.

There had been a similar kerfuffle in the United Kingdom a dozen years earlier, prompting the late, great Ian Woolridge of the *Daily Mail* to contact the MCC librarian at Lord's to unravel the tale behind the chinaman. Woolridge subsequently wrote that the chinaman first appeared in the 1930s courtesy of Mr Ernie Achong, a Trinidad left-arm wrist-spinner of mixed West Indian and Chinese parentage.

'He wasn't all that good but he did manage to dismiss R.W.V. Robins of Middlesex once. "Good heavens," Robins is supposed to have said. "Fancy being bowled out by a Chinaman."'

Still, it could have been worse. Robins might have been caught out in cow corner off a pie chucker.

Ron Lovitt's photograph of the Tied Test

An extraordinary photograph of an extraordinary match, the first Test to be tied and still considered by many to be the greatest Test of all time.

So, before we get to the photograph, let's say a word or two about the match. Cricket – Test cricket, at least – was in crisis ahead of the West Indies' tour to Australia in 1960/61. In 2004, to celebrate the 200th anniversary of the first recorded cricket match played in Australia, the *Melbourne Age* canvassed a selection of former players and commentators to pick its Fifty Greatest Moments of the Game Down Under. The Tied Test came in fourth, with the paper explaining to readers that 'it was part of a captivating series that revitalised Test cricket, often regarded as stodgy and uninspiring during the 1950s'.

Few series were as stodgy as the 1958/59 Ashes clash. In the first four days' play of the Brisbane Test between England and Australia – twenty hours of cricket in total – only 518 runs were scored, an average of 25 runs an hour. *Wisden* condemned the 'negative cricket', lamented 'an age of pushes and deflections' and worried about the future of Test cricket if the trend for 'dull and unenterprising play' continued.

Between England departing in February 1959 and Frank Worrell's West Indies arriving in December 1960, the Australian public had been starved of Test cricket. But was that a bad thing? The Sheffield Shield competition was becoming ever more popular and few expected the tourists to put up much of a challenge. The spin twins of Sonny Ramadhin and Alf Valentine were past their prime, there was no Everton Weekes or Clyde Walcott, but at least there was twenty-one-year-old Garry Sobers, and of course there was Worrell himself, the thirteenth captain of the West Indies, but the first who was black. Worrell proved to the world that a black man could lead just as well as a white; better in fact, in the case of the West Indies, because under his captaincy the islands for the first time put aside their differences and Barbadians, Trinidadians, Jamaicans and Guyanans played for the team.

> Spin twins Sonny Ramadhin and Alf Valentine were past their prime

After a warm-up match against Queensland, the West Indies arrived at the Gabba in Brisbane on 9 December 1960 for the first Test. Sobers got stuck into the Australians' bowling attack from the start, scoring 132 out of the West Indies' first-innings total of 453. The home side replied with 505, Norm O'Neill top-scoring with 181, and the tourists were then all out for 284.

Australia required 233 runs for victory in 310 minutes. They had the upper hand, but the West Indies had Wes Hall. The paceman ripped through the Aussies' top order, dismissing Bobby Simpson for 0, Neil Harvey for 5 and Norm O'Neill for 26. 'Half Australia were out for 57, and Hall had four for 37,' wrote E.M. Wellings in *Wisden*. 'Then a sixth wicket fell at 92, and those watchers who lived in Sydney were planning to catch the 5.45 plane.'

Meanwhile Australia's captain, Richie Benaud, joined Alan Davidson at the crease. 'Most batting sides, I think, would have tried to play for a draw in these circumstances,' commented *Wisden*. 'Australia did not. They had their captain at the wicket, and he and Davidson set off for victory.'

Davidson had already taken eleven West Indian wickets, and now he laid into their bowlers, smashing 80 runs as he and Benaud added 134 with one eye on the clock. With twelve minutes of the match remaining Australia required just 7 for victory. Easy.

Then came the most remarkable passage of play in the history of Test cricket.

Benaud called for a quick single. Davidson set off down the wicket. Joe Solomon picked up at mid-wicket. 'The secret is balance, to be four-square steady as I took aim,' recalled the West Indian fielder years later. 'I was an East Indian country boy from Berbice, in the sticks, and before we could walk we'd be pitching marbles.'

Solomon pitched the ball at the stumps and Davidson was run out. Australia 226 for seven. In came Wally Grout for the final (eight-ball) over. Benaud had a word with his wicketkeeper. No need to panic. Six runs needed, three wickets intact. Easy.

Wes Hall's first delivery hit Grout on the thigh and Benaud scampered through for a run. Five runs from seven balls needed. Hall fired his next one in short. Benaud edged it behind and was caught. The West Indians went wild. Five runs from six balls and two wickets intact. Grout had a word with Ian Meckiff. No need to panic.

Meckiff did as instructed, playing the third ball of the over 'quietly back to Hall'. Down to a run a ball. The fourth ball beat Meckiff but the batsmen ran through for a bye. Four runs from four balls.

Half a million Melbournians lined the city's streets

Grout skied the next delivery, but Hall dropped the catch. Australia needed three runs from three balls. The force was now with the home side. Meckiff cracked Hall's next ball towards the leg-side boundary. The batsmen ran one, they ran two, and then they chanced a third but Grout was run out.

Australia were down to their last man. Lindsay Kline played the penultimate ball of Hall's over to square leg. To Solomon. As Meckiff charged down the wicket, Solomon picked up the ball. He had just one stump to aim at, but that was all he needed.

Ron Lovitt captured the moment Solomon's throw hit the stumps in a photograph that was soon all over the world. Solomon, on the extreme left of the shot, still has his throwing arm extended, while Kline looks round desperately as Meckiff reaches out his bat

Australia were all out for 232, and for the first time a Test match ended in a tie.

The exquisite drama ignited the rest of the series – which Australia won two Tests to one – with 690,000 spectators attending the next four Tests. 'The kind of cricket that was played on that tour, I don't think I've ever seen it played before or after,' reflected Sobers. Half a million Melburnians showed their appreciation by lining the streets of their city on 17 February 1961 to honour the West Indians on an open-car parade.

The repercussions of the Tied Test were immense. Former Australian cricketer Jack Fingleton was so moved by the match he wrote a book entitled *The Greatest Test of All*. In it he claimed the match 'breathed new and lusty life into the ailing spectre of a once great game... a game that can be played as a game for the enjoyment of the players themselves and the enormous delight of those who pay at the gate.'

'Love Me Do' by
The Beatles

The year 1962 saw the release of the Beatles' first hit 'Love Me Do' breaking into the Top Twenty of the British charts in October. It was also the year that cricket lost a little piece of its past as the MCC abolished the game's amateur status.

No longer would there be a distinction in English first-class cricket between the amateur gentleman and the professional player; from now on there was only a cricketer, dressed all in white and trusted to play the game in a noble spirit regardless of how much he was earning.

The MCC took their decision in November, a month after the Fab Four were shaking their fringes at hysterical teenage girls. It's unlikely the men of the MCC paid much attention to Paul, John, Ringo and George, but they were doubtless aware that the country had changed post-war, particularly in the four years since they had last discussed abolishing cricket's amateur status in 1958. On that occasion the committee, chaired by the Duke of Norfolk, decreed that: 'The distinctive status of the amateur cricketer was not obsolete, was of great value to the game and should be preserved.'

But in 1962 attitudes were undergoing a seismic shift as the Swinging Sixties transformed urban Britain and the young and the working class found their voice, be it through the Beatles or John Osborne and the other Angry Young Men. 'Put simply, the era of social deference was

over,' wrote author and television producer Colin Schindler in
an essay for the 2012 *Wisden* (commissioned to mark the fiftieth
anniversary of the demise of the amateur). 'The wave of consumer-
spending encouraged by the Macmillan government... the rising
tide of immigration and the increasing influence of grammar
school graduates – all contributed to Britain's changing public face.'

Amateurs were thus viewed as archaic in modern Britain, even
though thirteen of the seventeen county sides were captained by
amateurs. One of them, Colin Ingleby-Mackenzie, had skippered
Hampshire to their first
championship title in
1961. But many of the
amateurs struggled
to support themselves
in an age when even
aristocrats were having

> All a first-class amateur
> received was a cleaning
> allowance for his
> flannels of £1

to work; rather as with an increasing number of stately homes,
the impressive exterior concealed the indigent interior, and it was
hard to make ends meet when all a first-class amateur received was
a cleaning allowance for his flannels of £1 and petrol allowance
of 6d a mile. England batsman Trevor Bailey was able to captain
Essex only by taking a paid job as the club's secretary, and other
amateurs were torn between turning professional or leaving the
game altogether to take up other occupations.

So in the end the MCC moved with the times and retired the
amateur, perhaps also tacitly acknowledging that if England
wished to remain strong in an increasingly competitive Test scene,
now that India, Pakistan and the West Indies had emerged from
the shadows, they required a more focused approach, one that
would more likely come from a professional and not an amateur
with other things on his mind. *Wisden* was unsure of the move,
fearing the decision had not been properly thought through.
'We live in a changing world,' it accepted. 'Conditions are vastly
different from the days of our grandparents; but is it wise to throw
everything overboard?'

The great England batsman Sir Jack Hobbs, who in 1953 had been the first professional to be knighted, saw both sides of the debate, remarking: 'It is sad to see the passing of the amateurs because it signals the end of an era in cricket. They were a great asset to the game, much appreciated by all of us because they were able to come in and play freely, whereas many professionals did not feel they could take chances. Now times are different, and I can understand the position of the amateur who has to make his living. You cannot expect him to refuse good offers outside cricket.'

Gillette Cup

So, as we've just seen, out went the amateur in 1962 and in came the Beatles. But not just the Beatles. Cricket witnessed this year the birth of a baby that would grow into an enormous figure, one that now wields huge influence and control and divides opinion within what the ICC like to call the 'global cricket family'.

The post-war cricket boom was over by the 1950s, and as football became increasingly popular thanks to television, floodlights and the introduction in 1955 of the glamorous European Cup, cricket attendances dwindled. The younger generation had more entertainment options by 1960 – not just sport but the cinema and pop concerts. Something had to be done, and the Advisory County Cricket Committee was established in 1961 to look into the matter. One person who contributed to the discussion was Mike Turner, at the time the young and innovative secretary of Leicestershire. Speaking to the *Guardian* in 2003, Turner reflected: 'By the early 60s we had reached the end of cricket's post-war boom. The crowds had declined and there was a need to make the game viable. These were parlous times and there were arguments about which direction the game should take.'

    Turner suggested a one-day knockout competition to be played in May 1962, during a gap in the fixture schedule, involving Leicestershire, Nottinghamshire, Northamptonshire and Derbyshire. 'I saw some gaps in the fixture list and phoned around,' explained Turner. 'My opposite numbers jumped at the chance.' It was agreed that each side would have sixty-five overs to make as many runs as they could, with bowlers allowed a maximum of fifteen overs each.

The BBC turned down the invitation to broadcast the competition, but a local television station agreed to cover the matches. Turner ferreted around in Leicester's second-hand shops until he found a suitable cup, which a local silversmith spruced up for the occasion and which Turner named the 'Midlands Knock-Out Cup'.

Now all Turner needed was some balmy May weather with which to launch his revolutionary idea. Alas, it was cold, very cold, and only around 1,000 spectators filed into Leicestershire's Grace Road ground to watch their boys beat Derbyshire. Over at Northampton's Wantage Road ground, the weather was just as bleak as the home side overcame Nottinghamshire.

Northants went on to win the final, earning their place in cricket history as the first winners of a one-day trophy. 'The crowds are not exactly flooding in,' conceded Brian Chapman in the *Daily Mirror*. 'But I believe they will when they realise the idea does produce bright and challenging cricket.'

The MCC agreed, and the following season the first official one-day competition was launched nationwide. Sponsored by Gillette to the tune of £6,500, the knockout competition was an unmitigated success, and naysayers held up their hands at the end of the season and admitted they'd misjudged the mood of the

> **Turner ferreted around in Leicester's second-hand shops until he found a suitable cup**

cricketing public. 'For years there was talk of introducing such a tournament,' remarked *Wisden*. 'Happily the modern generation decided to take the bold step.'

The tournament rules were the same as for Turner's Midland Cup competition: sixty-five overs per side with no bowler allowed more than fifteen overs. Captains had to ensure that there were not more than five fieldsmen on the leg side or six on the off, and a prize would be awarded to the player judged to be the Man of the Match.

Cricket had never before seen anything like it, and the 25,000 fans who flocked to Lord's to watch Sussex play Worcestershire represented the first all-ticket cricket match and the first time a game had been sold out before a ball was bowled. Not only that, commented *Wisden*, but 'supporters wore favours and banners were also in evidence, the whole scene resembling an Association Football Cup Final more than the game of cricket'.

Now all Turner needed was some balmy May weather

The final was far from a classic. On a cold, grey, rain-interrupted September day, Sussex set Worcestershire just 169 to win from their sixty-five overs, thanks to a battling 57 from Jim Parks, the only man to score more than 40 in the entire match.

But Worcestershire slumped to 154 all out, and Sussex fans celebrated the fall of the last wicket by invading the pitch.

Despite this heretical desecration of the outfield, everyone agreed the inaugural Gillette Cup had been a stunning success. 'No doubt the one-day knock-out match, contested by first-class cricketers, has come to stay,' declared *The Times* the following Monday. 'It has provided, with its brilliant fielding and interesting tactics and fast running, a happy diversion from three-day matches.'

But there were caveats to the praise. *The Times* expressed concern that Sussex had won the tournament by bowling only twenty-three overs of spin in its four competitive matches – the art of slow bowling, warned the paper, must not be allowed to wither for the sake of entertainment. *Wisden*'s worry was that too many captains were positioning their fielders 'around the boundary to prevent rapid scoring'.

Over the course of time both these worries diminished as sides realised the importance of spinners in tying down sides, and the lawmakers introduced rules restricting negative fielding. Instead more and more one-day competitions were introduced – in England and across the cricketing globe – as the craze caught on.

Cricket's next great one-day revolution came forty years
after the Midlands Knock-Out Cup, when the Twenty20 Cup was
sprung upon the English public. This time a new generation of
traditionalists spluttered in indignation and muttered about how
life was better in their day. It was left to former England all-rounder
turned *Daily Telegraph* cricket correspondent Derek Pringle to put
things into perspective. 'Modern one-day cricket bankrolls the
game, providing a bite-sized version desirable to TV as well as the
broader public,' he wrote. Pringle also described the one-day game
as the 'McDonald's' of cricket – unpalatable to some but a global
brand all the same that makes a whole heap of money.

Sobers' ball

No cricket ball had ever been as batted, battered and blasted as the one bowled to the great Garry Sobers one August day in 1968. That swashbuckling afternoon in Swansea, Sobers became the first player to strike six sixes in one first-class over of cricket.

Ten years earlier, batting for the West Indies against Pakistan, Sobers had scored 365 not out, a new record for an individual Test innings that stood until Brian Lara surpassed it in 1994. In 1964 *Wisden* elected Sobers their 'Cricketer of the Year', and in 1966 he scored 722 runs in five Tests against England, at an average of 103.14, also claiming twenty English wickets. He was – and remains – the greatest all-rounder in the history of cricket. Small wonder he was knighted in 1975 and crowned one of *Wisden*'s Five Cricketers of the Century in 2000. Cricket will probably never see his like again, and though others have subsequently struck six sixes in an over, Sobers will be remembered as the first and the finest.

Sobers was playing for Nottinghamshire at the time, arriving at the crease with his customary 'languid swagger... sleeves buttoned to wrists and collar turned up'. He batted stylishly but soberly early on in his innings as Notts reached 358 for five against Glamorgan. Then Sobers decided he should score some quick runs, set up a declaration and have a crack at the opposition. Having reached 40, he chose to launch his attack against Malcolm Nash.

Nash was actually a decent left-arm seamer who had

already taken four Nottinghamshire wickets in the innings. 'It was the first time I had played against Sobers in a first-class match, and I wanted his wicket,' recalled Nash years later. 'I was bowling orthodox slow left-arm spin, which I didn't do all that often. I was just trying to get him out, simple as that. There was no point in bowling wide to him, because then I wouldn't have got him out.'

Just as Nash ran up to deliver the first ball, the BBC Wales cameras at the St Helen's Ground were told to stop filming – they had all the footage they required. But the head cameraman asked producer John Norman whether they could film one final over because he wanted his cameramen to practise their cricket coverage. Norman agreed and told commentator Wilf Wooller to remain at his post.

So the first ball of Nash's over was captured on film, sailing over the Gorse Lane boundary as the left-handed Sobers pulled it for six. So too the second, landing in the stands, to the delight of the few dozen spectators. The third ball was smashed over the head of long-on and the fourth was dispatched over square leg, clattering into the terracing before bouncing back over the boundary rope.

'The idea of going for the six sixes only came into my head when I had got four and I was going for five,' reflected Sobers later. 'I was not thinking about it at all before that.'

The normally phlegmatic Wilf Wooller hollered 'He's done it!'

Nash's fifth ball pitched outside off stump, and Sobers sent it back over Nash's head towards Roger Davis at deep long-on. Davis shuffled to his right, eyes fixed on the plummeting ball, and took a tumbling catch to the dismay of the locals. But in landing Davis had touched the boundary rope and the umpires signalled a six. Dismay turned to delight among the Swansea supporters, now so excited that their loyalty went the same way as Nash's bowling.

One ball remained. Glamorgan captain Tony Lewis pushed his fielders back to the boundary. Nash decided he would 'bowl a medium-paced seamer up in the blockhole'. Sobers steadied himself. The ball was on middle stump, but a fraction short, what

Nash said later was 'the first ball I bowled all day that deserved to be hit for six'.

And it was. Sobers struck the ball a thunderous blow, and it disappeared out of the ground as the normally phlegmatic Wilf Wooller hollered: 'He's done it, he's done it. And my goodness it's gone way down to Swansea.' The ball was retrieved from a gutter in St Helen's Avenue, adjacent to King Edward Road, by a startled seventeen-year-old schoolboy, who later returned it to Sobers.

Nottinghamshire immediately declared and in went Glamorgan to bat. Nash's miserable match continued, as he was bowled for just 8 – by Sobers. Nash later emigrated to America, not to escape the embarrassment of his immortality but to help spread cricket Stateside. When he was tracked down by the *Daily Telegraph* in August 2008, on the fortieth anniversary of Sobers' six sixes, Nash was living in California and only too happy to reminisce. 'I reckon I get asked about it if not once a week then at least once a month,' Nash told the paper. 'It is never, ever far away or out of the limelight. I was just part of history and there was nothing I could do. It was just one over in my life. Would I take it back? Never. I just wish I got paid for it. It would have made me rich.'

The ball did make someone very rich. Having been presented to the Notts Supporters' Association at Trent Bridge, in 2006 it was sold anonymously at auction for £26,400.

Currant bun

'Anyone who would swallow that would believe the moon was a currant bun!' exclaimed the *Guardian* in its leader of 29 August 1968.

The reason for the paper's indignation was simple. The day before the MCC had announced the sixteen players who would represent England in the forthcoming tour to South Africa, and Basil D'Oliveira wasn't among the names. Yet five days earlier he had scored a match-winning 158 for England against Australia at the Oval. The *Guardian*, like just about every paper and person in England, suspected they knew why D'Oliveira had been left out of the squad – because the colour of his skin would be unacceptable to his hosts in South Africa. Not true! cried the MCC, a denial that drew forth the line in the *Guardian* leader.

It was a frivolous quip from the *Guardian*, but within days the mood darkened as cricket became headline news around the world. Suddenly it wasn't buns but bans being discussed as cricket finally confronted South Africa over the evil of their apartheid policy.

The trail that led to those momentous events began in Signal Hill, Cape Town, where Basil Lewis D'Oliveira was born in 1931. Under the apartheid regime he was classified as a 'Cape Coloured': permitted to play cricket, as long as it wasn't with whites, the only people who could play first-class cricket in South Africa. So in his desperation to play at the highest level, D'Oliveira wrote to the only man he thought might be able to help him – the BBC commentator John Arlott. 'Dear Mr Arlott,' began D'Oliveira. 'I daresay this is only a minor detail compared, I presume, to your other escapades, but I am sure that you would try your best and use your powerful assistance to help me...'

D'Oliveira had made the right choice. Arlott had connections in English cricket, and he also had an abiding dislike of apartheid. In 1960 he organised for D'Oliveira and his wife to come to England and play for the Middleton Club in the Central Lancashire league. Such was D'Oliveira's talent with bat and ball that in 1964 he was given a first-class contract with Worcestershire, thus becoming the first non-white South African in English county cricket. Two years later he made his bow for England in the Test-match arena, scoring 27 against the West Indies. In his second Test he scored a brace of half-centuries and in his fifth Test – against India – he made his maiden Test century.

Come the 1968 Ashes series D'Oliveira's form was a bit shaky. He was dropped after the Old Trafford Test but recalled for the final match of the rubber, where he scored (from the England selectors' point of view) the most unwanted century in Test-match history. 'Oh Christ, you've put the cat among the pigeons now,' chortled umpire Charlie Elliott, as D'Oliveira acknowledged the Oval applause on reaching three figures.

The cat was still running amok when the selectors met four days after that match to pick the tour party for South Africa. The minutiae of that meeting have never been fully revealed by those present, though chairman of selectors Doug Insole always claimed the squad was selected purely on cricketing merit. 'Let's forget about South Africa,' he is reported to have said at the start of the meeting. 'Let's pick a team to go to Australia. And that's what we did.'

D'Oliveira listened to the squad being read out on BBC radio, his Worcestershire teammates around him. When his name wasn't mentioned D'Oliveira 'fell apart. He put his head in his hands and wept.' John Arlott shared his friend's pain, writing in the *Guardian* that cricket's administrators must 'recognise that politics can no longer be shut out of the game'. He added that anger wasn't his overriding emotion at the decision but 'sadness, and that in the selection MCC have stirred forces – for both good and evil – whose powers they do not truly comprehend'.

The South Africans were jubilant, though the smirk was wiped off their faces a few days later when the *News of the World* announced that D'Oliveira would be reporting for them on the series from South Africa. Still, at least the cricketers would be all white, they thought. And then in September Tom Cartwright pulled out of the tour with a shoulder injury. He was a bowler but the selectors decided to replace him with a batsman – D'Oliveira.

The news was made public on 16 September, and the following day Prime Minister Vorster informed the MCC: 'We are not prepared to receive a team thrust upon us by people whose interests are not in the game, but to gain

Suddenly it wasn't buns but bans in discussion

certain political objectives which they do not even attempt to hide. The MCC team is not the team of the MCC, but of the anti-apartheid movement.' Britain reacted with fury to what the *Daily Mail* called Vorster's 'crude and boorish' speech, one designed purely to placate the right wing of South Africa. On 24 September the MCC called off the tour, but what couldn't be curtailed was opposition to South Africa in sport.

The events of the late summer were the spark for a firestorm of protest against South African sporting teams, not just in Britain but across the world. Though Australia toured the Republic in 1969/70, the MCC cancelled South Africa's tour to England in 1970, leaving what *Wisden* described as a 'bitter, emotional – sometimes hysterical – aura over English cricket'. In the same year the International Olympic Committee expelled South Africa and the ICC voted to suspend official matches with South Africa. Apartheid had turned to isolation, and South Africa would remain ostracised for twenty long years.

Packet of Rothmans

Apologies to the non-smokers out there, but there is no escaping this packet of Rothmans. Fair play to the cigarette manufacturer, they were the only company willing to stump up £5,000 to sponsor the first ever one-day international.

It was 5 January 1971 when Rothmans stepped into the breach, much to the relief of the Australian Cricket Board. The third Ashes Test in Melbourne had been a complete washout, not a ball being bowled in any of the first four days. Mind you, the cricket in the previous two Tests had been so tedious, so timid, that the *Guardian* was moved to warn: 'One more draw on the pattern of the first two could place the whole of international cricket as we know it in question.'

But in Melbourne the heavens opened, and for three days the rain fell, threatening to cost the MCG £80,000 in lost revenue. Something had to be done. What about an extra Test tagged on to the end? England pooh-poohed that idea. Then someone suggested staging a one-day match at the MCG on the Tuesday (the fifth day of the sodden third Test) – assuming the weather forecasters were correct in predicting an end to the storm. The match could be played 'on Gillette Cup lines' with both sides having forty eight-ball overs to score as many runs as they could. Rothmans said they would sponsor the game, even agreeing to chuck in £90 for the Man of the Match.

And so it was that on 5 January 1971 – ninety-four years after the ground had hosted the first ever Test match

– an Australia XI and an England XI contested the inaugural one-day international. Despite the fact the match was played on a Tuesday a crowd of 45,000 filed into the MCG, desperate to see some cricket and intrigued to watch the new format.

The players were sceptical about the venture, particularly the Australians, who had less experience than the English of limited-overs cricket. 'Everyone thought it was a Mickey Mouse game, just a bit of fun, really. We certainly didn't envisage it would be the start of something as big as one-day cricket,' reflected Australian batsman Doug Walters in an interview years later.

Australia won the toss and invited England to bat. The tourists made 190, losing their last wicket four balls short of their complement of forty overs. It was clear the English weren't sure how to approach the game. Geoff Boycott scored 8 from thirty-seven balls.

The Australian bowlers were similarly unsure what tactics to use. 'I recall bowling my normal line and length and the batsmen – mainly John Edrich and Basil D'Olivera – just put their front foot down the pitch and hit the ball back over my head,' said Alan Connolly, who finished with figures of 0 for 62 off eight overs. That, he reflected, 'was about as expensive as I'd ever been'.

> A crowd of 45,000 filed into the MCG, intrigued to watch the new format

When it was Australia's turn to bat they knocked off the runs without too much trouble, losing just five wickets in the forty-five overs it took them to pass England's total. 'We won it but we didn't really know what we were doing,' admitted Australia's captain Bill Lawry a few years later.

Reaction to the occasion was muted. Everyone agreed it had been a nice little filler, a chance for the players to stretch their legs, the crowd to see some cricket and the MCG to rake in AUS\$33,000 in gate receipts. But as to it being a groundbreaking moment in the history of the game? 'There is little doubt that the public will demand a match of this kind at least once a season,' was about the most enthusiastic comment in any of the Australian newspapers. And as Greg Chappell, one of the Australian players in the match, admitted on the fortieth anniversary of the game: 'We didn't probably appreciate the occasion at the time [but] looking back now it was quite a momentous occasion.'

The authorities similarly didn't appreciate the magnitude of what had been set in motion on that damp Melbourne day. In the next four years only a further eighteen one-day internationals were played, but despite that the men who ran the game had clearly glimpsed the promised land. In 1975 the inaugural World Cup was staged, and cricket would never be the same again.

In a 2003 article for *Wisden Asia Cricket* magazine, Sambit Bal wrote of the unstoppable march of the one-day format: 'The pace of the game quickened considerably; players became more athletic; they ran harder, between the wickets and after the ball; they leapt and they dived; they gave up pristine whites for bright team colours, and the sun for halogen lamps. Cricket, a connoisseur's preserve for more than a century, became a spectacle for Everyman.'

Lord Ganesha, the elephant-headed god of good fortune

We left Indian Test cricket in 1946 in the aftermath of its tour to England under the captaincy of the Nawab of Pataudi, a tour on which India tried hard but ultimately fell way short of the standard required to beat England in their own backyard.

In the quarter of a century since India had failed to win a Test match in England. Pakistan had, the West Indies had, but not India, who seemed unable to best their old colonial masters, losing fifteen and drawing four of their nineteen matches.

But India arrived in 1971 more confident than ever before. An unprecedented series victory in the West Indies had given them hope, and they believed that even the English in English conditions would struggle against their spin quartet of Bhagwat Chandrasekhar, Bishan Bedi,

Srinivasaraghavan Venkataraghavan and Erapalli Prasanna.

The first Test was drawn thanks to bad weather, the Indians looking on aghast from their dressing room as a snowstorm descended on Lord's, and the second match at Old Trafford also failed to produce a winner. So the rubber came down to the last of the three Test matches at the Oval, and it hadn't escaped the Indian players or their fans that the match coincided with Ganesh Chaturthi, a Hindu festival to honour the elephant-headed god of good fortune and destroyer of obstacles.

England batted first and made 355, and when India were dismissed for 284 in reply, a draw or a defeat for the visitors appeared the most likely outcome. But on the fourth day of play, Monday 23 August, Indian supporters arrived at the Oval with an elephant in tow to honour Ganesh Chaturthi. As the *Sunday Times* explained: 'Bella, a three-year-old Asian elephant from Chessington Zoo in Surrey, took to the field wearing a white cap with the words "Chessington Zoo XI". It proved a good omen.'

England collapsed from 23 without loss to 101 all out as Chandrasekhar took a leaf out of Ganesh's books and destroyed all obstacles in his path, finishing with figures of six wickets for 38 runs in eighteen overs. 'I have never been a bowler who planned things,' he told the *Sunday Times* later. 'Most of the time I bowled whatever I felt like, without giving much importance to the conditions or who I was bowling to. I always believed that if I bowled well, I could trouble most batsmen. That afternoon everything fell into place.'

> Chandrasekhar took Ganesh's lead and destroyed all obstacles in his path

But India still needed 173 for victory, on a pitch taking spin and with England able to call on their own 'deadly' spinner in Derek Underwood. At the close of play on the fourth day India had chipped away 76 runs from their target for the loss of just two wickets.

The fifth day was unbearably tense, not just for the small number of Indian fans in the ground but for the millions listening on radios back home. Progress was painstakingly slow as they eked out run after run, but wicketkeeper Farokh Engineer saw them home, scoring 28 of their last 40 runs. 'Those 28 I scored were like 128,' recalled Engineer.

The news of the victory, relayed to India on *Test Match Special*, blew the lid off Bombay, the spiritual home of Indian cricket. *Wisden* reported that 'unprecedented scenes were witnessed on the night of August 24... there was dancing in the streets. Revellers stopped and boarded buses to convey the news to commuters. In the homes, children garlanded wireless sets over which the cheery voice of Brian Johnston had proclaimed the glad tidings of India's first Test victory in England, a victory which also gave them the rubber.'

India returned home in triumph, the unofficial world champions having won a series in the Caribbean and now in England. But it was the latter triumph that stirred India's soul and inspired a new generation of fans. 'India was a colony of England, and to beat your masters at their own game was a bit of a feather in the cap,' reflected Engineer. 'Any victory in a Test series was joyous, but to beat England in England was a phenomenal feat at the time for us Indians.'

World Cup trophy

If you glance back past the elephant-headed god of good fortune you'll see that our fifty-ninth object was a packet of Rothmans. Four years on from that historic one-day international, the ICC launched the inaugural cricket World Cup.

Sponsored by Prudential and featuring eight countries (the six Test-playing countries of England, Australia, India, Pakistan, New Zealand and the West Indies plus Sri Lanka and East Africa), there were no fancy gimmicks. Players wore white, the ball was red and play began at eleven sharp.

No one knew who the favourites were because in the four years of international one-day cricket only eighteen matches had been played. But from the outset it was clear there were only four teams in with a realistic chance of lifting the cup: the West Indies, England, Australia and New Zealand. England's first match was against India, and the hosts crushed their visitors with ruthless disdain. Dennis Amiss scored 137 from 147 balls as England racked up 337 from their sixty overs. India had no idea how to respond, so Sunil Gavaskar played in the only style he knew, accumulating 36 runs from 174 balls as if he were batting for a draw in a Test match. It was, as former England captain turned broadcaster Tony Lewis later described it, 'a perverse moment of self-inflicted shame'. The knock remains the slowest strike rate for any ODI innings over 20 ever.

India finished their innings on 132 for two from sixty

overs, and they were soon on their way home. So too Pakistan, though they pushed both Australia and the West Indies to the wire in their pool matches. In the semifinals the English were routed by Gary Gilmour, the Australian paceman taking six for 14 in a devastating spell of bowling. All out for 93, the English fought back and reduced the Aussies to 39 for six. Then Gilmour did with the bat what he'd done with the ball, dashing English hopes as he plundered 28 from twenty-eight balls.

That set up a final against the West Indies, who'd had no trouble brushing past New Zealand in their semifinal. The stage was set, but would that fickle mistress of English cricket behave on the day? Yes. 'A capacity crowd and another hot shirt-sleeved day, completing the meteorological miracle which has blessed every single moment of this competition with blues skies and sunshine,' wrote Tony Lewis in *Summer of Cricket*.

The West Indies batted first, roared on by the hundreds of Caribbean supporters crowded at the foot of the Tavern Stand, blowing whistles, banging cans and dancing in delight as Clive Lloyd rescued his side. The giant West Indian captain loped to the wicket with his side in trouble at 50 for three. 'How often has he contradicted his studious appearance with thoughts of

> Lloyd lowered Australian heads with a series of mighty blows

violence,' mused Lewis, who sat back and watched as Lloyd lowered Australian heads with a series of mighty blows. A century in just 82 balls, 'and if figures do not persuade the world that something very special was happening, the inhabitants of London NW8 will tell how the mere sound of his bat, hammering out the music sweet to West Indian ears, destroyed their afternoon sleep!'

Lloyd's ton, and a half-century from Rohan Kanhai, took the West Indies to a vertiginous 291. Australia were game in their chase but not good enough, and they had no one to desecrate the West Indian bowling attack as Lloyd had done their own. But there was no shame in falling 17 runs short of a total inspired by a wondrous exhibition of batting. Lloyd took the Man of the Match award, and from the hands of HRH Prince Philip, President of the MCC, the Prudential Trophy, a prize he would lift four years later when this time Viv Richards unfurled his genius at Lord's against England.

'As a final it was all one could ever have hoped for a brave new venture in sponsorship,' wrote Lewis in the book he published at the end of 1975. 'A game which begins at 11am and ends at 8.42pm inevitably kills and rekindles hopes by the minute and by the hour; it chars the nerve-ends, bringing, eventually, the delirium of victory for one and that unwelcome stoicism to the other.'

A devil's pitchfork

The name Kerry Packer still makes many in cricket shudder. More than thirty-five years after he launched his World Series Cricket, opinion remains divided as to its effect on the game. A remark uttered by Packer encapsulated the bitterness that existed between his media organisation and cricket's governing body; it was a bitterness that tore cricket apart but which ultimately helped the game move into the twentieth century.

After a rancorous meeting with the ICC at Lord's to discuss broadcasting rights for his series broke up in June 1977 without agreement, Packer stormed from the famous old ground, pausing only to bellow at the waiting reporters: 'Had I got those TV rights I was prepared to withdraw from the scene and leave the running of cricket to the board. I will take no steps now to help anyone. It's every man for himself and the devil take the hindmost.'

The remark sent a chill down the spine of cricket, and for the next two years Packer caused the sport no end of hellish problems.

The genesis of what came to be called the Packer Circus began in the mid-1970s, a time when cricket in Australia was riding a wave of unprecedented financial success.

Australia's five state cricket associations grossed AUS$1.9 million in the 1975/76 season, an increase of $400,000 on the previous season, and Australia's six home Tests in 1975 grossed almost $1 million in gate money. Yet despite this surge in profit the players were being paid a pittance. In that same 1975 season they were earning just $400 a Test.

Players such as the fast bowling duo of Dennis Lillee and Jeff Thomson, wicketkeeper Rod Marsh and the Chappell brothers weren't happy; it was their talent, their charisma that brought in the crowds – and the cash – but it was the Australian Board reaping the benefit. Into this discontent swaggered Packer, at the time an Australian media entrepreneur and owner of Channel Nine. He had already revolutionised coverage of Australian golf and now he wanted to do the same for cricket, but for that to happen he had to secure the broadcasting rights then held by the Australian Broadcasting Corporation (ABC). When the Australian Board refused to negotiate with him Packer was convinced he had been the victim of the old boys' network and vowed to set up a rival international cricket brand.

To do that meant signing up the cream of world cricket to play in a series of Supertests between an Australian XI and a World XI. This proved easier than he imagined because of the anger felt by the players at what they were being paid. The first player to sign was Dennis Lillee, who put pen to paper in January 1977 in a deal worth $105,000. It was riches beyond the wildest dreams of international cricketers, and within months thirteen of the seventeen members of the Australian squad chosen to tour England that summer had signed up with Packer.

Packer's remark sent a chill down the spine of cricket

Other international stars followed, among them West Indies captain Clive Lloyd, the dashing Pakistani all-rounder Imran Khan and England captain Tony Greig, who signed a three-year deal worth $100,000.

Packer came to London in May 1977, arriving with the hope of reaching an amicable agreement with the ICC for his World Series, but negotiations broke down, and what followed was ugly and unedifying for anyone who cared about cricket. After a series of court cases Packer was forbidden from calling either his matches

Tests (so he called them Supertests) or his team Australia. The MCC also reminded Packer that they held the copyright to the Laws of the Game.

Undeterred, Packer launched his World Series Cricket on 2 December 1977 with a match between an Australian side and the West Indies at an Australian Rules ground in Victoria; at the same time in Brisbane, an official Test match got under way between Australia and India. The cricket was better in Victoria, but the crowds were bigger in Brisbane.

Packer was convinced he'd been the victim of the old boys' network

The crucial factor for Packer was the reaction of the Australian public. Would they throw in their lot behind him or remain loyal to the official Test team, a side of young inexperienced players led by the veteran Bobby Simpson, who had been coaxed out of retirement to lead Australia through the most turbulent season in their history? The public chose to support Simpson and his boys, as did the newspapers, who gave Packer a bad press. As the series with India unfolded into a thrilling rubber, so the crowds began to dwindle at the World Series matches.

In desperation Packer switched the emphasis from Supertests to one-day matches, introducing such concepts as coloured clothing and white balls. But it was the introduction of floodlights that brought the public back to Packer. The first day-night match was staged in Sydney on 28 November 1978 between the Australian and West Indian teams. Nearly 50,000 turned out – not just die-hard cricket fans but women and children and people who thought it would be fun to watch cricket under lights.

The World Series was back, and this time the Australian Board couldn't look to their Test team for help – they were being thrashed by England in one of the most one-sided Ashes contests in history.

By now Packer, the Australian Board and ABC were feeling the financial pinch, and in May 1979 a truce was declared. Channel

Nine won the rights to broadcast Test cricket, and the WSC players were welcomed back into the fold. The real winner, however, was the cricketing public.

In a short space of time Packer had revolutionised the game, and many of his innovations were quickly incorporated as one-day cricket caught on. Reflecting on the impact made by Packer in a 2012 article for the ESPN Cricinfo website, broadcaster Mark Nicholas described how the Australian 'changed the game irrevocably'. He continued: 'It is often overlooked that Packer loved cricket deeply, and that beneath the bluster was an unseen pastoral care for its roots and its people. He took the history of the game and revamped it for the future. His cricket was played with a shocking, gladiatorial intensity and at an immensely high standard.'

That's Packer for you, a devil to some, a deity to others.

Batsman's helmet

Our next object proved an overnight success when it first appeared in a 1978 Test match. Australia's Graham Yallop is the batsman first credited with wearing a helmet, but in fact one of modern cricket's most essential items of kit first saw the light of day forty-five years earlier.

It was the great Middlesex and England batsman Patsy Hendren who first came up with the idea for some sort of protective headgear. Legend has it that the Notts Express Harold Larwood promised Hendren's wife that he would 'knock his block off', and he almost did with a stream of short-pitched deliveries during a county game.

Hendren, by now in his forties and relying more on instinct than eyesight, knew he had to find a solution. In discussing the subject with cricket writer William Pollock, Hendren told him that 'he had had all the bangs in the head from fast bowlers that he wanted for the rest of his life, and that he had come to the conclusion that it was folly to bat against certain quick bowlers, particularly on the wickets at Lord's, without some kind of extra protection'.

Hendren experimented first with 'some rubber inside the cap' before enlisting the help of his long-suffering wife. According to Hendren's obituary in the 1963 edition of *Wisden*, what they produced was a normal cricket cap which 'had three peaks, two of which covered the ears and temple, and was lined with sponge rubber'. For nearly half a century cricket continued without helmets. Bowlers were still quick, batsmen still anxious, but no player dared run the risk of ridicule by striding to the crease covered up. Then in 1972 Australian all-rounder Graeme Watson took a ball in the face from Tony Greig while batting against a World XI. According to Melbourne's *Sunday Age*, Watson 'was in a critical condition in a Melbourne hospital for several days and received 40 pints of blood in transfusions. At one stage he stopped breathing and received heart massage and mouth-to-mouth resuscitation'.

Greig wasn't a quickie, but there were plenty who were in the 1970s, men such as Lillee and Thomson, England's Bob Willis and the fearsome West Indian duo of Michael Holding and Andy Roberts. The World Series seemed to add an extra yard or two of pace to these bowlers.

Batsmen's anxiety began turning to dread. England's Mike Brearley had started wearing a padded cap similar to Hendren's in 1977, but following Peter Toohey's destruction at Roberts's hands Dennis Amiss sought greater security, the Englishman wearing a motorbike crash helmet for the rest of the World Series. Though the helmet was hot and uncomfortable Amiss said it 'enhanced his confidence at the crease by removing the fear of being struck on the head'.

Trevor Bailey penned a classic 'Not-in-my-day' essay

Soon he was loaning out his helmet, until in March 1978 Graham Yallop walked out to bat against the West Indies in Barbados wearing a white helmet designed especially for cricket with a transparent visor. According to Indian cricket writer Arunabha Sengupta, Yallop was 'booed and jeered all the way to the wicket [but] the Victorian batted about two and a half hours and scored 42, and started a fashion that changed the game forever'.

Many of the game's old guard were less than impressed. In a classic 'Not-in-my-day' essay written for the 1981 edition of *Wisden*, former England captain Trevor Bailey poured scorn on the helmet, impugning the courage of the modern player and implying that his generation were made of sterner stuff. 'None of the [former] players I have mentioned required a helmet for protection, for either physical or mental reasons, which is, of course, why they are worn,' declared Bailey. 'Which leads to the question, has the pace of the bowlers increased dramatically? I don't personally think so.'

Bailey ended his polemic wondering 'whether the helmet is a sensible adjunct to batting, like pads and gloves, or merely a well-marketed gimmick and a modern trend'.

> **Bowlers, no longer able to rely on intimidation, enlarged their bag of tricks**

It was neither; it was a necessity, as South African batsman Jonty Rhodes discovered in 1994 when he was hit on the helmet by a Devon Malcolm bouncer. Doctors later said the ferocity of the blow would have probably killed Rhodes were it not for the helmet, which ended up in the hands of Tony Henson, a headgear manufacturer. 'We had an aerospace engineer assess the evidence and work out the speed of the blow and the force of the impact. And we used that information to improve our helmets,' recalled Henson in an interview four years later. 'Jonty's blow helped improve cricket helmets… The minimum figure for a helmet now is that it should reduce impact by 25 per cent. At the time Jonty's reduced it by about 17 per cent and that was enough to save him from serious injury. Now we aim to make helmets which reduce the shock of the blow by 40 per cent.'

There was much gnashing of teeth when helmets became widespread. While Bailey and his ilk tut-tutted at the timorous modern players, connoisseurs of the game worried that there would no longer be a place for cricket's pacemen. In fact studies have shown that between 1971 and 1978 (in other words, the pre-helmet era) quick bowlers took Test wickets at an average of 25.12 runs with a strike rate of 52.60; from 1978 to 1986 this average improved slightly to 24.82 with a strike rate of 53.89.

So batsmen may have felt more confident playing the quicks but it didn't mean scoring runs became easier. And the bowlers, no longer able to rely so much on intimidation, enlarged their kit bag of tricks, mixing up slower balls with slow bouncers and reverse swing. 'I'd like to see more intimidatory bowling in the current game, but the aim is to get batsmen out, not hurt them,' said Rodney Hogg, an Aussie paceman in the 1970s who once hit Viv Richards on the head with a 90mph bouncer. 'Helmets are the most sensible thing going. Why wouldn't you want to wear a helmet?'

Aluminium bat

Dennis Lillee is one of the greats of the game, a seriously fast Australian bowler who, in tandem with Jeff Thomson, wreaked havoc on a generation of English batsmen in the 1970s. Then there was Lillee's partnership with Australian wicketkeeper Rodney Marsh; ninety-five times a Test scorecard read 'Caught Marsh, bowled Lillee', a record combination for a bowler/keeper.

Lillee had much in common with England's Fred Trueman, outspoken men and superb fast bowlers both. Writing in 1984 in *From Larwood to Lillee*, a series of essays on great fast bowlers, Trueman, the first bowler to take 300 Test wickets, said of Lillee: 'Dennis has been blessed with all the attributes required to reach the peak of his particular art form. He is fast-bowling perfection... he possesses a fine running action worthy of an Olympic athlete. Couple the way he moves with balance, rhythm, fire in the belly, stamina and a big heart and you are close to greatness. The last piece in the jigsaw is the bowling action, which in the case of Lillee is superb. His action and timing cannot be bettered.'

Something else of Lillee's that couldn't be bettered was his temper. Dennis could be a menace when the mood took him, and that's exactly what happened on 14 December 1979 when Australia played England at the WACA in Perth. The Aussies batted first and were 219 for eight when Lillee strode to the wicket. Umpire Max O'Connell takes up the story: 'Ian Botham took the new ball and after about four balls, Mike Brearley [the England captain] came to me and said "have a look at this". It looked like a five-cent piece had been taken out of the ball and when I asked Brearley what caused it, he suggested I look at Lillee's bat.'

O'Connell summoned Lillee just as Australian captain Greg Chappell ordered Rodney Hogg, the twelfth man, to take a wooden bat out to the wicket. 'Excuse me, Dennis, Greg wants you to try one of these,' stammered a terrified Hogg. Lillee told Hogg to piss off, and Chappell too. Meanwhile O'Connell had realised that Lillee wasn't carrying a normal length of willow. 'From my end the bat looked normal enough,' he recalled. 'It was only up close you could tell the bat was aluminium and one piece.'

O'Connell told Lillee to change the bat. Lillee refused. England refused to continue unless Lillee did as instructed. Backed into a corner, Lillee lashed out, hurling the bat forty yards across the WACA before sulkily taking his guard with an old-fashioned bat.

The idea for the aluminium bat began a couple of years earlier, during World Series Cricket, when Lillee and Graham Monaghan, a club cricketer, opened an indoor cricket centre in Perth. Writing in his autobiography, Lillee recalled that 'Graham brought in a strange bat made from a piece of aluminium staircase which was smaller than a bat's width. He had cut it off at blade length and got a mate to weld on a bat handle, with a couple of grips around it.'

Lillee hurled the bat 40 yards across the WACA

Lillee had a go in the nets and liked the result so much he and Monaghan decided to go into business manufacturing the bats in conjunction with an aluminium company in Western Australia.

The bat Lillee took to the crease against England was a prototype, and as the Aussie explained: 'It was a marketing ploy. I'm not ashamed of that. It certainly attained total exposure.'

It did, particularly after Lillee later got both teams to sign the bat. Brearley wrote 'good luck with the sales', and for a time it appeared Lillee didn't need any luck. The bat sold in its hundreds, proving particularly popular in schools, which approved of its durability. But it proved less popular with the MCC, who in 1980 tweaked the laws of the game so that in future all cricket bats 'shall be made of wood'.

In recent years bat manufacturers have tried to outwit the game's governing body. In 2007 Kookaburra designed the Smart Cricket Bat, whose handle had been designed by eggheads at Melbourne's School of Aerospace, Mechanical and Manufacturing Engineering. According to a report in the *Daily Telegraph* the 'handle is equipped with electro-mechanical sensors and a vibration-absorbing synthetic material which converts shockwaves into heat and dampens vibration by 46%'.

> From aluminium bats to electro-mechanical sensors, cricket has come a long way

Once the MCC had decoded the boffin-speak in 2008, they banned that too, releasing an Appendix E in which it was stated in regard to Law 6: 'As a proportion of the total volume of the handle, materials other than cane, wood or twine are restricted to one-tenth for Grades A and B and one-fifth for Grade C. Such materials must not project more than 3.25in/8.26cm into the lower portion of the handle.' It was only the fifth time the laws regarding the bat had been changed since the first codification of the rules in 1744.

From aluminium bats to electro-mechanical sensors, cricket has come a long way in thirty years. Thinking about it, it's a pity some of that 'vibration-absorbing synthetic material which converts shockwaves into heat' wasn't around in the era of Lillee. It would have come in handy for umpires and opponents whenever 'the Menace' exploded.

Floodlights

Let there be light, decreed the International Cricket Council in July 1997, and lo and behold, four months later there was in Test cricket – in Perth, of all places, in the second Test between Australia and New Zealand.

On the final session of the second day's play, the lights came on and Mark Waugh basked in the spotlights, driving Kiwi spinner Daniel Vettori on to the roof of the five-tier Lillee–Marsh Stand. It was, declared local old-timers, probably the biggest six that the WACA had seen.

As *Wisden* later noted, in a decade in which Test cricket was struggling in several countries 'to justify its

existence as a commercial entity, the advent of Tests with supper intervals cannot be far away'.

In fact floodlights first came to cricket twenty years earlier, during a World Series match in Victoria in December 1977 between the World XI and Australia. John Woodcock of *The Times* sniffed that it was OK for Australians, what with them 'being always early with their evening meal'. Others were less dismissive. Alan Lee predicted that the concept would 'arouse the envy of the traditional authorities'.

It aroused only their indifference. As Rob Steen explained in an essay for the 1998 edition of *Wisden*: 'State funds provided pylons in Brisbane and Perth. English concessions to all this garish modernity were hesitant and fleeting.' India, on the other hand, pumped money from the 1996 World Cup it had hosted into installing floodlights at its major stadiums. Some English counties were more enthusiastic than others; Edgbaston hoisted some temporary lights within days of the ICC's ruling in 1997, and 15,174 spectators came to see Warwickshire play Somerset in a Sunday league match.

The traditionalists were mortified

But what held back the English was their fear of the weather. Floodlit cricket was suitable for Australia and the subcontinent, but not in Blighty, surely, where even in the summer sun a chill dampness lingers?

But as attendances for county matches continued to drop and the ECB searched around desperately for a way to bring back the fans (which ultimately would lead to Twenty20), so an acceptance seeped into the MCC that Lord's would have to move with the times. The traditionalists were mortified. Writing in the *Daily Mail*, Ian Woolridge shed tears of anguish which practically dripped on to the page as he informed readers that 'radical proposals [are] now under consideration to transform this historic territory into a pop venue or theme park'.

Temporary floodlights were installed at Lord's in 2007, and then in 2009 – after protracted negotiations with local residents, who threatened legal action if there was a 'visual intrusion' – work began to erect a set of permanent lights. They are state-of-the-art, retractable telescopic lights that are raised from their lower level of 97 feet up to 157 feet 6 inches by a hydraulic ram.

The floodlights were an immediate success, seeing the light of night for the first time on 27 May in a Twenty20 match between Middlesex and Kent.

Encouraged by the commercial success of floodlit cricket, the ICC announced in October 2012 that in the future countries will be permitted to schedule day–night Tests. 'Bring it on!' exclaimed former Australian wicketkeeper Rodney Marsh, a recent addition to the MCC's world cricket committee. 'People need to understand that during World Series Cricket we played Super Tests at night,' he added. 'There is no reason why this can't happen with Test matches today.'

What would need to change in order to accommodate Test cricket at night is the colour of the ball. Red would be impossible to see, agreed Marsh, who suggested they 'could use a red ball in the day time and white clothing, and then change to colours and a white ball in the evening session'.

But Marsh acknowledges that for such an innovation to happen the ICC will have to be 'courageous'. Or, to put it another way, they'll have to show balls.

The covers

This object is dedicated to Geoff Boycott, the bane of whose life, as every *Test Match Special* listener knows, is covered pitches, introduced into England at the end of 1980.

'When I played for Yorkshire for the first time... We played on uncovered pitches back then. Players today can't even comprehend what it was like – high quality bowling on a pitch which was touched by rain. When I say it was sporting, I'm using a euphemism. It was very, very challenging.'

Ask any player of a certain vintage who played in England on uncovered pitches and the answer is always the same – by heck, it was hard. Well, almost. Former Middlesex and England fast bowler Mike Selvey, whose first-class career spanned the years 1968 to 1984, commented in the pages of the *Guardian* (for which he writes) in 1991 that, 'Uncovered pitches made a difference, that much is true, but it is another modern misconception that, prior to 1980, all cricket was played on green puddings.'

Just ask Jim Laker who, as we saw with our forty-ninth object, took ten wickets on a dry and dusty strip at Old Trafford in 1956.

But hasn't cricket – faced with innovation – had a tendency to hark back to another age and imagine the game was all so much better then? When Edwin Budding patented a grass-cutting machine in 1830, it was inevitable the mechanical lawnmower would soon follow.

It did, in the early 1850s, but for thirty years the MCC refused to use such a machine on the hallowed turf of Lord's, fearing it would sully their noble game.

The invention and deployment of the lawnmower was a blessing to the likes of W.G. Grace, according to David Mortimer, author of *The Oval: Test Match Cricket Since 1880*. 'W.G. began his career just as pitches were going from rough scythed grass to much finer and rolled grass on which the reliability and predictability of the ball could be enjoyed. This gave rise to a greater variety of possible shots – of all of which W.G. was able to take advantage and transform the popularity of cricket for both players and spectators.'

So there you have it. The lawnmower – far from being a mechanical monster – was of enormous benefit to cricket. The 1880s also saw the introduction of a law permitting the batting side to have the wicket rolled prior to play on the second and third day of three-day county matches. Nearly fifty years later greybeards were still grumbling about this innovation, declaring that cricket should go back to the time when rolling or sweeping the pitch was allowed only on the first day of a match. *Wisden* ridiculed the objections in its 1928 editorial, reminding its readers that prior to 1883 'there was always great keenness to get one's opponents in overnight. Next morning bowlers were helped by worm casts and any other roughness which might have developed as the result of the weather during the night.' In other words, matches back then were too often decided not by the batsmen and bowlers but by the elements.

> The MCC refused to use a mechanical lawnmower on the hallowed turf

The clamour for a return to uncovered pitches in England reached a climax in the early 1990s when the national side lurched from one defeat to another. The great 'cover-up' of 1980 was to blame for the terminal decline in the English game, said a vocal minority, conveniently overlooking the fact that the previous decade had seen the likes of Gower, Lamb, Gatting and Gooch score plenty of runs.

'I was brought up on uncovered pitches,' the former England batsman Brian Bolus told the *Independent* in 1991. 'They turn batsmen into technicians and are also essential in the learning process for bowlers. Different conditions teach batsmen how to master length and line, play up and down it, but never across.'

Next morning bowlers were helped by worm casts

Three years later the respected cricket writer John Thicknesse used his column in the London *Evening Standard* to declare that the 'cover-up has cost us our place in the elite'. Only by returning to uncovered pitches, warned Thicknesse, could England restore their fortunes. 'My guess is that a large majority of those who played or watched county cricket in the Fifties and Sixties know that the start of England's decline was the switch to covered pitches in 1981.'

It was a fatuous theory, and Thicknesse's call for a return to covered pitches was dismissed by the players. 'Uncovered wickets would make the game a lottery,' said Derbyshire captain Kim Barnett, while Tim Curtis of Worcestershire (also the then chairman of the Cricketers' Association) explained: 'I know that uncovered pitches might add a bit of spice but I am still not in favour. They would involve an element of luck with the toss.'

Nowadays there are fewer calls for pitches in England to be uncovered. The generation who played the game in the 1950s and '60s is thinning, plus England are winning – so covers can't be all bad. Only Geoffrey continues to pine for the days when pitches were uncovered and corridors were more uncertain.

A stump

If Shane Warne is famous for having bowled the 'Ball of the Century' to Mike Gatting in 1993, then the accolade of 'Over of the Century' belongs to Michael Holding. They called the West Indian paceman 'Whispering Death', and the death he dished out to Geoff Boycott in Bridgetown, Barbados, on the afternoon of Saturday 14 March 1981 was slow, agonising and merciless.

So this object, a stump, is in honour of Holding, and in honour of Boycott, who did well to survive as long as he did.

Holding had previous when it came to petrifying batsmen, as Trevor Bailey wrote in 1983, in *From Larwood to Lillee*, a study of great fast bowlers. 'One of the greatest, possibly the greatest, piece of sustained fast bowling it has been my privilege to witness was by Michael Holding in the 1976 Test at the Oval,' said Bailey, who knew a few things about pace, having played against Ray Lindwall, the Aussie quick they dubbed 'Killer'. In that match, played on a featherbed track, Holding finished with figures of fourteen for 149, the best bowling figures in a Test by a West Indian.

Bailey was there in Barbados in March 1981, peeking out from between his fingers as Boycott was tortured by Holding. 'It was one of the very few occasions when I was rather glad that I was no longer playing Test cricket,' commented Bailey.

Also watching from the press box that day was Paul Weaver, who relived the over in an article for the *Guardian*

thirteen years later. The first ball hit Boycott in the chest. Holding
turned, ambled calmly back to his mark and ran in again, roared
on by a packed George Challenor Stand at the Kennington Oval.
'To the second and third deliveries he played and missed as the ball
whistled through to David Murray,' recalled Weaver. 'The fourth
crashed into his thigh pad.'

Watching dumbstruck from the non-striker's end was Graham
Gooch. 'It was 0–90mph in about 3.2 seconds,' he said later. 'Boycs
took several blows to the gloves and ribs.'

Weaver described Holding's fifth ball as 'a savage snotball' that
almost decapitated the Englishman. By now Boycott was befuddled.
'I never laid bat on ball,' he said years later in a television interview
with ESPN. 'One ball hit me in the chest, one on top of the thigh. I
missed a ball. Two I gloved out of neck, and then he knocked my off
stump over.'

Gooch recalled that the stump ended up twenty yards from
the wicket as Boycott stood stunned in his crease. 'Boycott looked
round,' wrote Frank Keating, 'then as the din assailed his ears,
his mouth gaped and he
tottered as if he'd seen the
Devil himself. Then slowly
he walked away, erect and
brave and beaten.'

The death Holding dished
out to Boycott was
slow, agonising
and merciless

Boycott spent the rest
of the day slumped in the
dressing room, his senses slowly recalibrating. At the close of play
he went to the press box and watched a replay of how he'd been
hung, drawn and quartered by Holding. Satisfied with what he
saw, he retired to his room almost content, writing in his tour
diary: 'For the first time in my life, I can look at a scoreboard with a
duck against my name and not feel a profound sense of failure.'

Boycott had simply been put to the sword by a great piece of
bowling, by a man he later described as 'a truly great bowler'. Yet
in the list of Test-cricket bowling records, Holding comes beneath
some of those other great quicks from the Caribbean – Malcolm

Marshall, Joel Garner, Curtly Ambrose and Colin Croft. They
may have been more economical than Holding with his average
of a wicket for every 23.68 runs conceded, but none of them ever
produced overs like the one he served up to Boycott – six balls that
shook the world. They may not have been as dashing as the six
that turned Garry Sobers into a legend, but they were a hell of a lot
deadlier.

Crown green bowl

For a man accused of having no balls, Greg Chappell might have appreciated the sight of a lawn bowl rolling gently towards him as he came out to bat against New Zealand in 1982. But a crown green bowl was the last thing the Australian captained needed to see, a reminder of the ghastly events of the previous year, events that sparked a diplomatic war of words and led to a change in cricket's rules.

The date was 1 February 1981, the venue the venerable Sydney Cricket Ground and the occasion the third in a best-of-five World Series final between the Aussies and the Kiwis. The hosts had batted first and totalled 235 for four, with captain Greg Chappell top-scoring with 90. New Zealand chased well thanks to a century from opener Bruce Edgar, and as Trevor Chappell came up to bowl the last of the fifty overs the Kiwis required 15 to win with four wickets remaining. Richard Hadlee drove the first ball for four but was trapped lbw by the second. Eleven needed, four balls to go and three wickets to get. Ian Smith came to the wicket, cracked four from two balls and was then bowled by Chappell.

In came Brian McKechnie, needing to strike a six off the last ball to level the scores and tie the match. 'McKechnie came in to bat, and I'd never seen him before,' Greg Chappell told the *Sunday Herald Sun* in an interview to mark the thirtieth anniversary of the incident. 'The fact that he was batting number 10 probably suggested he wasn't that good, but at that stage I didn't really care... I walked up to Trevor and I said: "How are you bowling your underarms?" and he said: "I don't know" and I said: "Well, you're just about to find out".'

Greg Chappell then strolled back to his position at deep mid-on, 'knowing it wouldn't be all that well received, but probably unaware of the furore it was just about to unleash'. McKechnie arrived at the crease, took guard and then watched in bemusement as umpire Don Weser, having consulted with his square-leg umpire, wandered down the pitch to inform him that Trevor Chappell would be bowling underarm – unethical, maybe, but not illegal. 'I think Brian almost dropped his bat when I told him,' remembered Weser.

Trevor Chappell ran up to the crease and bowled what Weser described as a 'a beautiful delivery all the way along the ground from stump to stump – as a lawn bowler myself these days, I rate it highly!'

A 'dumbfounded' McKechnie blocked the delivery and 'then tossed [his] bat away in disgust'.

According to McKechnie their initial anger soon subsided and 'a few jokes started to lighten us up and we were pretty jovial when we left the ground, mumbling about bowling fifty overs of underarms in our next match'.

But others weren't so amused. That evening Richie Benaud, one of cricket's most respected figures, ended his TV highlights show of the match with a stinging attack on the Chappell brothers. 'It was a very poor performance, one of the worst things I have ever seen done on a cricket field,' stormed the former Australian captain. 'We keep reading and hearing that the players are under a lot of pressure and that they're tired and jaded and perhaps their judgment and skill is blunted... perhaps they might advance that as an excuse for what happened out there today. Not with me they don't.'

Even more vitriolic was New Zealand prime minister Robert Muldoon, who called the underarm ball 'the most disgusting incident I can recall in the history of cricket' and added it was appropriate the Australian team wore yellow because 'it was an act of true cowardice'.

The Australian Cricket Board acted swiftly to ensure there would never been a repeat. As Henry Blofeld noted in the 1982 issue of *Wisden*, they 'at once agreed that the playing conditions should be changed to prohibit the use of underarm bowling in the remaining matches of the competition'.

Within weeks the fuss had died down and Greg Chappell was no longer the scourge of the sporting world. But though the New Zealanders had forgiven they hadn't forgotten, and when he walked out to bat a year later at Eden Park in a one-day international, a crown green bowl was rolled on to the grass from the stand. A joke that backfired as the Australian went on to score 108 off just 92 (overarm) balls

> When Chappell batted at Eden Park, a crown green bowl was rolled on to the grass

Reflecting on the controversy thirty years later with the *Sunday Herald Sun*, Chappell says he wasn't thinking straight when he ordered his brother to bowl underarm. Fourteen months of continuous cricket had taken its toll. 'Everything that was imperfect in the system after the World Series days impacted on us, me in particular as captain,' he explained. 'There was no manager, no media manger and we played all the double-headers in the one-dayers and twice as many Tests as usual. I felt it was all closing in on me – and I guess this was a cry for help.'

Asked if he and Trevor ever mentioned the incident, Chappell replied in the negative, and when the newspaper called Trevor for a comment they discovered that he was still not playing ball. 'I know it's the 30th anniversary coming up,' he said. 'But it is something that I don't like to talk about. I'd rather never talk about it.'

Betting slip

It was a more innocent age in the early 1980s, when a cricketer could lay a quiet bet without arousing suspicion. The betting slip that we present as our next object was placed by a couple of Australian cricketers at Leeds in July 1981. They won the bet but lost the match. They lost not because of any skulduggery on their part but because Ian Botham strode to the wicket and scored one of the most astonishing centuries in Test-match cricket.

That 1981 series has gone down in history as 'Botham's Ashes', and it's hard to think of another Test-match series that has been influenced by one player the way that remarkable rubber was influenced by Botham. There were other outstanding performances, of course, notably the bowling of Bob Willis and the captaincy of Mike Brearley, but Botham stood head and shoulders above his teammates.

Botham had started the series as captain, but a pair in the second Test at Lord's (which ended in a draw following Australia's victory at Trent Bridge) led him to resign from the role. Brearley stepped in and, putting an avuncular arm round Botham's broad shoulders, reassured him everything would come right in the third Test at Headingley. 'I think you'll get 150 runs and take ten wickets,' he predicted to Botham.

Botham began the match as if he meant to live up to Brearley's prediction. Australia compiled an impressive 401, but the man they called 'Beefy' took six of their

wickets in his best spell of bowling for ages. As for the runs forecast
by Brearley, Botham managed 50 as England laboured to 174
all out in their first innings. Australia enforced the follow-on,
and Graham Gooch fell to Dennis Lillee without scoring to leave
England 6 for one at stumps on day three.

Day four began badly for England. Brearley, Gower, Gatting, all
gone cheaply, and though Geoff Boycott and Peter Willey offered
some resistance, when the latter fell for 33 England were 105
for five and facing defeat by an innings. Botham joined Boycott,
and the pair took their side, slowly, to 133. Then Boycott and
wicketkeeper Bob Taylor fell in quick succession. England were 135
for seven, still 92 runs short of making the Australians bat again.
'The ground was nearer empty than full and the bookmakers left
no one in any doubt as to the way they saw things,' wrote Botham.
'Ladbrokes made England 500–1 and they had very few takers.
Those odds, however, were definitely too seductive for Dennis Lillee
to ignore.'

The odds offered by Ladbrokes were made on the advice of
former England wicketkeeper Godfrey Evans, who worked for the
bookmakers as a cricket adviser. 'He said England had no chance
and we marked up the 500–1,' recalled bookmaker
Ron Pollard, Evans' partner at Headingley, years
later. 'Quite truthfully, not a lot of people backed it
because it was an obvious no-chance.'

But Lillee did, along with teammate Rod
Marsh, having been alerted to the odds at tea by
their coach driver.

After tea Botham decided he had nothing to lose.
He might as well give it a blast, or, as Brearley described
it, indulge in 'pure village green stuff'. Aided by Graham Dilley,
Botham laid into the Australian attack, 'playing by pure instinct'
and producing shots that defied belief. As England's score mounted
the realisation dawned on Botham that he was putting his side
into a position from where they could have a crack at winning the
match. As it did on the Australians. As their frustration mounted,

so Botham dispatched the ball even farther, reaching 100 and going way beyond. Eventually he ran out of partners, leaving him stranded on 149 and England all out for 356. It was a lead of 129, not much of a lead, but a lead all the same.

Brearley gave the new ball to Botham and Dilley, leaving Bob Willis to seethe on the boundary. When England's fastest bowler was brought into the attack he was just about ready to bite off the Australians' heads. He confined himself to producing one of the greatest displays of hostile bowling ever witnessed in Test cricket. Australian never knew what hit them. As Botham recalled: 'Talk about rabbits caught in the headlights!' Australia were all out for 111 and Willis finished with figures of eight for 34.

That was the high point of the series for Willis, but Botham had only just begun. In the fourth Test at Edgbaston he won the match for England, taking five Australian second-innings wickets for just 1 run. In the fifth Test at Old Trafford he took five wickets in the match and scored a majestic 118, leading John Woodcock to ask in *The Times*: 'Was this the greatest Test innings ever?' Certainly Botham rated it better than his 149 at Headingley, which he called 'a slog'. Of his Old Trafford innings, he said it was one he would 'want to tell my grandchildren about'.

Lillee and Marsh at least had the consolation of returning home £7500 richer

Victory at Old Trafford wrapped up the series for England and established Botham as a household name. It was a fitting series with which to celebrate the biggest wedding of the century – that of Prince Charles to Lady Diana Spencer.

As for Lillee and Marsh, they at least had the consolation of returning home £7,500 richer than when they had left Australia, thanks to their £15 bet at teatime at Headingley. And Peter the coach driver didn't do badly either; the two Australians bought him a set of golf clubs and a return ticket to Australia.

A copy of the *Christian Science Monitor*

It says something about the state of the game when the *Christian Science Monitor* takes an interest in cricket. But in 1982 the American newspaper, which represents our seventieth object, felt compelled to comment about the 'rebel' tour to South Africa.

Another newspaper, this one not quite on the same spiritual plane as the *CSM*, dubbed the twelve English rebels the 'Dirty Dozen', and how could one disagree with the *Daily Mirror* after the players' decision to tour South Africa in defiance of their sporting isolation (see chapter 58)?

The twelve players arrived in South Africa in March 1982, each having first had their palm greased with an alleged £40,000 for four weeks' work. And this wasn't some hotchpotch side cobbled together from the county scene; nine of the twelve had just been on an official England tour to India and Sri Lanka.

It was, as the *Guardian* commented, a 'tactical coup' for South Africa, which had been trying for twelve years to lure an international side to the Republic. The tour had actually been a year in the planning, with Geoff Boycott acting as the England spokesman. Initially Ian Botham and David Gower were pencilled in as participants, but they pulled out at the end of 1981. Botham claimed later he refused to tour because 'I could never have looked my mate Viv Richards in the eye'; sceptics point to the lucrative contracts and sponsorship deals that came flooding in following his heroics in that summer's Ashes series. Either way, without Botham and Gower the tour was in jeopardy.

Then in February 1982 South African Breweries resurrected the tour with a pile of cash that tempted a dozen players. Three more would join the rebels in South Africa – the 'Filthy Fifteen', as the *Guardian* called them.

Boycott was captain and around him he had some truly fine players: Graham Gooch, Derek Underwood, Alan Knott, John Emburey and Dennis Amiss. But a lot of the tourists were the wrong side of thirty, and they were up against a South African side desperate to prove themselves. As a consequence hopes of a competitive series disappeared in the first one-day international as South Africa won comfortably by seven wickets.

In the first unofficial Test the rebels went down by eight wickets, and they ended the tour without a win from any of their eight matches.

The tour made headlines around the world, not just in cricketing countries but in Europe and even North America. The *New York Times* told its readers that South Africa had 'scored a major victory in its effort to combat the various sanctions imposed on it' by enticing the rebels, and explained that the ramifications could be enormous, 'disrupt[ing] not only the game of cricket but also other international sporting events, including the Commonwealth Games this year and possibly the 1984 Olympic Games'.

However, added the *NYT*, British prime minister Margaret Thatcher seemed unwilling to condemn the tour outright, reminding the House of Commons that 'Citizens of this country are free to travel, as far as we are concerned. There are no restrictions placed upon them.'

While the tour was still in progress, the Test and County Cricket Board (TCCB) announced that all the rebels would be banned from playing for England for three years, a decision that effectively ended the careers of several players, including Boycott. The players' union, the Cricketers' Association, supported the ban, and when they returned home they were – in the words of former England captain Tony Lewis – 'the richest, loneliest men in cricket'.

Yet did they deserve their pariah status? It was a question asked by the *CSM* in its edition of 3 March. 'Does a decision to play international sport with or in the land of apartheid help weaken that racial system – or does it serve to condone it and lend it an aura of respectability?'

Politicians such as Labour leader Neil Kinnock were in no doubt it was the latter, but Boycott insisted that many of the tour's critics – particularly those from the world of cricket – were hypocrites. 'It has always seemed deeply ironic to me that when I toured South Africa in 1964, under Donald Carr as manager, and played in front of crowds segregated by virtue of race and colour, and by high wire fences, I was a legitimate England cricketer, an ambassador even,' he wrote. 'Eighteen years later I played as part of a privately funded team in stadiums where there was no segregation and where cricket people were free to mix as they chose – and I was a "rebel".'

In the first unofficial Test the rebels went down by 8 wickets

The following season a squad of West Indians and a team from Sri Lanka took the same path as the English rebels. The West Indies players in particular were vilified back home, labelled everything from 'stooges' and 'traitors' to 'honorary whites'. In the summer of 1983, a couple of months after the West Indian rebels had returned home in disgrace, a right-wing pressure group called (somewhat ironically) Freedom in Sport – and led by the Conservative MP for Luton West, John Carlisle – proposed to the MCC that an official touring party should be sent to South Africa. The proposal was put to the vote – and defeated by 6,604 votes to 4,344. 'In the history of one of sport's most intractable crises, it will probably not be regarded as one of the most momentous decisions,' commented the editor of *Wisden* in 1984. 'In the history of one of sport's most famous and most powerful clubs, it may well have been.' Indeed, the MCC, so often ridiculed for being out of touch, had quashed the rebellion.

Sri Lankan flag

Wisden called England's two-week trip to Sri Lanka 'delightful', and by all accounts the tourists had a good time. Tagged on to the end of a tour to India, England were in Sri Lanka to offer themselves up as their hosts' first adversaries in a Test match.

Sri Lanka, where cricket was introduced by British planters and soldiers in the first half of the eighteenth century, had been accepted by the International Cricket Council as the eighth Test-playing nation in July 1981. It was a momentous moment in the country's history, according to *Wisden*, 'final confirmation of Sri Lanka's importance and standing as an independent nation'.

England were lined up as Sri Lanka's first Test opponents, though first there were six months of frantic preparation as the Sri Lanka Board spent £100,000 on modernising the Colombo Oval, expanding its capacity to more than 20,000. Other venues in Galle and Kandy were also given a makeover as the country awaited the arrival of England. When they stepped off the plane Sri Lanka was frothing in excitement. 'Banquets were being organised, special stamps and coins were issued, and businesses and shops were planning to shut on the first day of the Test,' described *Wisden*.

The first match was in the picturesque setting of

> **In July 1981 Sri Lanka was accepted as the eighth Test-playing nation**

Kandy, a match against a President's XI that ended in a draw, and there were back-to-back one-day internationals at the Sinhalese Sports Club. England won the first by 5 runs but lost the second 'amid a tumult of local joy'. It was a fully deserved win, wrote Frank Keating in the *Guardian*, and he had concerns for England ahead of the impending one-off Test match. 'It was a famous day for this dear little island and it was very good to be there. And after that, they were saying afterwards, you just wait till Wednesday.'

On the Wednesday Sri Lanka won the toss and decided to bat. They made a respectable 218 with Arjuna Ranatunga stroking a fine half-century. England managed just five more than their opponents in their first innings as Ashantha de Mel wreaked havoc among the English top order.

At the close of play on day three a major shock looked odds-on. Sri Lanka were 152 for two in their second innings, a lead of 147 on a pitch that was deteriorating. Alas, it was the Sri Lanka batting that deteriorated on day four as they lost their last seven wickets for 8 runs, England spinner John Emburey claiming five of them.

England knocked off the runs without trouble, but Sri Lanka had come out of their first Test with credit. As *Wisden* said, fourth-day collapse apart, they had done 'enough in their first Test to show they deserved elevation to full membership of the International Cricket Conference'.

But there was one cause for concern for cricket's yellow bible. Attendances at the Test match were low with the ground never near full on any of the four days, 'this being variously attributed to high admission prices, television coverage and, disturbingly, the public's preference for one-day cricket'.

They might have been cricketing neophytes, but already the Sri Lankan public knew what they wanted.

Photo of the Mike Gatting and Shakoor Rana row

A photo is worth a thousand words, but the snap of Mike Gatting and Shakoor Rana's little tête-à-tête in 1987 screamed just one word in the cricket world – CRISIS! Never before in the history of Test cricket had an umpire's authority been so brazenly challenged in the heat of battle.

Our story begins in Faisalabad in December 1987, the second Test of the series between Pakistan and England. There was bad blood between the two sides even before

the series began; the summer series in England had been riddled with rancour with the Pakistanis not only winning but also taking objection to the presence of umpire David Constant. He was, they declared, incompetent, as some of his decisions had proved.

This was the era before neutral umpires, and Pakistan believed 'that English umpires are no longer the best in the world'. England shrugged off the criticism, but they probably knew what was coming when they travelled to Pakistan a few months later.

In the first Test in Lahore the decisions got so bad that eventually Chris Broad snapped and refused to leave the crease when given out caught behind. Martin Johnson, writing in the *Independent*, said that 'at a conservative estimate' Broad's bat had missed the ball by 'the width of another bat'. Nonetheless, his refusal to leave the crease for nearly a minute was stunning. 'Not even the owner of the longest memory in the press box could remember anything quite like it,' wrote Johnson.

Pakistan demanded that Broad be sent home; England demanded an improvement in umpiring standards in time for the second Test. Neither demand was fulfilled.

Matters came to a head at the end of the second day of the second Test in Faisalabad. England had scored 292 in their first innings, and Pakistan were in trouble at 106 for five in reply. As spinner Eddie Hemmings trundled in to bowl his penultimate delivery to Salim Malik, England captain Mike Gatting decided to bring his deep square leg fielder in from the boundary to try to save the single so that the inexperienced non-striker, Aamir Malik, would have to bat out the final over of the day.

Abiding by the courteous code of cricket, Gatting informed Salim of his intention, which Salim acknowledged, but as Hemmings began his run-up Gatting, out of view of Salim, signalled to his incoming fielder to stop 'because I didn't want him too close'.

Gatting had done nothing wrong, and as the *Guardian* noted, the 'duty to inform a facing batsman of out-of-vision field changes lies with his batting partner'.

But the umpire standing at square leg, Shakoor Rana, stopped play to tell the batsmen what the English were up to. Gatting was furious. 'I told the umpire that I didn't think it was his role to interfere like that and he replied that I was cheating by what was going on,' said Gatting.

Rana claimed later that Gatting had called him a 'shit umpire'. Challenged on this by the press, Gatting replied: 'Well, you've all been watching.'

Rana, on the other hand, allegedly called Gatting a 'fucking cheating cunt', though it was the umpire who said he was shocked by the language employed by the England captain.

The next day Shakoor refused to resume umpiring until he had an unequivocal apology from Gatting for his alleged foul language. Gatting said he would comply provided Rana said sorry for calling him a cheat. Rana replied that he 'had merely warned Gatting of unfair play'.

As the Pakistan press clamoured for Gatting to be sacked, so the English press got behind their man. Acknowledging that Gatting had been 'wrong to question the umpire so openly and aggressively', the general consensus was: who wouldn't have cracked under such intense provocation?

For a day there was an impasse (and no cricket), though Rana stoked the flames by claiming Gatting had called him a 'bastard son of a bitch' and saying: 'In this country people have been murdered for less.' No one of Gatting's acquaintance had ever heard him utter such a preposterous phrase – on or off a cricket field.

There was bad blood between the sides even before the series began

Eventually Gatting was forced to apologise by the Test and County Cricket Board in what they called the 'the wider interests of the game'. He did as instructed, though Rana remained silent in return.

The England players were furious at what they viewed as their governing body's capitulation, but tour manager Peter Lush explained that they had no choice, and to sweeten them he arranged a 'hardship bonus' of £1,000 for each player. 'We hoped things could be settled with a handshake but it got beyond that,' said Lush. 'The action we took then of Gatting's unconditional apology was forced on us after we spent two days trying to find a reasonable solution.'

The spat even made the pages of the *New York Times*, not an organ known for its coverage of cricket. They called on former England captain turned broadcaster Tony Lewis for help in explaining the seriousness of the row: 'It sounds very British,' he told them, 'but you've got to do your duty and obey the umpire.'

Despite the gravity of the dispute, the ICC was (characteristically) slow to react, and ironically it was a Pakistan player – captain Imran Khan – who pioneered the selection of neutral umpires for Tests, inviting Englishmen John Hampshire and John Holder to Pakistan for their home series against India in 1989/90. The ICC eventually cottoned on to the idea in 1991, appointing first one neutral umpire and, ten years later, two. But as we'll see with object ninety-one, that still wasn't much help when Pakistan arrived in England in 2006.

The spat even made the ages of the *New York Times*

Beer can

If the early twentieth century was considered cricket's Golden Age, then surely the 1970s and '80s was the sport's Amber Age. Or amber nectar, to be precise, a time when linseed oil wasn't the only lubrication liberally applied by cricketers. So, before you take a swig from our next object, first hear why we've chosen a beer can.

Cricket has a long tradition of alcoholic excess, stretching back to William Clarke's All-England XI of the 1850s when Julius Caesar and George Parr were the best of drinking buddies. In 1876 a hangover caused Harry Jupp to miss the boat transporting the England squad to Australia while the great Yorkshireman Bobby Peel is reputed to have relieved himself in the outfield on one memorable occasion in the 1890s.

More recently England batsman Bill Edrich wasn't one for the tonic water and Australian Doug Walters liked the odd tipple or ten. But it was in the 1970s and '80s that cricket became beery, blokey and boisterous. It wasn't so much that the players had changed – though a generation of cricketers that included the Chappell brothers, Ian Botham, Viv Richards, Allan Lamb and Rodney Marsh was never going to be known for its early nights – rather it was the money that began flowing into the sport now that one-day cricket was attracting a new type of audience. Television and sponsors – and sexy ones at that – began throwing cash at cricket, and soon the likes of John Player, Benson and Hedges, Red Stripe and Fosters were all putting their name to the game. As a result the players, fit and aggressive young men, had cash on the hip and in many cases they felt obliged to live up to the sport's new image.

Few players lived it up as much as Rodney Marsh, the great Australian wicketkeeper whose walrus moustache often glistened with beer. In 1977 he is said to have drunk forty-eight cans of beer on a flight from Australia to England to contest the Ashes, a record that lasted twelve long years until broken by the 'keg on legs' in May 1989.

The keg in question was David Boon, an Australian cricketer who bore a close resemblance to Marsh in physique, moustache and thirst.

According to South Africa's *Sunday Mail*, Boon was assisted in his record-breaking feat by his teammates. 'It is believed a roster system was conducted whereby one team-mate would drink with Boon while the others rested. When his "shift" was over, another team-mate would start his shift.'

Few players lived up as much as Rodney Marsh

For twenty-six hours (including a five-hour delay) Boon moved slowly towards his half-century, getting them in singles, as George Hirst might have said. By the time the squad touched down at Heathrow Boon had reached fifty-two cans, allegedly prompting team-mate Merv Hughes to yell, 'Booney's done it, he's broken the record.'

According to Jim Woodward, a cricket journalist who travelled with the squad from Australia, Boon 'was a bit under the weather' when he disembarked from the aircraft, but by the time he appeared at the press conference an hour later he 'appeared to be all right'.

The *Sunday Mail* calculated that in drinking fifty-two cans, each one containing 375ml of beer, Boon had consumed 19.5 litres of alcohol in twenty-four hours. Curiously Boon himself never bathed in the warm amber glow of his achievement. According to the *Sunday Mail* article that appeared after the alleged incident, Australian tour manager Bobby Simpson had forbidden the players from talking about the half-century. Dr Curran's article received a stony response from Ian McDonald, the Australian Cricket Board's media manager, who muttered that 'the doctor should know better than to make comments like this on hearsay. It could end up being legally damaging.'

Nearly twenty-five years on, and Boon's record still stands, a testament to a bygone era, an innocent if more inebriated age, when summers felt more golden and beer more amber. In the intervening years cricket has undergone a cultural revolution. The money that began trickling into the sport in the late 1960s has become a torrent, and companies that are paying hundreds of thousands of pounds to be associated with

> **Cricket now expects its players to be role models not beer monsters**

cricket expect its players to be role models not beer monsters. Simultaneously the media demands its sportsmen to live like puritans, and even a couple of beers after a Test match is frowned upon. But what self-respecting cricketer would risk a beer these days, what with all the fitness testing they have to undergo if they're to keep their place in the team?

Writing in the 2006 edition of *Wisden*, former England all-rounder Derek Pringle pined for the early 1980s when players used to unwind with a beer after a hard day in the field. But he wasn't just mourning the death of debauchery; Pringle was also advancing his theory about alcohol's role in developing raw talent. 'Socialising with opponents was often the best way for young players, especially bowlers, to learn the secrets of the trade. Alcohol loosens tongues, and more useful information has been disseminated over a drink with an opponent than in a dozen sober net sessions with the coach.'

Cricket has changed, and so it seems has David Boon. In 2011 he fronted an alcohol campaign – for Canadian Club whiskey. 'It's shameful,' wailed Michael Madigan in Brisbane's *Courier Mail*. 'This man, this national treasure, this custodian of a laconic

Australian masculinity who is reputed to have set an Australian Cricket Team drinking record by consuming 52 cans of Victoria Bitter beer on a 1989 flight from Sydney to London... now prefers a distilled spirit to beer.'

But then, as Madigan concluded, these days 'any national sporting figure who drank 52 beers in a row would be swiftly dispatched to rehab'.

The 'Yabba' statue

He was called Stephen Harold Gascoigne, and he sold rabbits from a horse-drawn cart on the backstreets of Balmain. But it was on the 'Hill', the grassy bank below the giant scoreboard at the Sydney Cricket Ground, that Gascoigne found fame.

A life-size statue of Gascoigne was unveiled at the SCG in 2008, some sixty-six years after his death and seventeen years after the legendary Hill had been concreted over and later replaced with what one Australian cricket writer described as the 'the magnificently arranged but soulless Victor Trumper Stand where punters sip on mid-strength beer and are threatened with deportation if they incite a Mexican wave'.

Fans who fork out for a seat in the stand can gaze down on the statue while perhaps listening to tales from those who were there about what life was like on the Hill. To be sure it was rowdy, though not when Gascoigne first took up his position at the turn of the last century, plonking himself down in front of the old scoreboard with a round of sandwiches and a couple of bottles of beer.

Gascoigne waged war with his mouth, not his fists, barracking opponents with a seemingly endless string of one-liners. 'Send him down a piano, see if he can play that!' he once yelled to a bowler. 'I wish you were a statue and I were a pigeon,' he hollered at an umpire, and a batsman adjusting his box was informed that 'they're the only balls you've touched all day'.

Locals christened Gascoigne 'Yabba', and his reputation grew during England's acrimonious Bodyline tour. 'Make him taste it first, Don!' advised Yabba as an English fielder passed Bradman a glass of water during a drinks break. Then he spotted captain Douglas Jardine brushing away a fly as he stood in the field. 'Jardine!' screamed Yabba. 'You leave our bloody flies alone, they're the only friends you've got.'

Gascoigne waged war with his mouth, not his fists

Gascoigne died aged sixty-four in 1942, the Hill all the poorer for his passing. 'He could brighten the dullest match, and during his reign was as much a part of the game as the players themselves,' wrote Jack Pollard in his *History of Australian Cricket*.

Pale imitators took Yabba's place, less witty but just as knowledgeable about the game, but then in the 1970s a new breed of fan began to frequent the Hill. 'The advent of Kerry Packer's revolutionary day-night World Series Cricket games in 1977 led to an increase in alcohol-related violence on the Hill,' explained the *Advertiser* in a 1991 article. Spectators turned up the SCG not just to watch cricket but to drink lots of beer, the recent innovation of the portable cooler allowing them to come well stocked with cans. When these were empty, they would be banged together as the Hill roared in unison the names of Lillee and Thomson. Soon there would be chicken carcasses thrown on to the pitch, and more often than not punches thrown among fans. One of the more popular T-shirts in 1970s Sydney was the one with the legend: 'I spent a day on the SCG hill – and survived!'

When the trouble persisted into the 1980s the authorities decided to do something about it, concreting over the Hill and replacing it with the Doug Walters Stand. 'We have been consciously developing the ground into a comfortable, seated stadium,' announced SCG Trust general manager Noel Neate in 1991. 'The people will have a lot more substantial range of facilities – food, service outlets, toilets etc.'

They also had to pay substantially more for the privilege of watching a day's cricket as what had been an Aus$12 ticket rose to a $20 one. British cricket writer Frank Keating was horrified with the transformation when he arrived at the SCG two years later. 'It was sad to find the famous "Hill" has been obliterated for the sake of yet another serried acreage of plastic seating,' he wrote in

> It was strange, said the old-timers, to see Yabba so silent

the *Guardian*. 'The Hill for almost all the century has been a dusty knoll of scrubland grass which rose gently up to the scoreboard from the squarish third-man boundary. It was a "tanner bank", a cheap haven for the ordinary Joe.'

In 2007 the Doug Walters Stand was demolished and replaced with a new edifice named after the great Victor Trumper. In a bid to ingratiate themselves with the 'ordinary Joes' the SCG commissioned Cathy Weiszmann to produce a bronze statue of Yabba. 'Hat tilted at a rakish angle, hand providing a foghorn for his mouth, the old rabbitoh watched impassively as the cricketers went through their paces,' wrote Peter Roebuck in the *Sydney Morning Herald* the day after its unveiling.

It was strange, said the old-timers, to see Yabba so silent. Then again, perhaps he'd just found out the three-figure price of a ticket in the Trumper Stand. The cost of corporate cricket had done what no player ever could – left Yabba speechless.

Tiger Moth aircraft

Like a streaker cavorting across the square during an afternoon's play, our next object offers a little light-hearted relief. In fact the object in question, a Tiger Moth, did a little streak of its own on 21 January 1991, swooping out of the Australian sky as an England XI played Queensland at the Carrara Ground in Brisbane.

Yet this was more than just a prank, it was a last flight of frivolity, when tours were as much about enjoyment as they were about winning. The 1990s – as we saw with object seventy-three – heralded a new approach to cricket and sport in general. It now became a serious business – the emphasis on 'business' – and a win-at-all-costs mentality took hold of administrators, coaches and players. As the two Tiger Moths circled the Carrara Ground and then rose into the sky, they flew off into the sunset of amateurism.

At the controls of the two 1930 Moths were two experienced local pilots, but sitting behind them, goggled and grinning, were England cricketers David Gower and John Morris, who by a merry coincidence shared a birthday – April Fool's Day.

That was about all they shared, in cricketing terms, at least. Morris was a competent batsman, Gower one of the greats. Born in Tunbridge Wells, Gower grew up in Africa, where his father was in the colonial service. Schooled at King's School, Canterbury, he forsook his law studies at university to play cricket for Leicestershire. Soon he was playing for England, a batting artist, his bat a brush and the pitch his canvas. He flicked his first ball in Test cricket for four, and up in the press box old John Arlott murmured: 'What a princely entry!'

After witnessing one of Gower's eighteen Test centuries, Henry Blofeld was moved to write: 'If Shakespeare had been there he would have written a sonnet.'

Off the pitch Gower acted like the last of the amateurs, crashing a car on a frozen lake, whizzing down the Cresta Run and cutting short an England press conference because he was running late for a show in the West End.

The public adored the curly-haired playboy, less so the game's blazers. 'From early on, it was clear that Gower and England didn't quite hit it off,' wrote Ian Woolridge in the *Daily Mail* in 1992. 'They were professionals, Gower, for all the money he earned, was really the last amateur, a devil-may-care swashbuckler.'

But as long as Gower coloured his canvas with glorious strokes his skittishness was indulged. Until, that is, Graham Gooch came to power. Gooch, it is fair to say, is not one of life's artists. A grafter, yes, gutsy, without doubt, and one of England's greatest run-getters, but his narrow mind was ill equipped to deal with a maverick like Gower. When, in 1992, he wrote a book called *Captaincy*, Gooch dappled the text with buzz words that have since become part of the sporting vocabulary – 'commitment', 'passion', 'attitude' and 'respect'. Gooch replaced Gower as captain of England in 1990, forming a trinity of – dare one say it – tyrants alongside coach Mickey Stewart and Chairman of Selectors Ted Dexter. One of their first acts was to drop Gower and the equally gifted Ian Botham from the 1990 tour to the West Indies. 'I had no intention of wasting too much time trying to persuade Ian and David to throw themselves into the fitness training I would demand for everyone,' explained Gooch. 'They were set in their ways, and I wanted a fresh, dynamic attitude from all my players on that tour.'

Gower batted his way back into the squad in time for the 1990/91 tour to Australia, and he was still in good touch come the Test series. Going into the game in Queensland he'd scored a couple of centuries and one knock of 61: 94 more runs and he would surpass Geoff Boycott as England's highest-scoring Test batsman.

But if the runs were flowing then so was the mischief. The Tiger Moth stunt was conceived to celebrate the return to form of Robin Smith, who along with John Morris had scored a century against Queensland. Morris was out, but in on Gower's scheme, and the pair dashed to a nearby airfield and handed over $75 for a twenty-minute flight. 'I did think of asking Graham [Gooch] but I knew

> The public adored the curly-haired playboy, less so the game's blazers

he would be unhappy with us flying,' admitted Gower later. He was dissuaded by the pilots from dropping a water bomb on to the square, but he did talk them into buzzing the ground at only 150 feet.

The England management flew into a rage at the stunt. 'The management and captain considered it to be immature, ill-judged and ill-timed,' declared England team manager Peter Lush, before fining each of the pair £1,000. Gower was outraged, in his own inimitable way. '£1,000 for a 20-minute flight is not good... and in these days of deregulation it's scandalous.'

The British press was split on the issue, the tabloids feigning outrage at the irresponsibility of the pair, the more serious papers raising some awkward questions. Why, wondered former England bowler Mike Selvey in the *Guardian*, were Gower and Morris fined

£1,000 when Lush chose not to fine Chris Broad a penny when he 'refused to leave the crease in Lahore in 1987 after being given out'?

When Gooch published his book on captaincy the following year, the *Guardian* described it as a 'a monument to intolerance'. So what, the paper said, if 'Gower prefers claret to Gooch's Sanatogen multi-vitamins, if he is sceptical of the value of the track-suited job which includes one 50-metre fast burst every 30 seconds, if he shuns the meaningful self-criticism, the deep commitment, the chemistry, the bonding, and the rest of Gooch's dreary Stakhanovite rot'. The fact was (by this stage) he was his country's leading runs scorer in Test cricket and 'as beautiful and prolific a lefthander as has played for England in the last 50 years'.

If the runs were flowing then so was the mischief

Or as Australia's *Herald Sun* commented on the twentieth anniversary of the Tiger Moth flight: 'Happy anniversary, David Gower. The game still misses you.'

ANC flag

What a day 10 July 1991 was for South Africans.
Within the space of twenty-four hours the Republic
came in from the cold as the apartheid regime was once
and for all dismantled. First the International Olympic
Committee restored South Africa's Olympic status, then
the United States of America announced it was lifting
economic sanctions and to cap it all the International
Cricket Council voted at Lord's to reinstate South Africa
to world cricket after an absence of twenty-one years.

A four-man delegation
had travelled from
South Africa to present
their case to the ICC,
among them Ali Bacher,
managing director of the
United Cricket Board of
South Africa (UCBSA)
and South Africa's last
Test captain, and Steve Tshwete, the sporting official of
the African National Congress (ANC). It was the presence
of the ANC at Lord's that tipped the vote in South Africa's
favour, which is why the party's flag is object seventy-six.
Bacher described the decision as the 'the happiest day
of my life' and declared that the news would be 'a great
motivating factor in stimulating cricket in all sections
of our society. South African cricket has a great future
ahead, and the possibilities for our future Test team are
tremendous.'

Though Bacher praised South African president F.W. de Klerk for 'his courage and initiative in wiping apartheid from the statute books', Bacher's warmest words were reserved for Tshwete. 'Steve and the ANC have inspired us to bury our differences and he will go down in history as one of the true statesmen of world cricket,' he said. It was the ANC that had announced to the world earlier in the year that the legal abolition of apartheid and single sporting bodies was enough to justify the ending of sporting and economic isolation.

South African euphoria was dampened, however, when Colin Cowdrey, chairman of the ICC, said he felt they wouldn't be able to compete in the 1992 World Cup 'on logistical grounds'. The news came as a crushing blow to South Africans, who since the first tournament in 1975 had always believed the term 'world cup' was a misnomer as they weren't there to challenge for the trophy.

The presence of the ANC at Lord's tipped the vote in South Africa's favour

It was India who came to South Africa's rescue. The nation that had been the fiercest in denouncing cricket ties with the Republic under the old regime was the quickest to reach out a hand of reconciliation. When the question of whether South Africa should play in the tournament was put to a vote at a meeting of the ICC in October 1991, India's support swung it the Republic's way.

Within days of the announcement there was more good news for South Africa as India invited them to play three one-day internationals the following month. Ironically, the invitation was issued when Pakistan cancelled their own tour of India because of worsening relations between Muslims and Hindus. In issuing the invitation, Madhavrao Scindia, president of the Board of Control for Cricket in India, said: 'The tour is taking place with the full support of the African National Congress and its president, Nelson Mandela.'

As the South Africa squad drove from the airport to their Calcutta hotel the route was lined with thousands of people waving, cheering and holding placards on which were written messages such as: 'South Africa–India friendship long live'.

Before the one-day series began the South Africans had a brief audience with a frail Mother Teresa, the Roman Catholic missionary awarded the Nobel Peace Prize in 1979. 'I will pray for you, that your mission be successful,' she told South African skipper Clive Rice. 'Let your cricket be a work of love. Works of love are works of peace.'

The opening match took place at Eden Gardens in Calcutta on 10 November, twenty-one years and eight months since South Africa had last played in an official international match. It was also the first ever international match between the two nations. India won by three wickets, and the South Africans, quietly confident before the match, began to realise that their return to the international arena might not be as straightforward as they'd imagined.

Ali Bacher first tried to blame the ball, making an 'informal protest' about its condition and then admitted his boys might have let the presence of 90,000 fans get to them. 'They have never seen crowds like the one today,' he said. 'The boys appeared a bit overawed by the electric atmosphere and the importance of the match. But it was such a happy occasion, an occasion which will be memorable for the rest of our lives.'

White ball

Way back at the start of this innings (object seven, to be precise), we saw that in the eighteenth century cricket was played with a white ball. It became red some time during the early nineteenth century, so that when Charles Dickens wrote *Martin Chuzzlewit* in 1843 he likened a surface to being red 'like strong cricket balls beaten flat'.

One hundred and fifty years later cricket balls were white once again, at least in the World Cup. The 1992 tournament was the first to introduce the white ball, and almost at once there was more than a whiff of controversy. As the *Independent* noted: 'The difference is not merely cosmetic. For reasons that remain mysterious, the white ball swings more than the red one.'

The idea behind the introduction of the white ball was to make it easier for players and spectators to pick up the ball, particularly as the 1992 World Cup was also the first to stage day–night matches and coloured clothing. The latter may have upset the traditionalists most, but it was the ball that unsettled the players. 'They are definitely doing too much,' said West Indies captain Richie Richardson when asked about the white ball. 'It's taking away from the one-day matches a little bit.'

South Africa also found the ball hard to control, and soon it was swinging all over the place for England,

Pakistan and others. The ball's Australian makers, Kookaburra, claimed there was no difference in the manufacture of a white ball and a red ball, so former Middlesex bowler turned reporter Simon Hughes took up the case. Sure enough, he reported, the only difference between the two was 'that the polyurethane coating is cream instead of red'.

So why did it appear that the white ball was swinging more? First a quick word about the art of swing bowling. As Rabindra Mehta of the NASA Ames Research Center wrote in a paper entitled 'Cricket Aerodynamics: Myth versus Science', a cricket ball swings 'by a judicious use of the primary seam'. He continued: 'The ball is released with the seam at an angle to the initial line of flight. Over a certain Reynolds number range, the seam trips the laminar boundary layer into turbulence on one side of the ball whereas that on the other (non-seam) side remains laminar... By virtue of its increased energy, the turbulent boundary layer separates later (further back along the ball surface) compared to the laminar layer and so a pressure differential, which results in a side force.'

> The coloured clothing upset traditionalists, but the ball unsettled the players

Hard to understand? Well, fortunately Hughes's answer to the mystery of the white ball was easier to get to grips with. There was no difference, he concluded, it was simply a combination of two factors: the number of matches played in the cool moist atmosphere of an Antipodean evening and the fact that because the trajectory of a white ball was easier to follow than a red one it just appeared it was moving more, when it wasn't.

Yet despite Hughes's theory, and the claims by ball manufacturers that there was no difference between a red and a white ball, Rabindra Mehta disagreed. The former school friend of Pakistan legend Imran Khan has been studying the aerodynamics of cricket balls for over thirty years and is arguably the world's leading expert on the matter. He addressed the question in his paper for NASA and concluded that the curve of the white ball was caused by its topcoat. 'With the conventional red ball the leather is dyed red, greased and polished with a shellac topcoat,' wrote Mehta:

> *This final polish disappears very quickly during play and it is the grease in the leather that produces the shine when polished by the bowler. The finish applied to the white ball is somewhat different. The leather is sprayed with a polyurethane white paint-like fluid and then heat-treated so that it bonds to the leather like a hard skin. As a final treatment, one coat of clear polyurethane-based topcoat is applied to further protect the white surface so that it does not get dirty easily. As far as the aerodynamics is concerned, the additional topcoat covers up the quarter seam and the effective roughness due to it is therefore reduced. As a consequence, a new white ball should swing more, especially at the higher bowling speeds since a laminar boundary layer is more readily maintained on the smoother surface. Also, the harder surface stays smooth for a longer time; it does not scuff up easily like the red ball and so conventional swing can be obtained for a longer playing time.*

So there you have it, scientific proof that a white ball swings more than a red ball. But did we really need a boffin to tell us? The evidence was right there before us in 1992. As Martin Chuzzlewitt once said to Tom Pinch: 'My own eyes are my witnesses.'

Diamond stud earring

The ball left Shane Warne's right hand on the line of middle and leg, spun and dipped through the air, and landed six inches outside Mike Gatting's leg stump. The England batsman pushed bat and pad at the ball and then, his face a contortion of confusion, watched as the ball spun back two feet and took out his off stump.

It was, the papers all agreed the next day, 'The Ball from Hell', and little did they know that Shane Warne would be England's tormenter for the next thirteen years.

Shane Warne was a cricket phenomenon, a player who brought back the art of leg-spin after two decades when cricket had been all about pace, power and short-pitched bowling; suddenly Warne reintroduced finesse and thought to bowling. It was like switching from a constant diet of burgers to haute cuisine.

A week after the twenty-three-year-old Warne had bowled Gatting with his first Ashes ball, Christopher Martin-Jenkins profiled him in the *Daily Telegraph*. Comparing him with other spinners around, Martin-Jenkins wrote that: 'Each has different qualities but none gives the ball such a vicious rip as Warne does, and with his blond hair and diamond-studded ear, he should attract the young. He may look a playboy, and off the field he has certainly enjoyed himself on the way to being a national hero, but he is intelligent.'

That larrikin lifestyle of Warne's had cost him his place at the Adelaide Cricket Academy, their coaches judging him too indisciplined to ever go far in the game. But others saw through the cloud of cigarette smoke that invariably seemed to envelop Warne and recognised a rare talent. After only five first-class matches for Victoria, Warne was picked to play for his country against India in January 1992. In his debut Test he picked up one wicket and conceded 150 runs; in his second he finished with figures of 0 for 78. Warne was told to go away, lose weight and work on his art.

He lost 28 pounds and spent the winter in the net under the skilled eye of Terry Jenner, 'another ex-larrikin leg-spinner'.

The work paid off, and Warne began taking wickets. Eight in the 1992 Boxing Day Test against the West Indies and then seventeen in a three-Test series against New Zealand in early 1993. The great Kiwi batsman Martin Crowe was so astounded by what he saw he sent a word of warning to England ahead of their summer series against Australia. The news he conveyed to coach Keith Fletcher was that Warne 'is unusual in that he makes the ball turn across the right-handed batsmen, often from outside leg stump, rather than pitching middle-and-off or off stump like most of his kind'.

> It was like switching from a diet of burgers to haute cuisine

Thus England were warned, but it did them no good. Warne finished that 1993 series with thirty-four wickets. Fourteen years later, in January 2007, Warne was through with Test cricket, playing the last of his 145 Tests in Sydney against England. In thirty-six Ashes Tests he had taken 195 wickets at an average of 23.26; no one else has managed more than 167 wickets in the history of Ashes encounters.

But it wasn't just England who fell under Warne's spell. He bewitched every nation, in Test matches and in one-day internationals; for a spinner he achieved that rare feat of winning a Man of the Match award in a World Cup final, his four wickets against Pakistan in the 1999 final taking the honour. Writing about the 'freak' Warne in 1995, cricket writer Martin Johnson marvelled at the speed with which he had reached 145 Test-match wickets and surmised 'it is by no means fanciful to suggest he will end up with more than 500'.

Warne finished with 708 and the reputation as the greatest spin bowler the world has ever seen. No one batted an eyelid in 2000 when *Wisden* named Warne as one of its Six Cricketers of the Century, as selected by a panel of 100 global cricket experts. He was in some illustrious company, but who could argue that Warne's talent and influence weren't as great as those of Don Bradman, Garry Sobers, Jack Hobbs and Viv Richards? In attributing his greatness to the three elements of skill, novelty and drama, *Wisden* then detailed Warne's finest achievement: 'Warne's impact can never be understated. When he was first picked, cricket was under the tyranny of fast bowling and aching for another dimension. Soon enough, the world came to know that a man could take Test wickets by seduction as well as extortion.'

Thanks to Shane Warne, spinning became sexy and a stud earring became cool.

Merv Hughes's moustache

It's one of the most famous 'taches in cricket, worn above the lip of Merv Hughes. And boy, could the Aussie paceman be lippy.

As it's now known, 'sledging' – according to the *Daily Mail*, the word 'first graced cricket's vocabulary in Adelaide when a cricketer who swore in the presence of a lady was considered "as subtle as a sledgehammer"' – has been around for centuries. Indeed, one of Hughes's hirsute predecessors, W.G. Grace, was known for his banter, as was the great Australia leg-spinner of the 1930s, Bill O'Reilly. But few players have mastered the

art quite like Mervyn, the son of a schoolteacher. It was on Australia's tour to England in 1989 that Hughes came into his own in a side skippered by the steely-eyed Allan Border. As Simon Briggs wrote in his book *Stiff Upper Lips and Baggy Green Caps: A Sledger's History of the Ashes*, Hughes was the 'spearhead when it came to sledging'.

A young Mike Atherton had his sexuality regularly called into question, but it was the Hampshire batsman Robin Smith who really felt the rough side of the Australian's tongue. 'Mate,' Hughes informed Smith on one occasion, 'if you just turn the bat over you'll find the instructions on the back,' while another choice offering was 'Does your husband play cricket as well?'

But Smith could sledge back. 'You can't fucking bat,' snorted Hughes as he beat the outside of the Englishman's bat. The next ball went for four. 'Hey, Merv,' yelled Smith. 'We make a fine pair, don't we? I can't fucking bat and you can't fucking bowl.'

Periodically, cricket's authorities gnash their teeth, wring their hands and vow to eradicate sledging. Easier said than done. As former Australian player Mark Taylor said in 2008: 'The intention is good but it is going to be very hard to police... If you're going to ban sledging, you'll have to ban talking.'

Robin Smith regularly felt the rough side of Merv's tongue

Certainly the level of sledging today is minimal compared with what went on in the 1990s, when what was said on the field was as untamed as Hughes's moustache. Sledges were no longer witty one-liners, they were mean and menacing. 'Why does Merv Hughes think he has the right to run up to batsmen and give them the snarling, spitting routine,' asked Ian Botham in his 1994 autobiography, *Don't Tell Kath*. 'I am no saint and I've exchanged a few words with opponents in my time, but there is a line beyond which players know they shouldn't go.'

Today, stump microphones and television close-ups, allied to the hefty fines dished out, have forced most players to put a sock in their sledges.

So before the sledge becomes extinct we thought we would compile our sledging all-stars XI:

When England captain Douglas Jardine complained to rival skipper Bill Woodfull during the infamous 1932/33 'Bodyline' series that he'd been called a 'bastard' by one of the Australians, Woodfull demanded of his teammates: 'Which one of you bastards called this bastard a bastard?'

'There's no way you're good enough to play for England,' Australia's Mark Waugh told James Ormond when he walked out to bat in an Ashes Test. 'Maybe not, but at least I'm the best cricketer in my family,' replied Ormond.

'How are your wife and my kids?' Australian wicketkeeper Rod Marsh enquired of Ian Botham. 'The wife is fine,' came the retort, 'but the kids are retarded.'

Playing for Gloucestershire against Essex in 1898, W.G. Grace was still at the crease despite several confident appeals from the Essex bowlers. Finally Charles Kortright beat Grace all ends up, knocking down two of his stumps. Slowly Grace took his leave of the crease. 'Surely you're not going, Doctor?' exclaimed Kortright, well aware of Grace's inability to accept he was out. 'There's still one stump standing.'

'If you just turn the bat over you'll find the instructions on the back'

'Don't bother shutting it, son,' Fred Trueman told an Australian batsman as he opened the gate on his way out to the middle at Lord's. 'You won't be there long enough.'

'Why are you so fat?' Australian paceman Glen McGrath asked Zimbabwean batsman Eddo Brandes. Brandes' answer: 'Because every time I shag your wife, she gives me a biscuit.'

As Daryll Cullinan arrived at the crease in a match against Australia, Shane Warne told him he'd been waiting two years for another chance to get him out. 'Looks like you spent it eating,' replied the South African.

'Mind the windows, Tino,' cautioned England all-rounder Freddy Flintoff to Tino Best as the West Indian looked to hit spinner Ashley Giles out of the attack. Best then charged down the wicket, missed the ball and was stumped.

A deft piece of fielding from twelfth man Mike Whitney persuaded Indian batsman Ravi Shastri not to run a quick single in a match against Australia. 'Leave the crease and I'll break your fucking head,' snarled Whitney. 'If you could bat as well as you could talk,' said Shastri, 'you wouldn't be the twelfth man.'

During the 1991 Adelaide Test between Australia and Pakistan, batsman Javed Miandad told Merv Hughes he reminded him of a big fat bus conductor. A few balls later Hughes dismissed Miandad and ran past him yelling 'Tickets, please!'

'I can tell you why you're batting so badly', Aussie paceman Dennis Lillee liked to tell batsmen. 'You've got some shit on the end of your bat.' They would then inspect the toe of the bat, at which point Lillee advised: 'Wrong end, mate.'

Trinidadian flag

In the spring of 1994 Warwickshire were faced with a problem. They were going to have to make do without their South African fast bowler Allan Donald that summer, as he'd been selected to tour England with his country.

So as a replacement Warwickshire signed India's Manoj Prabhakar, a useful all-rounder who could swing the bowl sharply. 'It seemed just the thing to help the seamers out with their workload,' reflected Gladstone Small, the England fast bowler. 'I was definitely looking forward to his arrival.'

But then Prabhakar got injured, and the county was left needing a replacement at short notice. Small would have preferred a bowler, but instead Warwickshire signed Brian Lara, the twenty-four-year-old left-handed West Indian, then engaged in a series against England in the Caribbean. 'That caused me to rejig my mental strategy towards the season's bowling task,' admitted Small. 'It's a sobering thought when you suddenly realise that another 300-odd overs have got to be shared around the main bowlers.'

Warwickshire signed Lara at the beginning of April, a few days before the West Indies met England in Antigua. As luck would have it, the West Indies innings of that match coincided with the chairman's annual lunch at Edgbaston, and as the lunch progressed so did Lara's score, until he was within sight of Garry Sobers' thirty-six-year-old record Test innings of 365. 'Just as he was getting close to 365, we all piled into the committee room, opened up the drinks cabinet, and switched on Sky TV,' recalled Small. 'When he did it, there was so much rejoicing in that room that you would have thought that an Englishman had scored 375 against the West Indies, not the other way around. Hardly any of the guys had met him, but that didn't stop us giving high fives all round. He had introduced himself to us in the best possible way and Prabhakar was promptly forgotten.'

Lara's 375 was an individual feat that propelled him on to the front pages of newspapers from Darwin to Delhi to Dublin. The *Irish Times* reported the comments of Sobers, present to witness history being made. 'I could not think of a better person to break my record,' said Sobers. 'He is the only batsman today who plays the game the way it should be played with his bat. He never uses his pads, and it is always a pride and joy to watch him play.'

A month later Lara was playing for Warwickshire, who, as a result of his presence, had boosted their membership to over 8,000. Thousands of non-members packed Edgbaston to watch this small genius bat, leading the *Independent* to write that it wasn't just Lara's native Trinidad going gaga over one of cricket's greatest global stars. 'In England, too, he has transcended the boundaries of sporting stardom and entered the public domain,' said the paper. 'He has posed for Madame Tussauds – only the third cricketer to do so after Viv Richards and Ian Botham – he has had a poem about him commissioned by BBC TV's *On the Line*... and been made an honorary member of The Belfry [golf club].'

> Lara's 375 propelled him on to the front pages, from Darwin to Delhi to Durban

Lara's first match for his new county was against Glamorgan, and a fixture that would normally have struggled to pull in 400 punters had more than 4,000 people hanging on Lara's every move. They were rewarded with a faultless 147 from Lara, and neither he nor Warwickshire looked back. In his next game the West Indian scored a century in each innings against Leicestershire and another followed versus Somerset. Then in June Warwickshire hosted Durham in a four-day county match. The visitors batted first and posted a daunting 556, John Morris crafting a delightful double century. Lara led Warwickshire's response, and at the end of the second day he was unbeaten on 111. Rain washed out the third day so there was little to play for when Lara resumed batting. He began slowly, adding 27 runs in his first forty-one balls, but then, as if bored, he took the Durham attack apart, smashing 147 runs off just seventy-eight balls. At lunch he'd reached 285 not out, and Warwickshire captain Dermot Reeve wondered aloud if he shouldn't declare. Lara asked whether anyone knew what the Warwickshire batting record was. Small remembered Paul Smith interjecting and suggesting Lara aim for Hanif Mohammad's world record of 499. 'You think I can do that?' Lara replied. Then, turning to Reeve, he asked: 'Are you going to let me go for it?'

185 days later Lara took his record back from Hayden

Reeve did, and Lara did, smashing Mohammad's thirty-five-year-old record and finishing on 501 with a drive for four. 'I don't think I'm a great cricketer,' Lara said as the world once again went potty at his brilliance. 'Records are there to be broken and I'm happy to be the one doing it. If the records I have set are broken I hope I am the one doing it.'

Nine years after Lara's Test record of 375, Australia's Matthew Hayden surpassed it with a knock of 380 against Zimbabwe. Lara wasn't impressed. One hundred and eighty-five days later he took back the record, scoring an unbeaten 400 against England on the same Antigua ground. 'We all set out to achieve greatness, but he is a gifted, gifted player,' said England captain Michael Vaughan. 'He will go down as one of the greats of the game and it will take some player and some performance to beat his 400.'

A little dirt

Cricket can be a dirty business at times, as Michael Atherton showed in 1994 when television cameras caught him applying a little dirt to the ball during a Test between England and South Africa. But, though we've chosen dirt to illustrate our object, we could just as well have gone for resin, another substance that has been used in one of cricket's dark arts – ball-tampering.

It was way back in 1926 that Arthur Mailey, the Australian googly bowler, declared that it was 'quite in order for a bowler to use resin on his fingers as a means of imparting additional spin to the ball'. The then editor of *Wisden*, Charles Stewart Caine, asked around the English county circuit and discovered that others too used resin to produce a better rip from the fingers. Pressed on whether they thought this practice within the spirit of the game, the players told Caine that if sawdust was permissible to get a better grip on the ball, why not resin? Caine didn't buy that, writing in *Wisden* that 'sawdust is allowed after rain to restore the condition of the ball to normal; resin clearly brings about a condition that is abnormal'.

Mind you, that wasn't the only sharp practice exercising the mind of Caine in that year's issue of *Wisden*. During the 1925 season a bowler was reported to the MCC after he was seen lifting the seam of the ball. This prompted the MCC to issue a circular to all first-class umpires which reminded them that 'the practice of lifting the seam by a bowler is illegal and comes within Law 43'. If Caine was ambivalent about using resin to produce greater spin on the ball he was strident in his condemnation of lifting the seam. It was, he wrote, 'indefensible' and a scourge that must be stamped out.

It never was, murmurings and accusations never far from the surface during the next seventy years. Then in 1993 former Pakistan captain Imran Khan, one of the most widely respected figures in the game, revealed in his biography that once during a county match for Sussex he had 'used a bottle-top to roughen the surface of the ball', for which he was truly sorry. The furore that followed the 'bemused' Khan, who was trying to spark an intelligent debate on what constituted ball-tampering, forced him to resign from the ICC cricket committee. His parting shot was to write them a letter in May 1993 recommending that they rewrite the book on ball-tampering. 'Unfortunately,' says Khan, 'the ICC brushed the entire issue under the carpet.'

> Accusations of ball-tampering were never far from the surface

But if the ICC were hoping the issue would go away, television cameras were doing their utmost to bring the practice into the open. In 1994, in the first Test against South Africa at Lord's, England captain Mike Atherton was caught on camera dipping a hand in his pocket and then rubbing something over the ball. Some wondered whether it might be lip salve, as this had replaced resin as the bowler's substance of choice for altering the ball's surface so it would swing more.

Called to account at the end of play, Atherton vigorously denied he had tampered with the ball in an effort to get it to swing. 'The dirt in my pocket was used to dry my fingers because it was a hot and humid day,' he told reporters. Yes, he admitted, he was trying to get the ball to swing more but had kept within the laws. 'You need one side of the ball to remain completely dry,' he explained testily, a demeanour that soon earned him the sobriquet 'Captain Grumpy'.

Atherton was nonetheless fined £2,000 by Ray Illingworth, the chairman of selectors, though he refused to bow to pressure from the press to resign, insisting he hadn't cheated. Two years later ball-tampering remained a contentious issue, and Imran Khan used the *Daily Telegraph* to make an impassioned plea for the ICC to act before there was further controversy. 'The only way the controversy can be cleared is if the ICC make amendments to the ball-tampering laws,' he wrote. 'I propose that bowlers should be allowed to lift the seam or scratch the ball as long as they do not clearly alter its condition according to the standards set by the ICC... unfair play should only apply if an outside substance is used, such as a bottle-top, or Vaseline.'

Khan ended his article by warning that the ICC must act quickly so the 'the game of cricket will not have to suffer from a damaging controversy which has the potential to destroy cricketing relations between countries'.

The warning was ignored, and though it would take ten more years, the controversy that erupted in 2006, as we shall see in chapter 91, was more damaging than anyone could have foreseen.

St George's flag

The celebrated sports writer Ian Wooldridge wanted them gassed; the BBC's Christopher Martin-Jenkins wished they would be bombed and *Daily Telegraph* sports writer Matthew Norman dreamed of having them put 'on the first RAF transport to Helmand province'.

And to think all they'd ever done was support their country at cricket through thick and thin (mostly thin), while drinking beer and singing songs and turning redder than the cross on the St George's flag.

Few things in cricket in recent years have divided the sport's followers quite as much as the Barmy Army, England's travelling fans. Like Muttiah Muralitharan's bowling action, you're either for or against.

In the early days most people were against. The Barmy Army was first mobilised during England's 1994/95 tour to Australia when a core of fifty committed supporters began following Michael Atherton's team wherever they went and no matter how heavily they lost. It was during the fourth Test, when the fans took up position on the grassy mound at the Adelaide Oval, that the name was first used.

Some Aussie papers were more welcoming than others to this small group of fanatics they dubbed 'barmy'. In January 1995 a reporter from Melbourne's *Sunday Age* paper spent a day with the Poms, most of whom were decked out in St George's flags or sporting T-shirts emblazoned with 'We Came Here With Our Backpacks: You With a Ball and Chain, Ashes Tour 1994–95'. He

wrote admiringly of how the fans had packed in jobs to follow their team and how they livened up the quieter moments of Test cricket with their song-and-dance routines. 'The Poms have got variety,' wrote the reporter. 'Mass chants, question-and-answer routines, and the bouncy, nonsensical repetition of "Barmy Army", over and over, for up to 15 minutes at a time. By way of response "Aussie, Aussie, Aussie: Oi, Oi, Oi" is pathetically lame.'

Others were less impressed. A hysterical *Sun Herald* warned in a leader that the Barmy Army were nothing more than 'loud-mouthed yobbos... looking for trouble'. The paper then praised its own cricket fans for not sinking to the depths of the Barmy Army. 'We have a right to be proud of our feisty, competitive sporting culture,' sniffed the paper. 'Let's keep it as it is, and not allow its rich, tolerant traditions to be infected by the evil and violence that some UK sporting events generate.'

But worst of all were the comments of Wooldridge, who was all for violence as long as it was visited on the Barmy Army fans. Writing in the *Daily Mail*, Wooldridge recounted an alleged conversation he'd had with Graham Halbish, then chief executive of the Australian Cricket Board, in which the latter had said he wished the Barmy Army could be 'gassed but unfortunately that is not possible under Australian law'. Halbish later denied making the remark, accusing Wooldridge of employing 'journalistic licence'.

Licence or not, the alleged comments reflected the view of many people within cricket: the Barmy Army needed to be wiped out. Following that 1994/95 tour to Australia the Test and County Cricket Board issued a statement warning cricket fans that 'this kind of repetitive noise and chanting would be unacceptable on our grounds. We have regulations forbidding it, as well as the waving of banners and flags.'

The *Mail on Sunday* ran a piece in February 1995 in which it ordered the Barmy Army to disband because 'Your country does not need you'.

But they didn't disband, and the criticism from cricket's establishment acted as the army's best recruiting sergeant. In the years following its formation, the Barmy Army campaigned throughout the world, its ranks swelling year upon year despite the often sorry performances of the England team.

An estimated 75,000 cricket fans attached themselves to the Barmy Army during the 2006/07 Ashes series in Australia, a rubber that England lost 5–0. England's cricketers might have gone AWOL during the series but not their fans, who sang song after song to the point where Australian captain Ricky Ponting admitted: 'It was like being back at the [Kennington] Oval. I forgot where I was.'

> **Establishment criticism acted as the army's best recruiting sergeant**

When England returned to Australia four years later the Barmy Army's reputation had undergone a transformation every bit as astonishing as their cricket team. For the first time in twenty-four years England won an Ashes series Down Under, and their fans were feted wherever they went. 'The support of the Barmy Army has been outstanding,' declared captain Andrew Strauss, and to show how much they were appreciated players and army went barmy together in a raucous night of celebration following the fifth Test.

Even that most traditional of newspapers, the *Daily Telegraph*, was banging the Barmy drum. In its edition of 3 January 2011 the paper ran a piece that could have come from the army's own propaganda machine under the headline: 'From boorish beer swillers to money makers welcomed the world over; England's cheerleaders earn praise for their loyalty, their behaviour, their songs and their financial upside'.

No one was more delighted than Andy Burnham, the man who had co-founded the Barmy Army in the mid-1990s. Back then he had been a twenty-something backpacker indulging his love of cricket in Australia; in 2011 he was the full-time chief of the army, an organisation boasting more than 30,000 official members. Asked to explain why the Barmy Army had conquered the cricketing world, Burnham replied that it was simple: they all loved their cricket. 'We're actually traditionalists,' he said. 'To me, Twenty20 isn't proper cricket because you can only bowl one bouncer per over and the batsman can just get on the front foot and slog. Proper Test cricket is a drug, and I've been addicted to it since I was eight years old.'

Protractor

Muttiah Muralitharan is the greatest wicket-taker in the history of Test cricket. No other bowler in 136 years of international matches has taken more than the Sri Lankan spinner's haul of 800 wickets in 133 Tests.

Yet, as his biography says on Cricinfo, 'no cricketer since Douglas Jardine has polarised opinion quite like Muttiah Muralitharan'. The *Sydney Morning Herald* put it more succinctly in 2004: 'Murali is either a genius or a cheat, depending on your point of view.' Pass that protractor, this could get complicated...

Murali, as he was known throughout his eighteen-year Test career, was born with a deformed right elbow. That quirk, combined with incredibly supple wrists and explosively powerful shoulders, allowed him to turn the bowl more than any other finger-spinner had ever done. It was Murali's 'doosra' that proved virtually unplayable to a generation of batsmen, the ball delivered as a normal off-break but with the bowler's wrist cocked so that all the batsman can see is the back of his hand. On pitching, the doosra spins from leg to off to a right-handed batsman.

Murali made his Test debut against Australia in August 1992, picking up just four wickets in his first two Tests, but by the time of the 1995 Boxing Day Test in Melbourne doubts were being openly expressed in Australia about his action.

As Murali bowled his fourth over from the Great Southern Stand end of the MCG, he was no-balled by umpire Darrell Hair. Six more times in the next few overs the Sydney umpire stuck out an arm and bellowed 'no-ball'. Exasperated, the Sri Lankans switched Murali to the other end, where New Zealand umpire Steve Dunn remained silent. Sri Lanka were furious, believing it to be a 'conspiracy'. As the *Sydney Morning Herald* wrote: 'With some justification, they questioned why he needed to be humiliated before a big crowd on a huge stage.'

Hair's actions polarised the cricket world, except in Sri Lanka, where everyone threw their support behind Murali. A charming man, he was the side's only Tamil and a symbol of unity that the country desperately needed at a time of racial divisions in Sri Lanka. Writing in the *Guardian* a few days after the incident, former England bowler Mike Selvey called Hair's actions 'an absurd pretence'. He added: 'Muri is undoubtedly a highly skilled bowler, and his action a borderline case which, in technologically advanced times, leaves the umpires in an invidious position. What superhuman skills does the Australian umpire Darrell Hair possess to call Muri for throwing at normal speed, from four strides behind him, when an assortment of camera angles, with the benefits of slow motion, offer opportunity for detailed assessment?'

Murali's doosra proved virtually unplayable

Hair's supporters, and he had many, pointed out that the laws of cricket stated that the threshold for the amount of allowable elbow extension, or straightening, for a fast bowler was ten degrees and for a spinner five degrees. Yet biomechanical tests conducted on Murali revealed that because of his deformed elbow his arm couldn't be straightened past eleven degrees. In other words, he was outside the legal limit by six degrees. When he bowled the doosra, however, his elbow was at a fourteen-degree angle, almost three times the permitted amount for a spinner.

It was a conundrum. Murali wasn't deliberately throwing the ball, but nonetheless, because of his physiology, he would never be able to straighten his arm to conform to the laws of the game.

The ICC eventually cracked it in 2004 by relaxing the rules on illegal bowling actions, a move that caused as much controversy as

Murali's action. Now, all bowlers were allowed an elbow extension of fifteen degrees, well beyond Murali's eleven-degree range.

Geoff Boycott was in no doubt why the ICC had relaxed the rule. 'It's been brought in through pressure from Sri Lanka and Murali's supporters,' he told the BBC. 'It's a sad day for cricket that this pressure can allow Muralitharan to bowl whatever he wants.'

Boycott's view appeared to be borne out by the reaction of the Sri Lankan Cricket Board. 'We are very happy about it as it means Murali will be able bowl his "doosra". Sri Lanka Cricket appreciates it very much and we thank the ICC for making such a decision.'

The six years that followed the decision were the most prolific of Murali's Test career. In one nine-match streak between May 2006 and July 2007 he took eighty-six wickets, including ten for 115 against England and ten for 118 against New Zealand. He finished his extraordinary Test career in July 2010 with an eight-wicket haul against India.

The day after, an article appeared in the *Times of India* in which the legendary Indian spinner Bishan Singh Bedi wished Murali well. The Sri Lankan was, he said, 'a wonderful personality, a thinking cricketer and a crafty bowler'. But there was a 'but'. 'But he leaves behind a legacy of chucking.'

Hair's actions polarised world cricket

In Bedi's mind, as in the minds of millions of other cricket fans, Murali was not a legitimate bowler and certainly not worthy of comparison with the greats of the game. 'Comparing Murali with the likes of Jim Laker is preposterous,' he said. 'The ICC's experiments with leniency in elbow angles and subjecting Murali to bowling with a cast on his arm was a sham. A chucker can be spotted easily without technology as he has minimal follow-through. This is because the elbow, rather than the shoulder, comes into play. The shoulder doesn't follow the ball, hence no follow-through.'

Cricket's greatest spinner or the game's biggest cheat? You decide.

Duckworth-Lewis Method

Our next object requires of our readers a level of concentration the like of which was last seen when Geoffrey Boycott was in his pomp. It's a mathematical formula, cricket's very own Pythagoras' theorem, which has come to be known as the Duckworth-Lewis Method.

We'll come to the formula in a moment, but first a little about Messers Duckworth and Lewis, a couple of boffins who might not be much good with a bat or a bowl but know a thing or two about maths.

Duckworth first took up the challenge of devising a system of calculating an equitable target score in interrupted limited-overs matches shortly after the 1992 World Cup. That was the tournament when rain robbed South Africa of a place in the final. As they closed in on victory against England, South Africa's batsmen were forced from the field by a sudden shower needing just 22 runs from thirteen balls. When they returned after a brief delay South Africa required the same number of runs – but from just one ball. As the *Daily Mail* lamented, it was the 'victory that turned cricket's biggest tournament into a farce'.

'I recall hearing [BBC commentator] Christopher Martin-Jenkins on the radio saying "surely someone, somewhere could come up with something better" and I soon realised that it was a mathematical problem that required a mathematical solution,' recalled Duckworth years later.

At the time Duckworth was a research scientist and member of
the Royal Statistical Society (RSS), not to mention a cricketing buff.
Combined, the three facets of Duckworth's personality produced
a mathematical formula for target adjustment that he first aired
at the 1992 RSS international conference in Sheffield. Sitting
spellbound in the audience was Tony Lewis from the University
of the West of England, to number-crunching in the 1990s what
Shane Warne was to spin bowling.

Lewis and Duckworth teamed up to refine the formula, though
it wasn't until 1995 that the pair had what they've described as
their 'Waikiki Moment', a mathematical moment up there with
Archimedes' excitable shriek of 'Eureka!' as he stepped into the
bath.

It occurred, in all places, in a Hawaiian hotel, and within
two years the Duckworth-Lewis Method had been successfully
trialled during a one-day international between Zimbabwe and
England. In devising the formula Duckworth and Lewis sought to
avoid unrealistic targets
for the run-chasing second
innings while ensuring
that the team batting first
wouldn't be calculated out
of the equation. 'The whole
objective is that under

In 1992 rain robbed South
Africa of a place in the
World Cup final

the system a rain interruption will not alter the balance of the
advantage,' Frank Duckworth explained in an interview with the
Independent in 1997. 'So that when a team resume their innings
they have the same chance of winning as they would have done
before. The only quirk is that the impossible – say a team having
nine wickets down and still needing 100 to win – will become
completely impossible.'

The Duckworth-Lewis formula soon spread across the cricketing
world and was used in the 1999 World Cup – though incredibly,
considering the tournament was held in England, it wasn't required.
Two years later the International Cricket Council adopted it as their

official method, and fame followed for Lewis and Duckworth.

They released their autobiography, received MBEs from the Queen and were immortalised in song by an Irish band that called themselves the Duckworth Lewis Method (among their tracks was a number called 'Rain Stopped Play').

And yet, despite all the plaudits, a good proportion of the cricket population still didn't have a clue how the Duckworth-Lewis Method worked. The pair had tried to put it in laymen's terms over the years, patiently explaining to the unmathematically minded that 'you want a two-factor relationship between runs, overs, and wickets'. But that only made matters worse.

In an interview with the *Daily Telegraph* in 2011 Duckworth phrased the formula in more thickie-friendly terms. Referring to the traditional fifty-over game, he explained: 'If you had batted for 36 overs and lost three wickets, you would have 38.5 per cent of resources of the full innings remaining when you go off the field for rain. When you come back on, having lost two overs, this drops to 34.3 per cent. Look at the difference. Your target is then reduced by 4.2 per cent.'

Now it began to make sense. Except that in the same month Duckworth was enlightening us all in the *Telegraph*, Stephen Fleming, coach of the Chennai Super Kings in the Indian Premier League, was moaning: 'There's a real anomaly in Duckworth-Lewis. It's rubbish for Twenty20.'

Fleming's criticisms were echoed by V. Jayadevan, an Indian engineer, who has formulated a rival method specifically with Twenty20 cricket in mind called the VJD Method. Jayadevan says his system avoids the 'several silly mistakes' inherent in the Duckworth-Lewis Method.

We haven't got the time or the space, nor frankly the intelligence, to compare and contrast the two formulas. We'll leave the boffins to battle it out and simply give thanks for the Duckworth-Lewis Method. It might go over our heads, but then so do umbrellas, and they've also helped cricket combat the rain.

Snickometer

Protractors, mathematical solutions and now a Snickometer... and to think cricket used to be such a simple game involving a bat and a ball and a bad lbw decision. We dealt with the history of lbw in our ninth object, so now we come to its arch nemesis – the Snickometer, cricket's very own caped crusader, fighting injustice and ineffectual umpiring.

The Snickometer was debuted by Channel 4 at the start of the 1999 season to celebrate the launch of its coverage of English Test cricket. The *Independent* newspaper labelled the Snickometer 'sensational' and explained what it was to a television audience which had, in the course of sixty years, become accustomed to the benign tones of the BBC commentary team. 'It attempts to end controversies over whether a batsman has been caught behind by measuring sound at the crease,' said the *Independent*. 'Using a stump-microphone, a signal is sent via a computer to an oscilloscope and the viewer will see the soundwaves down the side of the screen.'

Leaving aside the fact that most British viewers thought oscilloscope was an Australian paceman, the Snickometer received a sceptical welcome when it made its international debut in the first Test at Edgbaston between England and New Zealand in July 1999. 'The sound is represented by a graphic on the screen which looks like a cross between an old advert for headache cures and the read-out from a lie detector and is probably about as scientifically reliable,' smirked the *Guardian*'s television critic, while the *Daily Mail* likened it to 'a pulse-like screen which detects an edge on the ball and would be more at home on the hospital series'.

But among the cricket fraternity there was a swift recognition that the Snickometer could revolutionise television coverage of the game. Matthew Engel called it a 'decent innovation' and the London *Evening Standard* said it was a piece of technical wizardry that could change the way sport in general was covered by broadcasters.

There was, however, a flaw to the Snickometer, as its inventor, 'a hair-brained scientist from Milton Keynes', Alan Plaskett, admitted. It was incapable of differentiating between a bat snick and a pad or body snick, as most people presumed it could. The sound wave will look the same, explained Channel 4, and 'if the bat and pad are close together it could be inconclusive'.

And like all omnipotent inventions, the Snickometer soon began to take on a terrifying and ever more powerful form. When Channel 4 unleashed the Snickometer on to an unsuspecting world, its purpose was to illuminate appeals for

> Each jagged line was a dagger thrust into the umpire's professional pride

catches behind the stumps. But soon the broadcaster found it had an even more controversial ability: it could be used in judging lbw decisions.

When England opener Michael Atherton was trapped lbw on 55 by Heath Streak of Zimbabwe in a 2000 Test he should never have been given out. Why? asked the *Independent*. Because 'the blur of jagged lines on the screen was evidence that Atherton had edged the ball on to his pad'. Alas, the paper had glimpsed the future, and it wasn't sure it liked what it saw. 'There is no stopping it, however. Here is another instance of the irresistible forward march of technology.'

Once Peter Willey, the umpire whose raised finger sent

Atherton on his way, would have been able to argue over a pint that night that he was sure the batsman hadn't got a snick – not any more. The Snickometer had revealed Willey's incompetence for all to see, each jagged line like a dagger thrust into the professional pride of the umpire.

Nonetheless, despite certain reservations that it would undermine umpires, the ECB kept faith with the Snickometer – and Channel 4's 'red zone', an electronic strip between each set of stumps to show whether the ball pitched in line – believing it to be a price worth paying in order to attract a younger audience to cricket. More technology arrived in time for the 2001 series between England and Pakistan as Channel 4 introduced Hawk-Eye. A computer system which traces a ball's trajectory to within less than $1/4$ inch, the Hawk-Eye system uses six computer-linked television cameras located around the ground. The computer reads the video in real time and tracks the path of the cricket ball on each camera. These six separate views are then combined together to produce an accurate 3D representation of the ball's flight. This groundbreaking technology won Hawk-Eye the BAFTA for Sports Innovation in 2001. It also embellished the lexicon of cricket, introducing such terms as 'Wagon Wheels', a graphic chart showing where on the ground a batsman scored his runs, and 'Beehives', a chart for the bowlers, showing where their deliveries pitched.

As we shall discover later, cricket technology has also brought distrust and defiance, but the people against it are in the minority. As the former Middlesex cricketer turned broadcaster Simon Hughes said in 2002: 'Television has illuminated and enhanced cricket. All the intricate skills and mysterious strategies of the game have been explained and explored, making it easier to understand and appreciate. Players young and old have benefited from the highlighting of their art. Ultimately, umpires will as well.'

Leather jacket

So much has been written and broadcast about Hansie Cronje in the thirteen years since his implication in one of sport's most notorious scandals that it seems superfluous to add much more. The bare bones of the case are these, that in 1996 the South African captain was introduced to an Indian bookmaker named Mukesh Gupta by Mohammad Azharuddin, then one of the stars of the Indian team.

Cronje was a national treasure at the time, described later by Ali Bacher, head of the United Cricket Board of South Africa, thus: 'In the new democracy he was seen as a young Afrikaner who had a vision to transform cricket, to transform the country.' As it turned out, Cronje was most interested into transforming himself into a very rich man.

During the third Test at Kanpur in December 1996 between India and South Africa, Gupta asked Cronje to throw the match on the last day. If he did he'd receive US$30,000. Cronje didn't mention the deal to his players, sure that the wickets would fall anyway on a turning wicket. They did, and Cronje pocketed the money for, in his own words, 'effectively doing nothing'.

On the same tour Cronje called a team meeting and offered $200,000 to his players to lose a one-day benefit match. According to a BBC radio documentary broadcast in 2012: 'Some of them walked out immediately, others stayed and suggested he asked for more from his bookmaker contact.'

Though the South African players refused to go along

with Cronje's scheme, it's said that over the course of the next four years the captain of South Africa received bribes of around $100,000.

Then on 17 January 2000 Cronje took a call from a South African bookmaker called Marlon Aronstam, a man he had never before met. Within hours of the call the pair were in a hotel room discussing 'a gift' in returning for fixing the outcome of South Africa's rain-affected Test against England. Cronje accepted, and the next day England captain Nasser Hussain, oblivious to his rival's ulterior motive, agreed to both sides forfeiting an innings, leaving England with a run chase on the last day. The tourists knocked off the runs and everyone agreed Cronje had done something splendidly sporting.

Cronje's greed and deception were laid bare

'Hansie did the game the biggest favour imaginable at the dawn of the new century,' exclaimed South Africa's coach Bob Woolmer, who, like Hussain, had no idea there had been 'gifts' involved in Cronje's decision.

Cronje's downfall came three months later when Delhi police revealed that they had a recording of a telephone conversation between the South Africa captain and a member of an Indian betting syndicate discussing match-fixing. At first Cronje ridiculed the claims, as did the United Cricket Board of South Africa. Four days later Cronje was sacked as captain when he admitted to Ali Bacher he hadn't been 'entirely honest'.

The extent of Cronje's greed and deception was laid bare in the King Commission that summer, each new revelation further stunning the people of South Africa. Asked what it had taken to fix the Centurion Test against England Cronje disclosed how easy it was to buy his soul – £5,000 and a nice leather jacket.

So there's our eighty-sixth object – one leather jacket, one previous owner. As investigations have subsequently revealed, Cronje (who died in a plane crash in 2002) wasn't the only one cheating back then, but he was the most brazen, the most shameless. No one abused his position of trust quite as much as the God-fearing boy from Bloemfontein.

Baggy green cap

The baggy green cap of Australia is arguably the most iconic item of clothing in cricket. There have been many legendary heads under the baggy green cap but we're focusing on one head in particular – Steve Waugh's.

Waugh captained Australia in fifty-seven of his 168 Test appearances, winning forty-one of those matches, a 71.93 per cent win rate, superior to that of all other Australians who have captained their country in more than twenty-five Tests. Waugh took over the captaincy from Mark Taylor at the end of the 1998/99 season. 'At first,' wrote Peter Roebuck in the *Sydney Morning Herald*, 'Waugh seemed uncertain of himself, a tentative tactician trying to echo his predecessors. Lacking direction, Australia fell back. In the nick of time, Waugh realised that he had to find his own voice, whereupon he set about conveying his ideas and ambitions to his players.'

Waugh was fortunate that some of those players were the best in the world, the best in fact in the history of cricket. Shane Warne and Glenn McGrath finished with 1,271 Test wickets between them, while wicketkeeper Adam Gilchrist and batsman Ricky Ponting boasted Test averages of 50 plus. Waugh's first success came in the 1999 World Cup when

Australia thrashed Pakistan by eight wickets in a one-sided final.
The Aussies made few friends with their crafty manipulation of
the complicated points systems in the pool stage, but, as Waugh
retorted to a journalist when asked about his approach: 'We're not
here to win friends, mate.'

This steely-eyed attitude – summed up by *The Times* journalist
Simon Barnes as 'cold-blooded and scientific' – was soon evident
in the Test arena. With John Buchanan appointed as coach after
the World Cup, Australia now had a man who aligned himself with
Waugh's ruthless pursuit of success.

The 1999/2000 season saw Australia win a one-off Test
against Zimbabwe and then whitewash Pakistan 3–0 in a Test
series, followed by similar scorelines against India and New
Zealand. The West Indies toured Australia at the start of the
2000/01 season and were humbled 5–0 in the rubber, in the
process the men from the Caribbean ceding the eleven-Test match-
winning streak set by their compatriots in the 1980s.

Waugh missed the third Test of that series, but he returned for
the last two, scoring centuries in the first innings of both matches.
Next up was India, what
Waugh called the 'final
frontier', and though
Australia won the first Test
in Mumbai to extend their
record winning streak
to sixteen they lost an
extraordinary game in the second Test in which India became only
the third side in history to win a Test after following on.

> **The Aussies made few
> friends with their crafty
> manipulation of
> the pool stage**

India won the third and final Test, but Waugh was back to lead
Australia to a 4–1 win over England in the 2001 Ashes series, a feat
he repeated when England toured Down Under in 2002/03. In the
fifth Test of that series, in his home town of Sydney, Waugh scored
102 to equal Don Bradman's record of twenty-nine Test centuries.

Waugh retired in 2004 and, in searching around for a
suitable figure to best analyse his impact on Australian cricket,

the eye of the *Wisden* editor alighted on Nasser Hussain. Hussain had captained England in seven Ashes Tests against Waugh's Australians; he'd won once. Hussain described Waugh as an 'ice-man', a remote individual who gave little away. Only once did he come close to getting inside his opponent's head, when the pair shared a beer in an Adelaide bar after the 1998/99 Ashes series. Waugh told Hussain that 'the most important aspect to him was body language'. Never let them see you bleed was the message, always let them see you're up for the challenge.

Never let them see you bleed was the message

In Hussain's opinion, Australia had become the greatest Test side of the era (perhaps, given their sixteen-match winning streak, of any era) because of three captains: Allan Border, in the 1980s, who eradicated the beery mateyness and replaced it with ruthlessness; Mark Taylor in the 1990s, whose subtle man management brought out the best in his players; and Steve Waugh.

'Steve Waugh combined all of this,' explained Hussain, 'and gave them that final ingredient, belief.'

Twenty20 Cup

Forty-one years separate objects fifty-six and eighty-eight. The first was called the Midlands Knock-Out Cup and lasted one season. The second is the Twenty20 Cup, and ten years after its inception it continues to grow.

It's disingenuous, of course, to sum up the Midlands Knock-Out Cup as a short-lived success. It was a trial competition from which sprang the Gillette Cup, cricket's first one-day tournament, which transformed the game. The Twenty20 Cup has been similarly revolutionary, a new format devised at a time when the game was in commercial trouble.

It was in 1998 that the England and Wales Cricket Board (ECB) first proposed a 'reduced form of cricket', a plan hatched in the face of falling attendances as football's Premier League surged in popularity and made cricket feel played out. The First-Class Forum, comprising the MCC and the eighteen first-class counties, knocked back the idea, and English cricket carried on in denial.

But attendances continued to plummet, and the ECB, now running scared, conducted dozens of focus groups to find out why. The answer was grim. More than two-thirds of the population were turned off by cricket, particularly women, ethnic minorities and people aged under thirty. Cricket had reached crisis point and something had to be done. By 2002 even the counties realised that the game, as they knew it at least, was up. In April that year the First-Class Forum voted in favour of short-form cricket, though they still weren't sure what that meant. But the ECB did.

As their marketing manager, Stuart Robertson, explained as he unveiled his Twenty20 project: 'The Twenty20 is not an end in itself, but a means to an end. The hope is that a 20-over game after work or school will be the first rung on a cricket-watching ladder that has the Championship game at its top.'

Robertson outlined his idea when announcing that the Twenty20 competition would start on 13 June. The essence of the exercise was clear: fast, frenetic and fun – and definitely not dawdling. Each team would have twenty overs to blast as many runs as they could; there would be just fifteen minutes between innings and each new batsman had ninety seconds to get to the crease. To develop more of a bond between players and fans, teams wouldn't be hidden away in the pavilion; rather, they'd be sat at the boundary edge waiting for their turn to bat.

The competition aroused a mix of emotions among cricket supporters and commentators: scepticism, suspicion, downright hostility but also a feeling that finally cricket might have hit upon a winning formula. Writing in the *Sunday Telegraph* five days before the inaugural competition kicked off, veteran cricket writer Scyld Berry scented success: 'Let's give it a go,' he declared. 'We cannot be so purist as to expect county cricket to survive unchanged on the annual hand-out of profits generated by the England team... When the Twenty20 competition starts on Friday, spectators of all ages and both genders will be welcomed, not just the middle-aged, middle-class males who have traditionally attended county cricket.'

> By 2002 even the counties realised the game was up

As Berry then reminded his readers, the cricket authorities in England for too long had done their utmost to outlaw 'atmosphere' at matches, as in their 'completely prattish decision' to ban musical instruments from Test matches from the late 1980s onwards.

Music was at the heart of the off-field entertainment planned for the start of the Twenty20 competition. Pop star Mis-teeq was hired to blast out some hits, and there was a slew of minor acts, not to mention a Jacuzzi, fairground rides, face painting and barbecue zones. But there was one factor outside the control of the organisers – the notorious English weather. The first matches were planned for Friday 13th – surely that meant rain.

But the summer of 2003 was a record-breaker for sun and heat, and come the day of the tournament the players and spectators basked in sweltering temperatures. The day was a success, and so too proved the whole concept of Twenty20. 'Surely something had to go wrong,' mused *Wisden*. 'But just as the sun seemed to shimmer all summer long, so the Twenty20 went from strength to strength.'

Everyone loved it – fans, players and officials. England batsman Vikram Solanki said: 'The guys have thoroughly enjoyed playing. There shouldn't be any tampering.' Graham Gooch, then coach of Essex and not a man known for his effervescence, exclaimed: 'This sort of cricket is good fun and you will see more of it in the future. It's here to stay and once players get used to the format they will keep improving.'

Twenty20 had captured the public's imagination like no other tournament in the history of cricket. More than 15,000 packed into Old Trafford to see Lancashire play Yorkshire. As *Wisden* noted wryly: 'No one could remember an occasion outside Lord's when so many had paid to see a county match.'

The competition culminated at Trent Bridge on 19 July (Lord's was ruled out as a host when Westminster Council refused to grant the ground a concert licence) with the semis and final. Surrey lifted the trophy, and on the following Monday the *Guardian* described Twenty20 as an undoubted success. But it still had its reservations, declaring: 'Nobody can be sure whether Twenty20 is merely a fad or the future.'

Ten years on and the 'fad' has become a permanent fixture in cricket – domestic and international. From England, Twenty20 spread throughout the world and met with similar crowd reactions. Curiously, the one man who got it all wrong was Mike Turner, the man credited with giving the game one-day cricket. Asked in 2003 whether he saw a future for Twenty20 he replied: 'I don't think the Twenty20 will alter the shape of cricket the way the one-day game did in the '60s and '70s. I can't see it becoming an international game.'

The original revolutionary had become a reactionary.

Open-top bus

It's not putting too fine a point on it to describe Test cricket at the end of 2004 as being in a similar situation to that in which it found itself at the end of 1960. It wasn't that the Test cricket being played at the start of the twenty-first century was 'stodgy and uninspiring', the description given to the extended version of the game in 1960, it's just that the new millennium brought with it a new format of cricket, Twenty20, which revolutionised the game in a matter of months.

Test cricket was an endangered species, the so-called 'Facebook Generation' accused by their elders and betters of lacking the attention span to survive five days of sport. Then came the 2005 Ashes, Australia arriving in England determined to continue their sixteen-year winning streak, just three shy of the record. But England were quietly, cautiously optimistic. Freddy Flintoff had at last fulfilled his early potential, Kevin Pietersen – badger haircut and all – was the sort of brash batsman their middle order had missed and in Steve Harmison, Matthew Hoggard and Simon Jones they had a trio of world-class fast bowlers.

England were quietly, cautiously optimistic

The stage was set for a series to remember, but England went and blew their lines in the first Test, losing at Lord's by 239 runs. Advantage Australia, but then Michael Vaughan's England did something so many of their predecessors hadn't – they showed backbone, winning a thrilling contest at Edgbaston by two runs. They even did it *despite* Shane Warne, whose ten wickets weren't enough to surpass the brilliance of Flintoff with both bat and ball.

The third Test at Old Trafford was drawn, though it went to the wire with the Aussie fast-bowling pair of Brett Lee and Glenn McGrath coming to the rescue of their side – with the bat. In front of a full house of 23,000 (with another 20,000 fans locked out), the duo defied the England attack to secure a draw on the final day.

England took the fourth Test at Trent Bridge, Flintoff and Warne once more waging a war within a war, and so it came down to the fifth and final Test at the Oval. England just had to avoid defeat to win the Ashes for the first time since 1989. Could they do it? The country was counting on them. Oh, how the country was counting on them. Because by now England was in the grip of cricket fever. Even though the football season had started, nobody cared. Not the papers, not the public and not the kids, who were playing cricket in the playground, pretending to be Freddie or Hoggie instead of Rooney or Lampard. Sales of cricket bats were going through the roof, one firm shifting £3,000 worth of equipment on a Saturday compared with £150 on the same date the previous year.

> Tens of thousands lined the streets to salute their heroes

With so much expectation on their shoulders, would England buckle? Warne once again did his best to break the England batting order, but not even his devious dexterity could deny England their date with destiny. A century from Andrew Strauss in the first innings and one from Kevin Pietersen in the second were enough to see England get the draw that they needed.

The Queen was one of the first to express her delight – well, she was old enough to remember the last time England had won back the Ashes after an inordinately long time, in 1953, when she was still new to the job. 'My warmest congratulations to you, the England cricket team and all in the squad for the magnificent achievement of regaining the Ashes,' she said in a message to

Michael Vaughan. 'Both sides can take credit for giving us all such a wonderfully exciting and entertaining summer of cricket at its best.'

On 13 September, the day after the series had finished, the England squad rode on an open-top bus from Mansion House to Trafalgar Square. Tens of thousands people lined the streets to salute their heroes on their nine-minute journey. There was a feel-good factor about British sport at the time; London had been awarded the 2012 Olympics two months before and memories of the 2003 England Rugby World Cup triumph were also fresh in the mind. There was a pride in waving the English flag, but there was also a pride among cricket fans at what the series had proved. *Wisden* summed it up best the following year, when it reflected on that wonderful summer: 'It was a triumph for the real thing: five five-day Test matches between two gifted, well-matched teams playing fantastic cricket at high velocity and high pressure with the perfect mix of chivalry and venom. Here was the best game in the world, at its best. And now millions more people know about it.'

Sequined shirt

Into the nervous nineties, and we find ourselves dressed to the nines in one of Mark Ramprakash's sequined shirts.

While the top players in India and Pakistan have been household names in their respective countries for years, in England only Ian Botham and perhaps Freddie Flintoff can be said to have reached that level of celebrity status in the last thirty years. That all changed in 2006 when thirty-seven-year-old Surrey and former England batsman Mark Ramprakash competed in the BBC's *Strictly Come Dancing*. Partnered by the lithesome Karen Hardy, 'Ramps' waltzed to the title in front of a television audience of twelve million. Described by the *Daily Mail* as possessing 'brooding, swarthy looks and a quiet, determined temperament filling that primetime space once occupied by Colin Firth's Mr Darcy', Ramprakash proved a natural on the dancefloor. 'You must have been a dancer in another life, and once again you ignited my fire,' gushed judge Arlene Phillips who, along with the rest of the panel, awarded Ramprakash (who averaged a modest 27 in fifty-two Tests) 40 out of 40 for his salsa in the final.

Ramprakash was actually the second cricketer to win the BBC's most popular reality television show, following on from Darren Gough's success the previous year. Gough was good, but Ramprakash was frankly in a different class. Asked by the BBC why it was that cricketers were proving a hit on the dancefloor, Ramprakash replied: 'Cricketers are a lot fitter than they were fifteen to twenty years ago.

You need agility, to be able to move your feet... as a batsman, I do work a lot on technique, and always think about balance, my arms, where the feet go and how far they move.'

In fact Ramprakash and Gough are just the latest in a long line of cricketers who knew the paso doble wasn't a West Indian all-rounder.

George Lohmann, who took 112 wickets for England in 18 Tests at the end of the nineteenth century, kept fit in the winter with ballroom dancing as he believed it helped his balance as a bowler, as did the famous English batsman Jack Hobbs and the man himself, Don Bradman. Even Geoff Boycott knew his cha-cha-cha from his tango. 'I never stopped dancing,' Boycott told the BBC. 'At the crease, it's fatal to become flat-footed, so I was like Fred Astaire.'

According to James Goodman (whose father, Les, was one of the *Strictly Come Dancing* judges), who runs an eponymous dance school in Kent, it's obvious to a professional why cricketers make good dancers. 'When fast bowlers run in to bowl, they have to make sure they don't plant their feet over the line without looking down. I've always believed that's why Darren Gough had such good footwork. Batsmen also possess excellent co-ordination and work a lot on refining their technique, paying attention to balance and positioning. And they're used to spending a lot of time practising one-on-one in the nets, so perhaps they respond better to that sort of coaching in the dancehall.'

> Even Geoff Boycott knew his cha-cha-cha from his tango

Ramprakash hardly heralded a new dawn for English cricket by winning *Strictly Come Dancing* in such a handsome fashion, but he made as much of an impact on non-cricketing Britain as the England squad had the previous year in winning the Ashes. And with Twenty20 attracting a new and younger audience to cricket, Ramprakash was further proof that the sport was no longer the preserve of big hairy men in flapping white trousers. 'Disappointing performances at national level mean that he was never truly a household name,' said the *Daily Mail* of Ramprakash. 'The relatively anonymous cricketer has catapulted himself into the national consciousness with his passionate manoeuvres.'

But we cricket fans weren't surprised, for, as C.L.R. James wrote in *Beyond a Boundary*: 'Cricket is first and foremost a dramatic spectacle. It belongs with the theatre, ballet, opera and the dance.'

Umpire's white hat

We've had a fair bit of headgear in our list, from a Roundhead helmet to the Iron Duke's hat via the baggy green cap of Australia. None has been associated with quite the furore that this white straw hat was in the summer of 2006.

It was worn by Darrell Hair, who, you might remember, we first met in 1995 when he no-balled Sri Lankan spinner Muttiah Muralitharan for throwing. You might also recall what we said about ball-tampering when presenting our eighty-first object, the dirt in Michael Atherton's pocket. Well, on the afternoon of 20 August 2006, during the fourth day of the fourth Test between England and Pakistan at the Oval, Hair and fellow umpire Billy Doctrove agreed that the Pakistan bowlers had been tampering with the ball. Showing a spot on the ball to captain Inzamam-ul-Haq, Hair claimed it had been deliberately scratched in an attempt to swing the ball. Inzamam was clearly angry at the accusation, and the fact that England were awarded five penalty runs and allowed to choose a replacement ball, but play continued for another sixteen overs until an early tea was taken because of bad light.

At 4.35 p.m. the umpires emerged, but the Pakistanis didn't. Even when the two England batsmen strode to the wicket at 4.55 p.m. the tourists remained in their dressing room. Five minutes later, at 5 p.m., the umpires removed the bails and returned to the pavilion, accompanied by the English batsmen. Half an hour later the Pakistanis did take the field, but the umpires didn't. Officials, including match referee Mike Procter, could be seen in earnest discussions with the Pakistan management, but no one had any idea what was going on. 'It sums up the ICC for me,' said Nasser Hussain, commentating on Sky Sport. 'You've got a major sporting issue here at the Oval, surely Mike Procter sits down with the main people and says, "Right, what's going on?" Do it behind the scenes and get a decision made and this would stop all these ridiculous scenes of players going up and down stairs.'

Sympathy, at least with the commentary team, lay with the Pakistanis. Television footage showed no proof of ball-tampering and word from the dressing room was that no player had been specifically accused. The general opinion was that Hair should have voiced his concerns to the match referee at the end of the day's play. Finally, at 6.15 p.m., play was officially called off for the day, and a quarter of an hour later Bob Woolmer, the former England player then coaching Pakistan, issued a statement: 'The team is upset by the inference they have been accused of tampering with the ball and therefore cheating,' he said. 'It is a no-win situation as the umpires refuse to come out.'

Later that evening the match was forfeited as an England win, the first time in history a Test had been decided in such a way. The following month Inzamam-ul-Haq was cleared of ball-tampering, but banned for four one-day internationals for bringing the game into disrepute by leading the protest. Pakistan cricket chief Shahryar Khan said the decision 'had removed a slur on the good name of our team, and our country'.

Hair, meanwhile, was stood down as an international umpire, and after dropping a case of racial discrimination against the ICC in 2007 he returned to Test umpiring the following year, officiating in two matches between England and New Zealand. It was a short-lived return. Public Enemy No. 1 on the subcontinent after the Oval incident and his no-balling of Muttiah Muralitharan, Hair retired.

But there was still time for one more twist in the Oval scandal. In the summer of 2008 the ICC overturned the result of the Test, from an England win to a draw, a decision that caused an outcry. Former West Indian bowler Michael Holding resigned from the ICC cricket committee in protest, saying that though Pakistan hadn't done anything wrong *with the ball*, their refusal to appear after tea was unconscionable. 'That game should never, ever be a draw,' said Holding. 'When you take certain actions, you must be quite happy to suffer the consequences.'

Six months later the ICC reversed its decision so that once more England were marked down as the victors. 'The ICC has already changed the result of the Oval Test two or three times in the past,' said a contemptuous Inzamam-ul-Haq. 'Maybe it would wake up tomorrow and decide that it was time to reverse it again.'

It didn't, but perhaps it will one day in the future. Anything's possible where the ICC is concerned.

Helicopter

What can we say about object ninety-two – other than sorry. Sorry that we had to include it and sorry that it stands for arguably the most shameful episode in English cricket. There have been a few of those over the decades, from Bodyline to rebel tours, but this shiny black helicopter which is our ninety-second object represents the day the game in England traded its soul for cash – and American cash at that.

Unfortunately for the England and Wales Cricket Board (ECB) the cash wasn't just cold and hard it was also fraudulent. But more of that anon. First let us return to that fateful day of 11 June 2008 when Allen Stanford arrived at Lord's in his private helicopter. Described by the *Observer* as a 'monogrammed chopper', the aircraft deposited the fifty-eight-year-old Stanford on the Nursery Ground – appropriate considering the ECB were there to greet him as if they were kids at Christmas awaiting Santa Claus. Also present was a clique of cricket reporters, including Angus Fraser, the former England bowler with the reputation in his playing days for hard and honest toil. Writing in the *Independent* the following day, Fraser admitted he was stumped to know which had been the tackier: 'The arrival of Sir Allen Stanford and his coterie in a private helicopter and the hierarchy of the England and Wales Cricket Board fawning over him, or the wheeling out of US$20m in $50 notes in a plastic crate.'

Stanford stepped on to the hallowed turf at Lord's as a long-standing opponent of Test cricket. 'Boring,' he called it, preferring instead the new Twenty20 game, which he saw as mirroring himself: loud, brash and exciting.

And that's why he had come to Lord's with a plastic crate containing $20 million. Once the fanfare, and the fawning, had subsided, Stanford announced that later that year a Twenty20 match would be held in on his own ground in Antigua (where he had lived for years) between the Stanford Superstars – or the West Indies in disguise – and an England side. It would be the first of five annual fixtures, and to the winning XI would go $11 million, plus $2 million to the backroom staff and unused players, while $7 million would be shared between the ECB and their West Indian counterparts.

Stanford's motivation was altruism pure and simple. As a lover of West Indian cricket he had been dismayed to watch their decline over the past two decades, and it was his fervent wish that the money should go towards re-establishing Caribbean cricket on the world stage. 'I am investing it in the future of West Indies cricket,' he told reporters. 'I have been in the Caribbean for 26 years and when you see something that you love so dearly fall to the bottom you want to see it get back up, and I am doing the best that I can.'

As for involving the ECB, Stanford said it was because 'they have the best organisation and structure in world cricket'. One or two of the reporters present wondered also whether it wasn't also because the ECB had the most money-grabbing officials in its ranks.

As Angus Fraser wrote, 'on the surface everyone seems to be a winner, and those on Stanford's payroll undoubtedly are. Cricket, like every sport, needs money and publicity and who wouldn't do a bit of shoe shining if a billionaire is handing out a portion of his fortune but, even so, there is something rather unappetising about the whole thing.'

What troubled Fraser was the fact the match would be unauthorised because Stanford insisted on teams using his own black bats, which didn't comply with MCC regulations. In other words the most lucrative game in the history of cricket would be 'nothing more than an exhibition match'. Others weren't taken in by Stanford, the *Observer* saying that the American's whole demeanour to any 'self-respecting sceptic screamed car salesman'.

But not to Giles Clarke, chairman of the ECB, who derided the sceptics and ridiculed history. 'What we are saying to them [the players] is this is the chance to show that you can really perform under pressure and make money that is beyond the dreams of some of their predecessors.'

Alas, few of the England team coped with the pressure, and Stanford's Superstars coasted to a ten-wicket victory that few enjoyed, except Stanford himself, who was photographed bouncing one of the wives of the England team on his knee. Three months later the only things bouncing were Stanford's cheques.

Arrested by American authorities in February 2009, Stanford was subsequently charged with a £4.4 billion financial investment fraud and ultimately jailed in March 2012 for 110 years. Giles Clarke, in his third term as chairman of the ECB, didn't want to revisit old ground when asked by *The Cricketer* magazine what he now thought of the American. 'I'm not going to talk about Stanford,' he replied. 'Stanford is a thing of the past. Stanford was a small, single matter.'

Small, single and sordid, but then at least Stanford did deliver the money, enriching each of the eighteen counties to the tune of £50,000, money that they didn't have to pay back to Stanford's American creditors.

As for the West Indies, they have re-established themselves in the global game by winning the 2012 Twenty20 World Cup, their first silverware in eight years. Crime may not have paid for Stanford but it did for the West Indies. 'It was unfortunate what happened afterwards, but the impact he had on West Indies cricket can never be forgotten,' said Darren Sammy, their victorious captain at the Twenty20 World Cup. 'His tournament in the Caribbean did wonders... there was a whole new energy in our cricket.'

Moochu Singh, brand mascot for the Rajasthan Royals

Considering the hype and hysteria that accompanied the launch of the Indian Premier League in 2008, it was only fitting that the final was a nerve-shredding thriller. Chasing the Chennai Super Kings' 164, the Rajasthan Royals knocked off the runs with the very last ball of their twenty overs. The players, the fans, even the Royal's mascot, a lion called Moochu Singh, were wild with excitement.

Moochu Singh, our ninety-third object, was just one of the novelties introduced to the world's most lucrative cricket competition. From the moment the forty-four-day tournament was launched by the Board of Control for Cricket in India (BCCI) in early 2008 it grabbed headlines with the big names involved and the huge money on offer. Of the eight franchises, the Rajasthan Royals were the cheapest with a player budget of US$67 million, unable to compete with the likes of

Chennai, who, in February's player auction, bid $1.5 million for the services of M.S. Dhoni, or Hyderabad, who got Australian all-rounder Andrew Symonds for a mere $1.35 million. The players, it was reported, were being paid more than £500,000 for six weeks' work.

Symonds was just one the stars on show when the first of fifty-nine matches began on 18 April with Bangalore facing Kolkata in Bangalore. Shane Warne, Glenn McGrath and Adam Gilchrist were involved, so too a trio of South Africans in all-rounder Jacques Kallis, fast bowler Shaun Pollock and national team captain Graeme Smith. The best players from West Indies, New Zealand and Pakistan were also represented; in fact the only nation not involved was England, because the tournament clashed with its domestic season and its top players were contracted to the ECB. Only Dimitri Mascarenhas, an England player but not on a central contract, took advantage of the riches on offer, leaving his teammates to mutter about the inequity of it all. 'It's silly to think that you're losing up to a million [dollars] over six weeks,' Kevin Pietersen told *The Times*. 'It's definitely something that the hierarchy needs to fit into our fixtures.'

The ECB promised to look into the matter and sent a delegation to India to study the tournament, muttering vaguely about setting up a rival competition more in line with the English season. Later they would ensure the loyalty of their stars by offering them each substantial win bonuses reported to be as much as £2 million.

In India, meanwhile, no one gave a hoot what the English thought. They were too busy picking a franchise as the tournament got under way. With so much hype the IPL had a lot to live up to, but it fulfilled every expectation. 'The IPL has had everything,' said Kanishkaa Balachandran in an article reviewing the tournament for ESPN Cricinfo. 'Shiny uniforms and big money, controversy and comedy, dancing girls and dancing down the track. And, lest we forget, lots and lots of big hitting.'

When it all ended with the Royals' victory over Chennai on 1 June opinion was divided about what it meant for the future of the game, as it had been thirty years earlier when Kerry Packer came to town with his World Series Circuit. 'Twenty20 has become the central financial pillar of cricket,' wrote the *Sunday Times*. 'In infancy, it was a diversion and an entertainment; in maturity, it is the bread-winner. The sport has never been so wealthy as it is right now... everything to do with Twenty20 is measured in millions. Every stakeholder – from cricketers to counties to countries – is reassessing their priorities and business plans. The game may be cash-rich, but many of its well-wishers are confidence-poor. They fear the unknown final destination of this vast gravy train.'

Cricket writer Rob Steen struck a more optimistic note, asking: 'How can anyone who cares about the game's future not be delighted that the upshot, properly handled, might be millions of additional apostles and disciples?' He added, however, that he foresaw difficulties ahead. 'Turning on, or even up to, a match to see Glenn McGrath re-cross swords with Sachin Tendulkar will be all well and good, but who, beyond India, will care whether they play for Mohali or Mumbai – let alone who wins? Even in India, persuading the public to care about a team's fortunes, that barest of necessities for a spectator sport, may prove an insuperable hurdle.'

And that's proving to be the case. Despite the fact that in November 2012 Pepsi bought the IPL sponsorship rights for five years for approximately $71.77 million (almost double the original title sponsorship deal of 2008), television audiences are on the wane. Ratings figures for the first sixteen games of 2012 were down 8.75 per cent on the same stage the previous season, with the cumulative figure decreasing from 127.40 million to 122.44 million. As brand analyst Santosh Desai told Cricinfo, sentiment is key to audience viewing habits and sentiment can rapidly change. 'When the tide turns, then it can turn dramatically,' he warned.

In Steen's opinion the best option for the IPL, and cricket in general, would be for the ICC to join forces with the IPL and 'rebrand it as the World Cricket League' with sides from every major cricket-playing city in the world. 'Who knows, it might even excise the word "burnout" from the players' dictionary.'

Coming Back to Me
by Marcus Trescothick

In 2001, seven years before our next object was published, the results of an international study revealed that English cricketers were almost twice as likely to take their own lives than the average male and also had a suicide rate higher than that of players of any other sport.

The study, carried out by David Frith, one of cricket's best-known writers, shone a light into an area of the sport that for far too long had remained in darkness. And it wasn't just England where cricketers were suffering. In fact, the 1.77 per cent suicide rate among English cricketers (compared with the national average of 1.07) was small compared to the other nations included in the study. In South Africa 4.12 per cent of players committed suicide, in New Zealand 3.92 per cent and in Australia 2.75 per cent. The findings shocked Frith. 'Cricket has this dreadful, hidden burden,' he explained. 'It must now answer the very serious question of whether it gradually transforms unwary cricket-loving boys into brooding, insecure and ultimately self-destructive men.'

Cricket has always had a history of

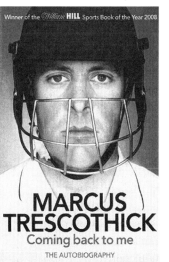

Winner of the *William* **HILL** Sports Book of the Year 2008

MARCUS TRESCOTHICK
Coming back to me
THE AUTOBIOGRAPHY

suicide, stretching back 100 years or more, when such greats of the game as A.E. Stoddart, Arthur Shrewsbury and Albert Trott killed themselves. The formidable South African googly bowler, Aubrey Faulkner, took his own life in 1930, and in recent years former England wicketkeeper David Bairstow and Nottinghamshire batsman Mark Saxelby have committed suicide.

According to Frith, cricket is predisposed to suicide more than any other sport because of its unique nature. 'It is the uncertainty, day in and day out, that plays a sinister beat on the cricketer's soul,' he said. 'Golfers, footballers, tennis players and boxers all have an assurance that they have a chance to recover from early defeat in the game but cricket embodies uncertainty on the grand scale and on a relentless daily basis.'

There are other factors also at play. As Tasmanian batsman Ed Cowan said in a 2011 article: 'Despite being a team sport, it is perhaps the only game where one's contribution is entirely objective. There is no escaping the black and white of failure – among other things, it is statistically tangible.' And the statistics can taunt, causing players to brood and turn inwards, fretting about where the next run or wicket will come from. Finally there's the time spent away from their family. 'On a professional level, no sport takes you away from home for extended periods without your support network like cricket does,' explained Cowan. 'In the next three years Australian cricketers will spend on average 44 weeks a year away from their own beds.'

It was this last factor that ultimately proved too much for Marcus Trescothick. The Somerset opener made his England debut in 2000 and was never dropped in his six-year career. He was a wonderful Test batsman to watch, reinvigorating the English side at a time when it was still racked by insecurities. Ironically, however, confident as he looked at the crease, Trescothick was hearing the first flappings of what he would call in his autobiography the 'black wings of depression'. That was on

England's 2004/05 tour to South Africa, though it wasn't until eighteen months later that Trescothick finally succumbed to the anguish when he toured India. In prose that is almost unbearably candid, Trescothick describes in his autobiography *Coming Back to Me* how he was tormented by thoughts of his wife and child back in England. 'In bed with the covers pulled tightly over my head, I would try to hide from the thoughts. Then, sometimes out of bed, almost blind with fear, I tried to run from them... this was not a life. It was a living death and it was just too dreadful to put up with.'

Trescothick pulled out of the tour and returned to England, reunited with his family but still in great torment. Eventually he was diagnosed with depression. He was stunned. He had played over seventy Tests for England, scored over 5,000 runs, helped win back the Ashes in 2005. What could he be depressed about? 'Depression? Surely that was for weak people?' Trescothick wrote in his autobiography. It was this attitude that prompted Trescothick and England initially to conceal the real reason for his departure from India, instead blaming it on a bug. Only later, as Trescothick realised he had nothing to be ashamed of, did he come clean. 'I had always been someone who coped. But depression doesn't care who it attacks: if it wants you, you cannot beat it off with a CV or a bank balance.'

> Trescothick's honesty finally forced depression into the open

Though Trescothick's illness ultimately finished his England career, his honesty in discussing his depression finally forced the issue into the open. In recent years a number of cricketers, including Trescothick's former England teammate Freddie Flintoff and New Zealand seamer Ian O'Brien, have admitted that they too have suffered from depression. In the middle of the 2011 World Cup England left-arm spinner Michael Yardy returned home with depression. This time there was no cover-up. 'It was agreed Yardy should return home immediately to receive the best possible advice and support as he seeks to overcome an illness he has been managing for a prolonged period of time,' said an England statement.

In September 2012 the Professional Cricketers' Association launched a series of six online 'Mind Matters' tutorials to help its members deal with issues such as alcohol, gambling and suicide. Yardy contributed to the project as did Trescothick. 'We are leading the way, be that in dealing with drugs, gambling, depression or anxiety, there is a massive difference from just a few years ago,' he said. 'It has helped the process of breaking apart the taboo that sports people have to be mentally infallible. We can do more to make things better again but it is 100% better than it was a few years ago. It is less and less of a taboo.'

News of the World

This object is no longer with us, having departed this life in July 2011. The ins and outs and explanations as to the demise of the *News of the World* (*NoW*) are not for this book, but, whatever one thought of Britain's most scurrilous Sunday tabloid, one of its last significant coups did cricket a huge service.

As we saw with object eighty-six, the cancer of match-fixing had first been detected in the late 1990s, though if we're being historically thorough cricketers have been fiddling matches for 200 years, ever since William Lambert, the outstanding cricketer of his day, was accused of using his position as captain of Nottinghamshire to fix a match against an England side in 1817.

But following the Cronje affair the International Cricket Council (ICC) thought the growth had been removed but, as *Wisden* pointed out, 'the myth that the cancer of match-fixing and manipulation was in remission was exploded by events' in 2010.

Those events began on 26 August, during the third over of the first day of the fourth Test between England and Pakistan. Mohammad Amir ran into bowl to Alastair Cook and was no-balled by umpire Tony Hill. As the Sky Sports commentary team noted, it was 'an enormous no-ball, a good half a metre over the line'. On the last ball of the tenth over Mohammad Asif also no-balled, though his error of judgement was a mere 2 inches. The following day, a Friday, Amir was at it again, overstepping his mark by a foot. What was going on? Even though Amir was only eighteen, this was his fourteenth Test. He shouldn't be making such errors. Perhaps he was overawed by playing his first Test at Lord's?

The *News of the World* gave us the answer on Sunday in what it described – for once without need for tabloid hyperbole – as 'the most sensational sporting scandal ever'. Video footage filmed a fortnight earlier and posted on the newspaper's website showed sports agent Mazhar Majeed in a hotel room with an undercover reporter from the *NoW*. Between them was a table on which was £140,000 in used £50 notes. The money was for Majeed. In return he told the reporter that the first ball of the third over of the England innings would be a no-ball; so too the sixth delivery of the tenth over.

Intoxicated by the money on show, Majeed – claiming to represent Indian bookmakers specialising in cricket – told the *NoW* reporter that he represented six of the Pakistan squad and wielded great influence because of his relationship with captain Salman Butt.

When the story broke the storm that engulfed cricket was huge. The term 'spot-fixing' was being discussed in homes, pubs, offices and schools across the cricketing world. Most people unfamiliar with the inside of a bookmaker's had to be educated in what exactly it was. It wasn't fixing the outcome of a match; rather it was a form of gambling in which small, subtle elements of matches were manipulated by players for the benefit of gamblers: no-balls were a particular favourite as opposed to hitting a six or dropping a catch because the corrupt bowler has the opportunity to deliver the 'goods' at the required moment.

That Sunday at Lord's was one of the strangest in the history of Test cricket. The Pakistan squad arrived at the ground hours after their team hotel had been raided by the Metropolitan Police. They questioned the implicated players – Butt, Amir and Asif – and found a quantity of money whose serial numbers matched those handed to Majeed in the hotel room a fortnight earlier.

Not surprisingly, the tourists' minds weren't on the cricket. They slumped to an innings defeat with Vic Marks in the *Guardian* describing them as 'ashen-faced and unsmiling'. Then, in possibly the most surreal moment ever seen at Lord's, Amir was presented with a cheque after being named Pakistan's Player of the Series. At least he'd be able to put it towards the cost of his impending legal fees.

Faced with mounting criticism from the cricket world, the Pakistan government and Cricket Board withdrew the three players from the one-day series. Then acting captain Shahid Afridi issued an apology on behalf of the Pakistan squad 'to all cricket lovers and all the cricketing nations'.

The apology did little to quell the growing anger in the cricketing world as police interviewed a fourth Pakistan player about spot-fixing, and Pakistan's Federal Bureau of Revenue opened an investigation into the personal finances of past and present players. The ICC then said it had suspicions about 'certain scoring patterns' in the Pakistan innings during one of the one-day matches.

> That Sunday at Lord's was one of the strangest in the history of Test cricket

After a lengthy investigation into the *NoW* sting, with the players continuing to protest their innocence, the ICC announced its verdict in February 2011. To the widespread relief of everyone involved in cricket, the sport's governing body had taken the firmest of lines. As the *Independent* said, 'the game was at last standing up to its responsibilities'. Salman Butt was banned for ten years, with five suspended; Asif banned for seven with two suspended; Amir's youthful promise was cut short with a five-year exclusion.

The ICC tribunal concluded its judgement with a melancholic assessment of the damage inflicted on the sport by the trio, saying: 'We cannot leave this case without exercising our regret at the events that led to it. In the Black Sox Scandal of 1919, sometimes described as the Sporting Scandal of the Century, the famous American baseball player "Shoeless" Joe Jackson was found to have thrown a match. A distraught fan uttered the memorable words "Say it ain't so, Joe". We too wish in this case that it was not so.'

Indian flag

India were the main hosts of the 2011 World Cup, and they were all too aware that history was against them if they wished to end twenty-eight years of hurt and win cricket's showpiece event. No nation had ever won the World Cup in their own back yard in the thirty-six years of the tournament, and it felt for the whole of the competition that the entire country was holding its collective breath as it waited to see if M.S. Dhoni's boys could finally emulate the success achieved by India in the 1983 World Cup.

India showed glimpses of brilliance in the pool stages but also glimpses of vulnerability, losing by three wickets to South Africa and tying a thrilling game with England. Still, they qualified for the quarterfinals and a clash with their nemesis – Australia. The Aussies had reigned supreme at the World Cup for twelve long years, and they began the match in confident mood, posting 260 for six in their fifty overs with a century from Ricky Ponting. India needed a knock from veteran Sachin Tendulkar, and the 'Little Master' duly delivered, scoring a half-century along with Gautam Gambhir and Yuvraj Singh.

Outside the ground the Indian military were on full alert

That set up an explosive semifinal in Mohali with Pakistan. Though Pakistan had lost their four previous World Cup matches to India, this was more personal than ever before. Pakistan had been scheduled to host fourteen of the tournament's matches, but after the Sri Lanka team

were attacked by terrorists in 2009, the ICC had reallocated eight of those games to India and the others to Sri Lanka and Bangladesh. The Pakistan Cricket Board reacted furiously, claiming they would lose US$10.5 million as a result and muttering dark threats about legal action. That never came to pass, but the semifinal offered them a chance for revenge.

The pressure going into the game was immense. As touts sold tickets outside the ground for ten times their face value, the prime ministers of both nations took their seats and an estimated one billion people – most benefiting from an official public holiday – settled down in front of the television. Meanwhile, the Indian military were on full alert outside the ground, even deploying anti-aircraft missiles in case of an audacious terrorist attack.

Mercifully, all the action took place inside the stadium with India winning the toss and electing to bat. Tendulkar was far from his best but he still had the class – and the luck – to make 85, a total that enabled India to set Pakistan a challenging but by no means impossible 261 to win. Though the visitors started well, reaching three figures for the loss of two wickets, the five-pronged Indian bowling attack was just too remorselessly accurate. Pakistan fell 30 runs short of the target, and the whole of India erupted in joy. 'The quality of cricket didn't really live up to the occasion,' admitted the *Times of India*, 'but the ebb and flow of emotions – from exuberance to unease to disappointment to hope to joy to sheer mad exultation – more than compensated.'

So India were in the final and ready to face Sri Lanka after their easy defeat of New Zealand. It was the first time the final would be an all-Asian affair, and the sense of occasion was heightened with the knowledge that this would be the last opportunity for Tendulkar to finally get his hands on the World Cup. Ever since the 1992 tournament he had been trying, and surely he wouldn't be denied at the sixth attempt – not on home soil in front of his adoring public? Not only that, but the thirty-seven-year-old Tendulkar needed just one more ton to become the first batsman to score 100 international centuries. Was it too much to ask for two miracles in the same match? wondered Indians.

Surely Tendulkar wouldn't be denied at his sixth attempt, not on home soil?

There were 33,000 spectators in Mumbai's Wankede Stadium for the final, nearly all of them watching through their fingers as Sri Lanka thumped a daunting 274 in their fifty overs. When the home side lost Virender Sehwag and Sachin Tendulkar early on in reply, the whole of India seemed ready to run off a cliff. But then Gautam Gambhir and Dhoni came together and steered India home, Dhoni choosing the final to play himself back into form with an unbeaten 91.

'They are happy tears, so I don't mind crying,' said Tendulkar as he cradled the trophy that had eluded him for nineteen years. 'As a young boy I grew up dreaming of lifting the World Cup some day and I always wanted to do that... I felt it was extremely important to chase my dreams and my biggest dream was this. So I continued to chase my dream and here we go. The team has managed to win this cup for the nation.'

Hotspot

India just won't have our next object, no matter how hard the International Cricket Council or anyone else tries to persuade them to accept the Decision Review System (DRS). As we saw with object eighty-five, technology has illuminated cricket for billions of people with its Snickometer, Hotspot and Hawk-Eye. The culmination of all this innovation was the DRS, officially introduced into international cricket in November 2009 for the first Test between New Zealand and Pakistan in Dunedin.

The ICC had decided to embrace the technology in the belief it was better to do so than continue to allow broadcasters to replay umpiring decisions that undermined their authority by showing up their errors. 'With the improvement of technology, umpires' mistakes are exposed and scrutinised like never before,' said Dave Richardson, the ICC general manager, in unveiling the DRS. 'This system will help alleviate the problems created when mistakes, which appear obvious on replays, are made.'

The ICC had been thorough in creating a system that harnessed all of the technological resources available while minimising the time spent confirming decisions. 'The system allows television technology to be used in a way that will not result in too many delays, will not de-skill the umpires and will take some pressure off the umpires,' explained Richardson. 'The fact is that trials showed that the system improved player behaviour and led to a significant reduction in the number of umpiring errors.'

Under the DRS each team is allowed two unsuccessful reviews per innings with the fielding side calling on the system to dispute a 'not-out' call and the batting side referring a dismissal to the third umpire if they believe the batsman was not out. Captains have fifteen seconds in which to decide whether to ask for a review. If they do the on-field umpire asks the third umpire to study a replay of the incident, using Hotspot, the Snickometer and Hawk-Eye, to judge whether the original decision was correct.

Like so much in cricket, DRS soon divided opinion in the cricket world. Aleem Dar, the ICC's Umpire of the Year in 2009, was an enthusiastic backer, saying: 'I support the introduction of this system... It's a tough job out there nowadays, and the review system is helpful for the umpires.'

Some batsmen soon came to loathe the DRS, none more so than England's Kevin Pietersen. During England's disastrous series against Pakistan in 2012 in the United Arab Emirates he managed just 67 runs in the three Test series and was given out lbw on three occasions. Each time the decision was referred to the DRS and twice he was given out when the ball-tracking technology showed the ball would just have clipped the stumps.

Technology has illuminated cricket for billions of people

'Because of the new DRS, there are definitely technical issues you have to look at in order to save yourself,' explained Pietersen. 'Batters are not getting the benefit of the doubt any more. Umpires are giving a lot more lbws. It just has to be clipping and you're out. Two, three, four years ago you were never, ever out. I have had to change my game.'

Pietersen's comments prompted cricket writer and broadcaster Simon Hughes to examine whether the DRS did favour bowlers, left-arm spinners in particular, who had become Pietersen's bogeymen under the new review system. In an article in the *Daily Telegraph* in March 2012, Hughes's findings did indeed back up the England batsman's claims. In the three Test series between England and Pakistan, forty-three batsmen were given out lbw, representing 42 per cent of the total dismissals for the series. That, said Hughes, was about twice what it usually is in Test cricket.

Why was this? He didn't believe it had anything to do with the quality (good or bad) of the bowling or batting. His conclusion was that umpires were becoming 'trigger-happy'. He explained: 'The introduction of Hawk-Eye to help adjudicate lbws has enabled, even persuaded umpires to give batsmen out when the ball was predicted to barely graze the top or outside of the stumps.'

Left-arm spinners had become Pietersen's bogeymen under the DRS

Hughes said that because of Hawk-Eye the wicket had become higher and wider in the perception of umpires, increasing the bowler's potential target area by an astonishing 70%. Good news for bowlers, bad news for batsmen. Of course, Hughes, a former bowler himself, didn't have much sympathy for batsmen. In the days before the DRS the batsman got the benefit of the doubt; the bowler got annoyed at what he saw as legitimate lbw appeals turned down by umpires.

So while batsmen like Pietersen work on changing their technique, playing straighter and keeping their legs out of harm's way, the debate over the DRS continues.

Nearly four years after the DRS was first introduced into international cricket it has not been universally applied, much to the chagrin of the ICC. They claim that tests carried out by Dr Ed Rosten in 2012 to test the accuracy and reliability of ball-tracking in Test matches had 'concluded that the results were 100% in agreement with the outcomes produced from his assessments'.

But India didn't care about the accuracy of the tests. 'The BCCI continues to believe that the system is not foolproof,' explained Sanjay Jagdale, the secretary of the Board of Control for Cricket in India. 'The board also sticks to its view that the decision on whether or not to use the DRS for a particular series should be left to the boards involved in that series.'

The Indians' decision came back to haunt them a few months

later when they played a series against England. On one day alone the umpires made six wrong calls, all of which could have been righted if the DRS had been available. At one point India captain M.S. Dhoni admonished one of the officials with an angry wag of the finger after another lbw appeal had been (incorrectly) turned down. He didn't get much sympathy from the English. 'There's technology that can help in making split-second decisions so why wouldn't you use it?' asked wicketkeeper Matt Prior. 'We've seen it in a number of series now where it's worked very well. It's not about trying to sneak wickets using technology. It's about eradicating major errors that can happen.'

Tendulkar waxwork

If only they could have bowled at the waxwork and not the real Sachin Tendulkar, a generation of fast bowlers wouldn't have had their reputations sent crashing to the boundary. The real Tendulkar has been a slayer of Test bowlers for nearly twenty-five years; the waxwork has stood for four years in London's Madame Tussauds museum, the bat held aloft in an all-too-familiar pose.

The pose was actually modelled on the moment in October 2008 when, against Australia in his 152nd Test, Tendulkar broke Brian Lara's record for the most runs in Test cricket. Not only did the 'Little Master' surpass his

West Indian rival, Tendulkar also became the first batsman to score 12,000 Test runs.

Since then the records have continued to tumble like fielders trying to cut off a Tendulkar cover drive. In February 2010, against South Africa, Tendulkar scored the first double century in one-day international history. Later that year he overtook Australia's Steve Waugh to become the most capped player in Test history, playing his 169th match for India against Sri Lanka. He ended a remarkable 2010 with another unprecedented feat, 100 against South Africa, the first batsman to score a half-century of Test-match tons.

In 2011 Tendulkar finally got his hands on the World Cup and he also became the first batsman to pass 15,000 runs in Test cricket. Then in 2012 came probably the most momentous of Tendulkar's myriad achievements – his 100th international century, scored in a one-day match against Bangladesh. 'Enjoy the game and chase your dreams,' he said as he soaked up the adulation.

The records have continued to tumble like fielders trying to cut off a Tendulkar cover drive

No other player has ever come close to scoring a century of international centuries (Ricky Ponting of Australia is second in the list with seventy-one), but then no player in the last fifty years has come close to matching Tendulkar's extraordinary run-scoring. As 2012 ended, Tendulkar had amassed 15,645 Test runs in 194 matches at an average of 54.32. No other batsman has scored more than 13,500 runs.

The powers have undoubtedly dimmed in recent seasons as Tendulkar, who turned forty in April 2013, discovers that not even he can overcome Old Father Time. In an attempt to prolong his Test career he announced his retirement from one-day international cricket in December 2012 after a record 463 matches.

The day will soon come when Tendulkar retires altogether, and then the comparisons with Don Bradman will begin in earnest. It's a debate that has already raged for more than a decade. Tendulkar's supporters say that though his Test average is substantially lower than Bradman's 99.94, several factors must be taken into account: the little Indian has played nearly four times as many Tests as the Australian; he has faced the world's best bowlers in all types of conditions whereas Bradman only ever played Test cricket in Australia and England; Bradman never had to contend with the rigours of combining Test cricket and one-day internationals, instead he could focus solely on the five-day game; finally, there's the weight of expectation that Tendulkar has faced in an age when the media often appear to delight in piling pressure on the shoulders of its sport stars. Australia expected much of their 'Don', but in a far less intrusive and hysterical manner.

Fans of Bradman, however, while accepting these points, ask that if batting was so much easier in his day – and bowlers less skilful – then why didn't other acknowledged greats of the game, who were Bradman's contemporaries, such as the English trio of Wally Hammond, Len Hutton and Herbert Sutcliffe, rival his astonishing average? Sutcliffe is the only other Test batsman to play more than fifty Tests and finish with an average above 60, but his 4,555 Test runs at an average of 60.73 pale into insignificance when set beside Bradman's.

Then there's the question of uncovered pitches, which exposed batsmen of Bradman's era to all of nature's vagaries, not to mention the inferior quality of the bats used in the 1920s and '30s.

The arguments will continue to rage long after Tendulkar has retired. Perhaps in time another batsman will emerge to challenge the greatness of both Bradman and Tendulkar. What remains certain, however, is that though Tendulkar's waxwork may in time be melted down, many of his records will stand for decades to come.

Umbrella

As we discovered when discussing object fifty-three, cricket has given us many colourful phrases over the years, whether it be 'tickling one down to fine leg' or 'dabbling in the corridor of uncertainty'. Yet if there's one sentence guaranteed to strike dread into the heart of every fan, to make his or her shoulders collapse like the England middle order, it's the hated 'Rain Stopped Play'.

Our magnificent game has given us some enduring partnerships in the last 100 years, from Sutcliffe and Hobbs, to Ramadhin and Valentine, to Lillee and Thomson, but none has endured quite like the alliance between cricket and our next object – the faithful umbrella.

They come in all shapes and sizes and just about every colour under that rainbow that often appears as the ground staff work feverishly to drain the outfield of surface water.

Fortunately for cricket lovers, umbrellas are an ancient invention, so they were available to our forebears in 1879, reputedly the wettest summer in the second half of the nineteenth century. More than 580mm of rain fell in the five months from May to September, and Hubert Lamb, writing in *Climate, History and the Modern World*, described this summer as the 'coldest in the long instrument records for England... the decline of English agriculture, which lasted for fifty years, dated from this time'.

The next English summer when the heavens remained open was 1903, the wettest in London since 1697, according to records. It was also the coldest, with the average June temperature in the capital down to minus two degrees centigrade. Not that the adverse conditions had much effect on W.G. Grace; he scored his 200th innings of 100 or more runs in first-class and minor cricket, though by this stage of his career his physique, as well as his beard, was of such generous proportions that it afforded him much-needed insulation.

Grace had retired by the time of the next calamitous season, that of 1912, when the summer produced a record 384.4mm of rain (the average is 241mm). August alone saw 193mm of rainfall – not so much the 'Golden Age' as the 'Sodden Age'. Yorkshire, the county champions, lost an estimated £1,000 in gate receipts because of all the cancelled matches, and the Triangular Tournament (see object thirty-two) proved a damp squib on account of the rain. Still, at least umbrella manufacturers were happy, as they were in 1924. That summer had just about everything: torrential rain, biting cold and, in Somerset on 18 August, 238.8mm of rain and hail in a twenty-four-hour period. Three years later *Wisden* labelled the 1927 season 'one of the worst in the history of cricket' and reported that competitive cricket lost approximately £20,000 in revenue to the rain.

> **Within two hours of the deluge, the teams were out playing**

In recent years clubs have come up with ever more sophisticated methods to combat the rain, beginning with Warwickshire's 'Brumbrella', a 200-yard cover which was unrolled to protect most of the Edgbaston ground from the rain. First introduced in 1981, the Brumbrella survived for twenty years before it was outlawed by the ECB's insistence on flat covers.

For the MCC the key in defeating the rain lay not in what they put on the surface of Lord's but what they did underneath. So in 2002 work began on a new drainage system at the home of cricket, one which involved digging up the outfield, removing the clay to a depth of 80cm (20,000 tonnes in total) and replacing it with a fine-sand mix. It cost the MCC £1.25 million, but that sum was recouped in one very wet July day in 2007. On the second day of the first Test against India it rained with a ferocity that Mick Hunt, the MCC's head groundsman, hadn't experienced in his thirty-eight years at Lord's. But was Hunt worried? 'Even when I saw the water pouring down the slope off the covers towards the Tavern Stand side I wasn't that concerned because our filtration rate is two inches per hour, so I knew all that water would go away,' he explained to the *Daily Telegraph*.

Within two hours of the deluge the teams were out playing, and the MCC weren't obliged to fork out the £1.2 million in ticket refunds that they would have if no play had been possible.

But sometimes even twenty-first-century technology is powerless against the merciless might of the English summer: 2012 was the wettest summer for a century, with 370.7mm of rain, not to mention a miserly 413 hours of sunshine up to the end of August, making it the greyest since 1987. The rain eased a little in August, allowing the touring South Africa to beat England in the Test series, but the County Championship was the dampest of damp squibs. No side suffered more than Yorkshire, who lost 138 hours of play to rain out of a maximum of 384 (36 per cent), while seven more counties saw more than 100 hours washed out in the Great British summer.

According to the BBC a jet stream, a fast-moving band of air high in the atmosphere which came from America, was responsible for all the rain.

Typical. Americans don't even play cricket, but they still find a way to rain on our parade.

A teapot

Give yourselves a standing ovation, we've reached our ton. And why not celebrate with a cup of tea?

Is there anything more civilised in sport than the cricket tea of a Test match? A ham sandwich here, a sticky bun there and a nice cup of tea to finish before it's back out for the final session. It's what separates our great game from other less refined pastimes, without mentioning names. But might the cricket tea, the staple of Test cricket for 136 years, be facing a sticky ending of its own?

In April 2011 Sri Lanka fast bowler Lasith Malinga retired from Tests at the age of twenty-seven, an age when most fast bowlers are coming into their prime. But Malinga called it a day in the five-day arena because he wanted to ensure he was in tip-top condition for the 2015 World Cup. 'The heavy workload of Tests could lead to permanent injury,' he said, leaving no one in doubt where his priority lay in international cricket.

The news alarmed England coach Andy Flower, who saw it as another sign that international cricketers are more focused on one-day games than Test matches. 'The ICC has to address that as a serious problem looming in the future,' warned Flower, who called on the ICC to guarantee that Test cricket retained its place as the premier form of international cricket and was not sacrificed for short-term financial gain. 'They have to act very responsibly and make decisions on what's good for the game in the future,' said Flower. 'I'm not sure that's the case at the moment.'

Flower's fears appeared well founded later in 2011 when the ICC announced that the first Test Championship involving the top four countries, expected to take place in England in 2013, would not now take place before 2017 at the earliest. ICC chief executive Haroon Lorgat blamed the postponement on a lack of 'support and consent' from the ICC's broadcast

The cricket tea is what separates the great game from less refined pastimes

partner, who it was clear didn't think much of Test cricket as a spectacle. The MCC described the announcement as 'a setback for Test cricket' and wondered whether the Test Championship would be quietly shelved in favour of the money-spinning fifty-over ICC Champions Trophy.

That prompted Lawrence Booth, the editor of *Wisden*, to write a heartfelt and thought-provoking editorial in the 2012 edition. Warning that international cricket 'stands at a precipice', Booth bemoaned the rise of Twenty20 cricket at the expense of Test cricket. Money was to blame, he said, and to that end India was most guilty of devaluing Test cricket. 'Too often their game appears driven by the self-interest of the few,' he wrote, before pleading: 'India, your sport needs you.'

Even the staunchest Indian supporters of their team found it hard to criticise Booth. In the Test series against England that summer, India – the one-day world champions – were thrashed four Tests to nil, losing the last two matches by an innings. Apart from the redoubtable Raul Dravid no Indian batsman made more 300 runs in the series. Was this proof that the constant diet of Twenty20 and one-day internationals had left Indians able to play with panache but no patience?

If future generations of cricketers the world over grow up without the mental strength to play long innings, then surely Test-match cricket, and its glorious tea, is doomed to go cold.

It will be the end of cricket as most of us know it, certainly as W.G. Grace saw it, when, in 1888, he offered some advice to budding young cricketers: 'The capacity for making long scores is not a thing of a day's growth,' he said. 'It may be years before strength and skill come and enable the young cricketer to bear the fatigue of a long innings... great scores at cricket, like great work of any kind, are, as a rule, the results of years of careful and judicious training and not accidental occurrences.'

Grace has been dead for nearly a century, but let's hope that 100 years from now his words about building a long innings will still ring true. A game that can be done in a day is fun, but a match that can produce five days of nail-biting tension is unforgettable.

Bibliography

A Fourth Innings with Cardus, Neville Cardus (Souvenir Press, 2011)

A History of Cricket, Gordon Ross (Arthur Baker, 1972)

Arlott on Cricket (Collins Willow, 1991)

Autobiography, Neville Cardus (Collins, 1947)

Basil D'Oliveria, Peter Oborne (Little, Brown, 2005)

By His Own Hand: A Study of Cricket's Suicides (ABC enterprises, 1990)

Can't Bat, Can't Bowl, Can't Field, Martin Johnson (Collins Willow, 1997)

Cardus on Cricket, Neville Cardus (Collins, 1949)

Coming Back to Me, Marcus Trescothick (Harper, 2008)

Cream of Cricket, William Pollock (Metheun, 1934)

Cricket, A.G. Steel, R.H. Lyttleton (Longmans, 1888)

Cricket Heritage, W.J. Edrich (Stanley Paul, 1948)

Don't Tell Kath, Ian Botham (Collins Willow, 1994)

Encylopaedia of Cricket, Maurice Golesworthy (Robert Hale, 1962)

Fields of Glory, Gavin Mortimer (André Deutsch, 2001)

Gone to the Test Match, John Arlott (Green & Co., 1949)

History of Cricket, H.S. Altham and E.W. Swanton (Allen & Unwin, 1938)

History of Indian Cricket, Mihir Bose (André Deutsch, 2002)

In Quest of the Ashes, Douglas Jardine (Hutchinson, 1933)

Jack Hobbs, Ronald Mason (Hollis Carter, 1960)

Lamb's Tales, Allan Lamb (Allen & Unwin, 1985)

Lord's: Cathedral of Cricket, Stephen Green (NPI Media, 2004)

MCC 1787 to 1937 (The Times Publishing, 1937)

More than a Game: The Story of Cricket's Early Years, John Major (Harper Press, 2007)

Old Trafford: Test Match Cricket, David Mortimer (Sutton, 2005)

Oval: Test Match Cricket (Sutton, 2004)

The Boundary Book: Second Innings, ed. Lesie Frewin (Pelham, 1986)

The Don, Roland Perry (Macmillan, 1995)

The Theory and Practice of Cricket, Charles Box (Frederick Warne, 1868)

The Men in White Coats, Teresa McLean (Hutchinson, 1987)

The Slow Men, David Frith (Allen & Unwin, 1984)

The Spirit of Cricket: A Personal Anthology, Christopher Martin-Jenkins (Faber & Faber, 1994)

Wisden Almanack 1864 to 2012 (A. & C. Black)

Wisden Papers of Neville Cardus, ed. Benny Green (Hutchinson, 1989)

Picture credits

Acknowledgments

I'd like to thank my father, David Mortimer, for granting me access to his considerable cricket library, as well as proofreading the text with his customary diligence. A round of applause to the staff at the British Library for making my research of old newspapers as painless as possible, and thanks to Pete Ayrton, Nick Sheerin and Ruthie Petrie at Serpent's Tail, not only for going with the idea but for their excellent edits and advice along the way.